Environmental Conflict Management

SAGE was founded in 1965 by Sara Miller McCune to support the dissemination of usable knowledge by publishing innovative and high-quality research and teaching content. Today, we publish more than 750 journals, including those of more than 300 learned societies, more than 800 new books per year, and a growing range of library products including archives, data, case studies, reports, conference highlights, and video. SAGE remains majority-owned by our founder, and after Sara's lifetime will become owned by a charitable trust that secures our continued independence.

Los Angeles | London | Washington DC | New Delhi | Singapore | Boston

Environmental Conflict Management

Tracylee Clarke

California State University Channel Islands

Tarla Rai Peterson

University of Utah

Los Angeles | London | New Delhi
Singapore | Washington DC | Boston

Los Angeles | London | New Delhi
Singapore | Washington DC | Boston

FOR INFORMATION:

SAGE Publications, Inc.
2455 Teller Road
Thousand Oaks, California 91320
E-mail: order@sagepub.com

SAGE Publications Ltd.
1 Oliver's Yard
55 City Road
London EC1Y 1SP
United Kingdom

SAGE Publications India Pvt. Ltd.
B 1/I 1 Mohan Cooperative Industrial Area
Mathura Road, New Delhi 110 044
India

SAGE Publications Asia-Pacific Pte. Ltd.
3 Church Street
#10-04 Samsung Hub
Singapore 049483

Printed in the United States of America

*Cataloging-in-publication data is available from the
Library of Congress.*

ISBN 978-1-4833-0303-1

Acquisitions Editor: Matthew Byrnie
Editorial Assistant: Janae Masnovi
Production Editor: Olivia Weber-Stenis
Copy Editor: Elizabeth Swearngin
Typesetter: C&M Digitals (P) Ltd.
Proofreader: Jennifer Grubba
Indexer: Terri Corry
Cover Designer: Candice Harman
Marketing Manager: Liz Thornton

This book is printed on acid-free paper.

15 16 17 18 19 10 9 8 7 6 5 4 3 2 1

Brief Contents

To Leslie Agustus Clarke

Detailed Contents

List of Boxes

Preface

Environmental Conflict Management (ECM) is an interdisciplinary textbook focused on the process of managing environmental conflict. It provides not only an introduction to environmental conflict management and policy development, but also lays out a process for understanding and managing conflict and a review of the most relevant laws and policies.

We provide a theoretical framework grounded in the direct application of concepts to case studies through exercises, worksheets, and role plays, including techniques for public involvement and community outreach, strategies for negotiating options, and methodologies for communicating concerns and working through differences. We also include additional references so you may explore the conceptual foundations more deeply.

Environmental conflict management is a process that begins with an assessment of the situation and continues through ratification of agreements. Our textbook is organized in the same format that collaborative management of an environmental conflict is conducted. We begin with introductory chapters and then move through the process of managing and resolving environmental conflict. Each chapter is organized by first introducing and explaining a specific concept or process step and then providing exercises and cases that guide you through the application of what you are learning. Chapter 1 has an overview of environmental conflict and its relationship with the larger field of conflict studies. Chapter 2 previews the concept of collaboration and explains how it guides our approach to conflict management. Chapter 3 summarizes the history of environmental laws, policies, and basic principles of environmental policy formation and implementation in the United States (i.e. NEPA, ESA). It also provides a sampling of relevant international laws and policies. Chapter 4 outlines the first step in an environmental conflict management process, or initiating a process. A general overview of a collaborative process is given and the benefits of using a third-party neutral are discussed. Chapter 5 focuses on assessment of environmental conflict for an analysis of collaborative potential. Chapter 6 outlines how to design a collaborative process and engage stakeholders in policy development. Chapter 7 explains how to design a public involvement strategy to engage the general public. Chapter 8 explains some of the techniques for working with stakeholders, developing a group charter, and how to plan for and manage meeting dynamics. Chapter 9 reviews the process of decision making from goal setting to the ratification of an agreement. Chapter 10 reviews necessary techniques for communication capacity building as well as addressing critical cultural dynamics. Chapter 11 focuses on implementation of a ratified agreement and evaluation of the process. Finally, Chapter 12 discusses the importance of sustaining positive relationships after the conclusion of the formal process.

Acknowledgments

This book is a culmination of years of practice, research, and teaching that involved engagement, support, and contributions from many people.

First of all, we would like to acknowledge and thank the graduate and undergraduate students who have helped us refine some of our ideas, especially Paulami Banerjee, Rena Barbosa, Kendall Barrett, Leigh Bernacchi, Kaitlin Dawson, Sequoia Hill, Cristi Horton, Sarah Ip, Lacy Lopez, Chara Ragland, Jo Ann Roettgen, Adrienne Strubb, Joseph Vasquez, and Erica Von Essen.

Our families have provided multiple different kinds of support throughout this process. We are so very appreciative of Chad Clarke, Darren Clarke, Doug Clarke, Kenny Clarke, Rick Clarke, Telesa Steedman, Velma Clarke, Leslie Clarke, Markus Peterson, Nils Peterson, Wayne Peterson, and Scott Peterson.

We especially appreciate the colleagues who gave generously of their time to provide the "Voices From the Field" cases placed throughout the book. Their insight helped contextualize many concepts and ideas in real time. Other academic colleagues whose contributions have been especially helpful include Hanna Bergeå, Anabela Carvalho, Christine Oravec, Steve Daniels, Danielle Endres, Andrea Feldpausch-Parker, Cristián Alarcón Ferrari, Lars Hallgren, Hans Peter Hansen, Leonard Hawes, Robert L. Ivie, Todd Norton, Kaisa Raitio, Donald Rodriguez, Michael Salvador, Julie Schutten, Susan Senecah, Jessica Thompson, Nadarajah Sriskandarajah, and Gregg Walker.

A book such as this one requires its authors to draw from a broad spectrum of experience extending beyond the academy into various societal organizations. Numerous organizations have provided us with opportunities to further refine the practices described in this book. They include both government agencies responsible for managing natural resources and nongovernmental organizations that advocate for various environmental policies.

We are grateful to the following reviewers for their insight and guidance as our manuscript came together:

Deserai A. Crow, University of Colorado Boulder

Stephen Depoe, University of Cincinnati

Larry A Erbert, University of Colorado Denver

Florian Fiebelkorn, University of Osnabrück

Rebekah L. Fox, Texas State University

Jeffrey W. Kassing, Arizona State University

Richard Kotter, Northumbria University

Bonnie McEwan, The New School

Jane Bloodworth Rowe, Old Dominion University

Robbie Smyth, Griffith College Dublin

Leah Sprain, University of Colorado Boulder

Finally, we have received institutional support from colleagues in the Environmental Communication Program at the Swedish University of Agricultural Sciences and the Communication, Environmental Science and Resource Management, and Political Science Programs at California State University Channel Islands. Development of this book was funded in part through numerous internal grants from the Arts and Science Division and Project Vista at California State University Channel Islands and we are grateful for their financial support.

We feel fortunate to have been able to meet and engage with many wonderful and insightful people through our work in environmental conflict. While they have been generous with their time and knowledge, all errors that remain in this manuscript are the authors' alone.

CHAPTER 1

Introduction to Environmental Conflict Management

Environmental conflict is among the greatest challenges facing humanity in the 21st century (Peterson & Feldpausch-Parker, 2013). As society has become increasingly aware of environmental issues, the challenge of structuring appropriate decision-making processes and public participation opportunities becomes a central concern for many natural resource agencies, industries, interest groups, and the general public. These conflicts range from relatively simple and localized disputes to highly complex and international disputes. For example, in Uppsala, Sweden, most people look forward to the balmy weather and long days of June. Although residents enjoy many different plants, birch trees are special. The municipality has responded to public desire for a rich supply of birch branches for spring bouquets, wreaths, and hair adornments by planting rows of the trees along many streets. On the other hand, many people suffer from allergic reactions to birch pollen in the spring and claim there are too many birches. The municipality has responded to conflicts over what to do about the trees by publishing regular reports of pollen levels and reminding people that the inconvenience will only last a few weeks.

In the United States, confined animal feeding operations (CAFOs) illustrate a more complex environmental conflict. These operations tend to move to areas with lax environmental regulation, which is not the same thing as *lack* of environmental regulation (Sullivan, Vasavada, & Smith, 2000). The lax enforcement situation may have resulted from minimal efforts, lack of institutional capabilities, or lack of financial resources to enforce the law. Whatever the reasons, community members usually have not perceived a need for environmental regulation. But when local residents start noticing unpleasant smells, conflict arises between those who push for stricter enforcement (on the grounds that enforcement will push the CAFO to relocate and stop degrading the community's quality of life) and those who prefer to continue as in the past (on the grounds that the threat of stricter enforcement will push the CAFO to relocate, thus damaging the community's economy). Although this environmental conflict is deeply important to both the CAFO owners/operators and to community members, it is relatively straightforward compared to conflicts over climate change policy. First, there is the question of whether anthropogenic climate change is even occurring. Despite strong empirical evidence that has produced agreement among scientists, there are still individuals who choose to ignore the evidence, and claim that the phenomenon is something that "liberals" have manufactured. Even if a policy maker is able to ignore the small but well-funded group of naysayers, conflict remains. Some people believe that a rapidly warming planet is not something that requires public policy changes. They remain at odds with people who believe a rapidly warming planet presents problems that require a public policy response. Even if we reach agreement that dealing with the results of anthropogenic climate change requires public policy responses that does not mean there is agreement regarding what kind of policy would be most useful, who should coordinate it, or what its specific goals should be (Carvalho & Peterson, 2012). All three of these examples, as well as many conflicts that fall someplace in between them in terms of **complexity**, indicate that environmental conflict touches our lives, both in the personal and public realms.

Conflict and Communication

Let's start by defining conflict as a communication process (Oetzel & Ting-Toomey, 2013) that includes "incompatibilities, an expressed struggle, and interdependence among two or more parties" (Putnam, 2013, p. 5). We agree with a common assumption among communication scholars that social interaction is fundamental to conflict. Even if we start with the idea that communication is central to conflict, there are numerous ways to theorize and practice conflict management. For a wide variety of approaches to the ways human communication contributes to conflict, we recommend books such as John Oetzel and Stella Ting-Toomey's *The SAGE Handbook of Conflict Communication* (2013).

One aspect of conflict that is especially relevant to environmental conflict is the relationship between values and policy. Environmental conflict puts people, who would not otherwise meet, in direct contact and often into situations where they are competing for the same resource (Peterson & Feldpausch-Parker, 2013). For example, people who live on the headwaters of a creek may not even be aware of other people who live miles downstream and since they are unaware of the downstream residents, they are unlikely to consider the needs of those distant people. At the same time, the runoff from upstream lawns, golf courses, and car washes directly impacts those who live downstream. Even if both groups of people share common values, conflicts are likely to occur when attempting to translate those values into environmental policy (Layzer, 2012). Because we are especially interested in conflicts that not only relate directly to values (Peterson, Peterson, Peterson, Lopez, & Silvy, 2002) but also require decisions about policy, we will focus on conflicts that demonstrate an "expressed disagreement among people who see incompatible goals and potential interference in achieving these goals" (Peterson et al., 2002, p. 947). This definition emphasizes the importance of communication (expressed disagreement), pluralistic desires (incompatible goals), and perceived threats (interference) from other participants who may seek different benefits from a particular environment.

Although conflict can contribute to creative alternatives for difficult situations, people tend to fear and avoid it. We recognize that, if it is not handled properly, conflict can damage social relationships and even lead to physical violence. Although there are many negative aspects of conflict, we suggest that more effective conflict management can be achieved if participants realize that conflict also has productive dimensions. It can promote communication between diverse groups of people, encourage problem solving, and stimulate positive change.

The final point we need to introduce is the idea that conflict is a normal part of human interaction. One of the most important contributions that early communication researchers made to conflict studies was to question the assumption that conflict was an aberration, or an abnormality (Putnam, 2013). They suggested that, rather than an interruption of normal interaction, conflict is the norm whenever people work or play together. People who are responsible for developing and implementing environmental policy live with perpetual conflict. Although some are more comfortable with this reality than others, all of them can benefit from more effective conflict management and resolution.

Environmental Conflict: What Makes it Special?

Environmental conflict will never cease to exist, but it can be productively managed and the productive management of environmental conflict is the focus of this book. Environmental conflict refers to a long-term division between groups with different beliefs about the proper relationships between human society and the natural environment. It refers to conflict concerning environmental elements, meaning the interconnected biophysical, economic, political, and social systems encompassing both natural and human systems (Dukes, 2004). There are numerous ways of categorizing environmental conflicts. For example, in their book, *The Promise and Performance of Environmental Conflict Resolution*, O'Leary and Bingham (2003) classify environmental conflicts as *upstream, midstream,* or *downstream.* Upstream environmental conflicts involve planning or policy making and may involve creating and implementing governmental policy at the national, regional, state, or local level and are often larger in scope. Midstream environmental conflicts are more site-specific and involve administrative permitting for actions impacting the environment. Downstream environmental conflicts are often about compliance and enforcement, and most often involve the ways that people use land, allocate or distribute natural resources, or site industrial facilities. Typically downstream conflicts involve the prevention or cleanup of pollution. Others have classified environmental conflict by referencing the scope of the dispute from formal decisions to recommendations, site specific conflicts to policy level disputes (O'Leary, Durant, Fiorino, & Weiland, 1999).

We suggest that, whatever classification system makes sense to you, there are several characteristics that make environmental conflict distinctive. These factors add to the complexity of environmental mediation and management and must be understood if conflict is to be addressed in an appropriate and timely manner.

Complex Interdisciplinary Issues

Environmental conflict rarely deals with one issue but often addresses multiple, overlapping issues. Working through these issues can complicate a process and make finding a solution challenging (Daniels & Walker, 2001; MacNaughton & Martin, 2002; O'Leary, 1995; O'Leary & Bingham, 2003). Further, the **interdisciplinary** and interdependent nature of environmental issues adds to the complexity of a given conflict (Dewulf, Francois, Paul-Wostl, & Taillieu, 2007; Jeffrey, 2003; Ravnborg & Westermann, 2000; Speth, 2004). Single disciplines are ill equipped to deal with issues that are both technically and socially complex, and also interdependent. For example, a conflict over a proposed timber sale is not just about harvesting a particular board-foot quantity. It includes issues of forest health, fire management, worker safety, vegetation, habitat, soils, recreation, visual quality, economic development, and viability. In order to address this issue, an interdisciplinary insight from a variety of fields is needed. Likewise, in a conflict concerning the relicensing of hydroelectric facilities by the Federal Energy Regulatory Commission in Bear River Idaho, environmental issues included meeting demands of energy production; the passage of anadromous fish; the movement of sediment and gravels critical to fish spawning; water quality including turbidity and temperature; riparian health; terrestrial health, including the free movement of wildlife across 40 miles of canals; and water flow impacting recreational use. Each issue is dependent on the other and a solution must adequately address each concern.

Multiple Parties With
Different Identities, Values, and Goals

Given the complex context of environmental issues, there will always be a myriad of government, public, and private interests with a stake in environmental conflicts. They often involve government officials at the local, county, state, and/or federal level; public interests represented by environmental advocates, community residents, interest groups; and private interests such as industry or commercial; and academic interests such as scientists, researchers, or technical consultants. Environmental negotiations are characterized by multiple parties, or stakeholders, most of whom have competing interests, goals, and values (Crowfoot & Wondolleck, 1990; MacNaughton & Martin, 2002; O'Leary & Bingham, 2003), or what Dietz and Stern (2008) refer to as ways of knowing. Varying ways of knowing or worldviews in regards to a proper relationship with the environment can cause conflict among interested parties (Elias, 2008, 2012). In fact, Crowfoot and Wondolleck (1990) identify the different values placed on our natural resources (intrinsic value or resource) as the root cause of most environmental conflict. Often these values and interests get pitted against each other and environmental conflict intensifies. For example, in the spotted owl controversy in the Northwest, the issue quickly became one of people (economy) versus owls (environment). Because of the underlying, fundamental values held by each side, the debate became extremely polarized and difficult to resolve in an effective manner.

In addition to differing values, the personalities or decision-making styles of participants may also influence the environmental conflict. Daniels and Walker (2001) discuss the various styles of decision making and argue that these differences can vastly impact how a conflict is perceived and approached. For example, a resource manager from one agency may have an open decision-making format, which welcomes comments and shared decision-making with others. Another resource manager may prefer hierarchical decision making where one person makes the final decision. Understanding various approaches is the key to understanding the conflict situation.

The perceived personal **identity** of the parties and its relation to an environmental issue can also influence a particular environmental conflict (Clarke, 2008; Rothman, 1997). Rothman (1997) argues that although most environmental conflicts appear at first glance to be primarily resource based, they are almost always identity based. These identity conflicts occur when people's essential identities, as expressed and maintained by their primary group affiliations, are threatened or frustrated. People feel they lose face when they perceive that their identity claims are being challenged or ignored and this impacts their approach to a given conflict or issue. For example, during a conflict concerning wetland mitigation in northern Utah, a member of a local Nongovernmental Organization (NGO) who had dedicated his life to a particular field felt threatened and personally attacked when the proposed solution did not take into account his years of service.

Diverse Cultures

It is important to understand that environmental conflict is often characterized by the varying cultures of participants. As environmental issues bring together various people, different cultures are often represented at the table of negotiation. These cultures have not only possibly different values regarding environmental issues but different communicative approaches and patterns of interaction as well (MacNaughton & Martin, 2002). "Environmental and natural resource conflicts emerge from differences in values and worldviews and conflicting interests influenced by culture. Culture is most often defined by ethnicity; however, culture can also be characterized in different ways, such as the culture of ranchers in a particular region. For example, Peterson and Horton (1995) argue the conflict over the golden-cheeked warbler habitat is replete with missed opportunities for understanding the cultural perspectives of Texas ranchers and landowners. Understanding the cultural ways of local stakeholders could have enhanced the constructive management of environmental disputes regarding the warbler (Peterson & Horton, 1995).

Validating cultural knowledge is an important part of understanding culture. **Traditional knowledge** (both indigenous and local) should be respected as much as formal scientific knowledge. Voices from local communities deserve to be heard and their understanding of an issue should be considered along with those of scientists (Lejano, Ingram, & Ingram, 2013). Sometimes, this contributes important environmental information. For example, for years Sami reindeer herders in Sweden tried unsuccessfully to persuade biologists that wolverines were killing reindeer by first leaping onto their backs and that this justified the Sami practice of killing the endangered wolverines. Biologists maintained that it was not possible for wolverines to perform this acrobatic feat, until a field researcher observed it for himself. In another case, coastal villagers in El Salvador tried unsuccessfully to persuade sea turtle researchers that some turtles spent their entire lives in close proximity to their nesting sites, rather than swimming countless miles in between nesting seasons; they claimed to recognize some of the "local" turtles. When researchers were able to fit a small number of turtles with transmitters, they learned that the villagers were correct, which led to revisions in management priorities. How to validate and include cultural knowledge without ignoring formally recognized scientific knowledge is one of the most difficult challenges associated with environmental conflict management.

Considering Culture

Addressing the Material, Symbolic, and Relational Dimensions of Environmental Conflict

In their book *Conflict Across Cultures: A Unique Experience of Bridging Difference*, LeBaron and Pillay (2006) outline the three **dimensions of conflict**: material, symbolic, and relational. The material dimension is the concrete issues or the "what" of the conflict. The symbolic dimension is the meaning the issues are given by those involved especially those meanings that resonate with people's identities, values, and worldviews. The relational level is the way in which conflict plays out among the participants. Every conflict involves all three dimensions. For example, a conflict regarding the storing of nuclear waste on a Native American reservation is not just about nuclear waste or sovereignty (material) issues; it is also about acknowledgment, representation (symbolic), legitimization, and survival (relational) (Clarke, 2010).

All three dimensions of conflict—the material, symbolic and relational—are underscored by culture as culture is deeply connected to all. The authors define culture as shared, often unspoken understanding in a group that shapes ideas about what is important and animates our behaviors. Culture is not a topic that relates to conflict, it is an integral part of all interaction and thus, all conflict. It can, but does not necessarily, cause conflict but is inextricable from conflict. Culture assigns meaning to conflict and in turn conflict stimulates cultural responses. Culture and conflict are intertwined, constantly shaping and reshaping each other in an evolving interactive process. "Looking at conflict through an intercultural lens encourages us to question the limited answers and understandings we have of conflict" (LeBaron & Pillay, 2006, p. 9). It provides insight into addressing all dimensions of an issue.

To be successful, conflict resolution must change at the material level, but recognition that it is shaped and influenced by the symbolic and relational is critical. The symbolic and relational emphasize the need for relationship building as a precondition to and a product of conflict resolution, so resolving issues at a material level first requires effort and time to address the deeper symbolic and relational issues below the surface. For example, in the mid-90s South Africa began its transition from the apartheid. Had the conflict resolution just focused on the laws, structures, and policies it would not have been as effective. Relationships had to be built across cultural divides. Large-scale nation-building efforts by The Truth and Reconciliation Commission to establish a racially representative government of national unity, and the efforts of various grassroots organizations that supported interaction between cultures made the structural change meaningful. Material efforts had to be anchored in efforts to build relationships that resonate with the symbolic meanings and identities (LeBaron & Pillay, 2006).

Technical Complexity and Scientific Uncertainty

Environmental conflict has a high level of scientific and technical **uncertainty**. Oftentimes, there is little or no supporting science to guide decisions. Other times there is contradicting science and decision makers are placed in a vulnerable position when finalizing agreements (Booher, 2004; Dewulf et al., 2007; Dietz & Stern, 2008; O'Leary & Bingham, 2003). Even when there is strong empirical evidence supporting one claim, environmental conflict always retains some uncertainty. Think back to the climate change example at the beginning of the chapter. Although scientists are more certain that modern industrial processes are contributing to today's rapid rates of climate change than they are that smoking cigarettes contributes to lung cancer, some degree of uncertainty remains and conflict persists. Therefore, we cannot rely on removing uncertainty to resolve conflicts about the appropriate policy response. In addition, environmental conflicts have both historical and future significance, further complicating any given issue. The history of an issue influences and intensifies the present condition. Likewise, the time frame of decisions in environmental negotiation is long-term. Thus, this requires serious consideration of future generations. Scientific uncertainty and the potential of long-term outcomes can make agreement between parties difficult. For example, Jordan Valley Water Conservancy District (JVWCD), whose charge is to provide water for their constituents in the Salt Lake Valley, Utah, wanted to increase their water supply by using a reverse osmosis water purification technology process. Reverse osmosis removes the salt and other effluent materials from seawater, or in this case salt water, from the Great Salt Lake. A challenge of this desalination process is what to do with the selenium by-product. JVWCD intended to release the selenium by-product from the process into the Great Salt Lake but uncertainty and controversy surrounding the appropriate levels of selenium in the Great Salt Lake ecosystem ignited conflict with local environmental groups. Those who opposed it argued that the scientific uncertainty regarding current and future impact of increased levels of selenium in the lake's ecosystem outweighed the need for an increased water supply.

High Public and Political Profile

Because of the significance of environmental decision making on present and future conditions, environmental conflict has become an important focus of the public's eye. Media interest and scrutiny are often greater on environmental issues. Thus, the public is more aware of environmental issues and is becoming increasingly concerned. In addition, lobbyists (either for ecological or business interests) try to influence policy on both the national and intergovernmental levels making environmental issues of high political concern (O'Leary, 1995; O'Leary & Bingham, 2003; Saarikoski, Raitio, & Barry, 2013). For example, a resource management plan conducted by the Bureau of Land Management (BLM) in Moab, Utah (a tourist and biking community of interest to local, national, and international communities), received much media and public attention, which impacted both the process and the final planning document. Articles and editorials in both local and national papers drew attention to issues surrounding the draft resource management plan (RMP) and comments on the RMP came from all over the United States, Canada, and parts of Europe.

Discrepancy Between Issues and Political Boundaries

Environmental phenomena rarely respect political boundaries and often require solutions that are beyond the scope of one organization's judicial reach (MacNaughton & Martin, 2002). Subject matter that crosses spatial and professional boundaries requires not only an interdisciplinary approach, but an inter-agency or inter-organizational one as well. This can add complexity when defining issues or developing options as different agencies have contradicting mandates. For example, in the state of Texas, the different missions of different agencies sometimes result in conflicts over how to manage land on the border between the United States and Mexico. The US Fish and Wildlife Service, which is responsible for protecting endangered species, may support maintenance of natural lighting and native plants that provide critical habitat for endangered wildlife. The US Department of Homeland Security, however, is responsible for securing the nation's borders. They may prefer to mow down all plants, because they could provide cover for people attempting to enter the country illegally. They also may prefer to install huge spotlights to further deter illegal entrance into the country. At the same time, the Texas Railroad Commission may simply see the border as a potential flood zone, and prefer to manage the space to minimize flood damage to adjoining property. Even after policy decisions have been made, institutionalizing them becomes difficult as implementation continues to involve a number of agencies and organizations. This dynamic becomes even more challenging when the issue is on a border between two countries with different environmental laws. When endangered birds nest in the demilitarized zone (DMZ) between North and South Korea, it is difficult to achieve satisfactory resolution to conflicts about how best to conserve their habitat (Choi, 2011; John, 2003)

Environmental Law and Policies

In the past 50 years, a considerable body of laws, executive orders, regulations, and legal precedents define environmental regulations and agency policy, dictating what is acceptable interaction with the natural environment. Environmental management and negotiation must adhere to these laws and it can sometimes be challenging. For example, water laws in the eastern United States (Saarikoski et al., 2013) do not provide for a potentially depleting water supply. Any collaboration surrounding water rights, access, or mitigation requires working within this framework or making attempts to change it. Often environmental laws create differing forums and arenas for decision making and stakeholders must learn to work within differing legal parameters (Layzer, 2002). Chapter 3 of this book outlines the most common environmental laws and regulatory requirements.

Conflict Industry

Daniels and Walker (2001) used the term **conflict industry** to describe those individuals or organizations whose job security depends more on the perpetuation of the environmental conflict rather than a settlement. The political and legal landscape around natural resource management is populated by a number of advocacy organizations whose roles are to fight for preferred outcome of some constituency. Their personal and organizational interests are better served by the perpetuation of a competitive approach to environmental policy. As many are paid to fight a good fight, they have little or no incentive to find lasting solutions. The very philosophies or mission statements of some organizations do not allow them to enter into agreements with government agencies or to use a consensus-based decision-making process. These organizations argue that engaging in such a process would undermine their mission or objectives, and may fear that participation would decrease public support or the need for their organization's presence in the community.

Activity

Identify the Characteristics of Environmental Conflict

Please read the following case study. Referring to the environmental characteristics mentioned above, identify and discuss the characteristics of this conflict and what makes it unique.

In August of 1997, the Southern California Steelhead was placed on the endangered species list. Since then, steelhead populations within the Southern

(Continued)

(Continued)

California Steelhead distinct population segments (DPS) have virtually collapsed, from estimated annual runs totaling 55,000 adults to less than 500 returning adult fish. Populations from over half of the 46 watersheds historically supporting steelhead runs are now extinct. All of the four largest watersheds (Santa Maria, Santa Ynez, Ventura, and Santa Clara Rivers) in the northern portion of the DPS have experienced declines in run sizes of 90% or more. Adult steelhead have been documented in only 3 watersheds since the original listing of the Southern California Steelhead DPS, one of which is the Santa Clara River watershed.

In early October of 2008, California Trout, an environmental group, announced that they plan to file suit against the United Water Conservancy District (UWCD) and the U.S. Bureau of Reclamation claiming that the water agencies are not doing enough to protect the federally endangered steelhead in the Santa Clara River. California Trout contends that UWCD's fish ladder that goes around the Freeman Diversion, which diverts water from the river to the Oxnard Plain for farming and local communities, does not work. Representatives from California Trout believe that immediate actions are needed, such as keeping more water in the river for the steelhead and fixing or building a new fish ladder to help steelhead get around the Freeman Diversion. California Trout argues this claim is supported by a Biological Opinion developed by the National Marine Fisheries Service that states that such dams are the major impediment to steelhead access to their traditional spawning grounds further upstream.

Representatives from UWCD believe they are doing what they can to protect the steelhead and that the call to build or fix a new ladder and decrease water diverted from the river is unnecessary. They argue the Freeman Diversion ladder is not an impediment to steelhead as their research indicates only a small amount of steelhead return in wet years. Further, they believe that actions suggested by California Trout would have a devastating impact on the region's economy, as farms will go dry and cities will not receive the necessary water to send to businesses and homes.

The conflict over the steelhead trout and the Freeman Diversion fish ladder represents a number of community interests and important subissues including, a) steelhead population risk, b) fish ladder capability, c) competing science, d) water diversion impact on farming and local communities (resource, economic implications), cultural iconic status of steelhead (indigenous to area) and farming (agricultural community). In the controversy over the Southern California steelhead trout, the environmental health and economic livelihood of Ventura County are at stake. This issue has polarized the community pitting organizations and agencies against each other as the conflict has been characterized as fish versus farming.

Key Terms

complexity	identity	uncertainty
conflict dimensions	interdisciplinary	
conflict industry	traditional knowledge	

CHAPTER 2

Collaborative Approaches to Environmental Conflict

The Need for a Collaborative Approach

Until recently, the prevailing notion was that the best public policy decisions were made through technocratic governance and professional experts. Decisions were left up to technical experts who use their knowledge to analyze a controversial situation and implement their proposals. Society has become increasingly aware of environmental issues, however, and has expressed a desire to participate in deciding how to resolve these issues (Peterson & Feldpausch-Parker, 2013). This awareness and interest means that the challenges of structuring productive participation opportunities, identifying appropriate stakeholders, and constructively incorporating public recommendations have become central concerns for government agencies, industries, and interest groups.

Conflict researchers argue that "governance grounded in conventional bureaucratic rationality too often produced results grounded in adversarial rather than deliberative processes" (Durant, O'Leary, & Fiorino, 2004, p. 4). Although technical expertise remains a necessary part of the policy development process, relying solely on professional expertise can often result in conflict over which expert should make the final decision and which scientific evidence to rely on. Further, communication with the public of such decisions often takes on a "decide, announce, defend" approach (Henry, 2004). Without involvement of the public in the decision-making process, public acceptance and adherence is minimal or nonexistent. This often leads to dissatisfaction among stakeholders and the public, perpetuating the division between the government and the public (Daniels & Walker, 2001). Inadequate **representation** of interested and affected parties is one of the leading criticisms of these traditional processes (Dietz & Stern, 2008b).

If decision makers involve the public through formal public involvement processes such as the National Environmental Policy Act (NEPA), they often conceptualize communication as one-way transfer of information from experts to public.

Although community members and organizations are invited to comment at public meetings during the issue surfacing/scoping and on the draft document, participants are dissatisfied and distrustful as they feel their input has little or no impact. Critics suggest that such procedures often give only the appearance of participation, since the agencies may not seriously consider the comments and testimony when they implement policy. Many feel this approach could be characterized as inform, invite, and ignore. Further, participants feel that public meetings become venting sessions motivated out of generalized resentment and mistrust of public officials, doing little to help make sound policy (Daniels & Walker, 2001).

Because of this dissatisfaction with public participation processes, many organizations or individuals rely on the traditional legislative process. But many environmental advocates cannot participate effectively in the legislative arena because they lack adequate financial resources or staff to engage in lobbying. This compounded legislative and administrative failure often means litigation will ensue. There are a number of criticisms of litigation as a dispute resolution process for environmental conflicts. First, litigation usually does not allow for adequate public participation in important environmental decisions. The costs of litigation are often prohibitive for interest groups, especially groups that are small or represent local interests. In addition, litigation can be extremely time-consuming, frequently requiring months or even years before a case comes to trial. After accounting for appeals, the entire litigation process can take several years increasing litigation costs for all parties involved. Further, litigation is often ineffective in resolving the core issues at stake in environmental disputes because the courts are constrained by the narrow legal issues presented to them. They are limited from addressing the substantive dimensions of an environmental conflict and instead decide cases primarily on procedural grounds. As a result, many of the underlying controversies remain unresolved.

With the complexity of environmental conflict, increased dissatisfaction with traditional forms of policy development, and the ineffective nature of litigation, there is an increased need for an approach that does the following:

1. Welcomes diversity and advocates acceptance of multiple perspectives

2. Values public involvement

3. Enhances **collaboration** and communication skills

4. Provides opportunities for **deliberation** and **dialogue**

5. Promotes creative thought and constructive debate

6. Involves effective implementation of proposals

7. Encourages joint problem solving and inclusive decision making

8. Forges relationships between different stakeholders involved in conflict

9. Creates a forum for shared voices

10. Urges continual progress

11. Advances social responsibility on the part of participants

Collaborative methods of problem solving provide an attractive alternative to technocratic conflict management, one whose outcomes achieve a high level of both technical competence and social discourse. Effective management of environmental conflict must embrace more consistently a user-driven, stakeholder-engaged approach to policy development, selection, and evaluation.

Collaborative methods of solving environmental conflict have grown exponentially over the past 30 years, with increasing use at the local, state, and national level. It has many labels, including environmental dispute resolution (Bingham, 1986), **consensus** building (Susskind, Levy, & Thomas-Larmer, 1999), collaborative learning (Daniels & Walker, 2001), environmental mediation (Bingham, 1986), collaboration (Dukes, Firehock, Leahy, & Anderson, 2001), collaborative planning (Innes, 1999), collaborative natural resource management (Conley & Moote, 2003), community-based collaboration (Dukes, Firehock, & Birkhoff, 2011), deliberative democracy (Durant et al., 2004), and community-based conservation (Berks, 2004). In this book, we use "collaborative environmental conflict management" to encompass multiple approaches that attempt to (1) engage key stakeholders to (2) work together to (3) find common ground and (4) develop options for improving the situation, even when they cannot fully resolve environmental differences.

Collaborative Approaches to Environmental Decision Making

Effective environmental policy includes addressing and resolving conflicts that often limit the options available to decision makers. Reviewing the literature on sound policy, Daniels and Walker (2001) found that sound environmental policy is adaptable, relies on appropriate science and technology, is implementable, and has low **transaction costs**.

Is an Adaptive Process

The complex and dynamic nature of environmental problems requires flexible decision making. Policy makers must recognize that all decisions are inevitably field experiments and must be open to adaptation and change. The complexity of environmental issues calls for decisions that can account for new scientific understandings of changed social or physical dynamics. Many settlement agreements now include ongoing monitoring and sideboards, within which changes in implementation can occur. For example, the Edwards Aquifer Habitat Conservation Plan (Bodie, Cyr, Pence, Rold, & Honeycutt, 2012), which was approved in 2013, grew out of a public process that included state agencies, cities, farming organizations, consumer protection groups, scientists, environmentalists, recreationists, and others. The stakeholder group met for 8 years before their habitat conservation plan (HCP) was approved. The historic HCP is designed to manage water to simultaneously support recovery of a suite of endangered species, the needs of a rapidly growing city, and numerous other human needs. During those meetings, **facilitators** and mediators helped stakeholders hammer out their operating procedures, including sideboards that specified how the group would adapt to various contingencies that they might be faced with. Those sideboards were important in helping the group continue moving forward in the face of political and legal events that could easily have halted progress.

Uses the Most Appropriate Science and Technology

Sound policy must be based on both local and technical scientific knowledge (Fischer & Young, 2007; Reed, 2008; Yearly, 2000). By tapping into local knowledge, more complete information can lead to more robust solutions. Daniels and Walker specifically use the word *appropriate* instead of latest or best to communicate the idea that often the most advanced or latest science is not always the most suitable. "There are certain cases where the most advanced technical solutions to policy problems are not the most appropriate, particularly when their costs are too high, or they result in policy recommendations that are not culturally or politically viable" (pp. 2–3). Policy recommendations that are not culturally, politically, or geographically viable do little to address the unique characteristics of environmental conflict. The environmental impact statement for the Utah Department of Transportation Legacy Parkway project in Salt lake City, Utah, was challenged legally because of the application of the hydrogeomorphic wetlands assessment model (HGM). Although the HGM model is new and widely used, it was not the most appropriate model for the situation, because it had not been calibrated for the region and it did not account for wildlife impacts.

Is Implementable

Sound policy must be historically informed and easily applied to a given situation. Also, it must yield tangible results that meet the original goal. In the city of Portland, Oregon, the Planning and Sustainability Division wanted to encourage recycling. They developed policy that increased garbage collection rates while making recycling free. The result was not an increase in recycling but, rather, in illegal dumping. The policy was not implementable and their original goal was not met.

Incurs Low Transaction Costs

Transaction costs are the expenses that society incurs to implement a policy. The cost of implementation must be worth the benefits of the policy. If a policy can avoid high administrative costs, then it is more effective than one that incurs those costs. For example, the removal of 100% of the combined sewer overflows in the city of Portland, Oregon, would have cost the city billions of dollars, whereas an 80% removal solution was environmentally effective and incurred lower transition costs.

In addition to the preceding four elements, we argue that effective environmental policy requires appropriate funding, measurability, and social **legitimacy**.

Has Appropriate Funding

Policy development initiatives must be properly and appropriately funded. It is imperative to identify and set aside the necessary funds for its implementation. The term **unfunded mandates** emerged in the late 1970s and 1980s in response to the growth of federal regulations that state and local agencies were forced to implement. Budgetary pressures have limited the ability of states and localities to raise revenue sufficient to meet regulatory goals. These top-down burdens add to the complexity of issues faced by environmental agencies and organizations (O'Leary, 1995).

Is Measurable

Success of any policy requires some means of measuring important changes. In order for measurement to be useful, the policy being measured must have a transparent purpose, clearly articulated assumptions, easily identifiable responsibilities, and well-defined outcomes that can be evaluated. This means that environmental policy must be measurable and include a capacity for evaluation to help determine effectiveness and identify possible areas where policy can be modified to better meet the environmental goals. Measurable outcomes can encourage members of the public to become supporters of environmental policies, because they understand the benefits of these policies. For example, sportsmen and women in Texas became strong supporters of a temporary ban on turkey hunting when they were shown that the ban was part of a program that brought about measurable increases in the state's wild turkey population. Many of them became strong supporters of a management program that eventually led to a healthy population of wild turkeys and one that is sufficiently robust to support hunting.

Is Socially Legitimate

It is crucial that policy is considered legitimate in the eyes of those it affects. Social legitimacy is achieved through accessibility to information, opportunities for public input, and a transparent and easily understood process (Berardo & Gerlak, 2012; Mann & Adsher, 2014). Arnstein (1969) argues that public input into policy development is essential to the redistribution of power from government to citizen. As citizens are the best judge of their own interests, the ability to participate in a democratic system of government reduces public feelings of powerlessness and alienation and increases the legitimacy of the government (Arnstein, 1969). If the process provides accessibility to information and the opportunity to voice concerns, it is more likely supported by those it will impact (Bingham, 2006). When community members participate in the policy development process, they are more likely to buy into the terms of the policy and support its implementation. In downtown Salt Lake City, Utah, the Utah Department of Transportation (UDOT) built two modes of public transportation, the city bus and TRAX (the city's above ground subway system). However, these do not receive equal use. Statistics show that community members will leave their cars at home to use the TRAX but not the bus because of the social stigma attached with riding the bus. Had UDOT involved the public in their policy decision-making process, they might have received this information, modified their policy, and appropriated their funding accordingly.

If public sentiment is not taken into account, not only will public support of a policy be compromised, if segments of society view a policy process as lacking legitimacy, they are likely to coalesce into interest groups intent on impeding or preventing its implementation. For example, many Texas ranchers subscribe to the 3S doctrine regarding endangered songbirds that may inhabit their property. Property owners who follow the 3S approach plan to "Shoot, Shovel, and Shut up" if they see one of the endangered birds.

The concepts of effective policy development and social legitimacy are foundational for our approach to environmental conflict management. In the next section, we review the literature on collaborative environmental policy development to set the stage for the remainder of the book.

Required Conditions for a Collaborative Approach

Scholars and practitioners have identified certain characteristics or required conditions that distinguish collaborative processes for other conflict management procedures. These characteristics include the following:

Representation of Multiple Interests

For a process to be truly collaborative, all interests and parties must be represented at the negotiation table. In fact, inadequate representation of interested and affected parties is one of the leading criticisms of traditional public processes (Dietz & Stern, 2008). Because of the nature of environmental issues, decision making that embraces a diversity of knowledge and values is imperative. Further, those acting on behalf of organizations or constituents must represent those constituents rather than their own self-interest (Cox, 2006; Dietz & Stern, 2008; Dukes, 2004; Innes, 1999; O'Leary & Bingham, 2003). Participants must have political equality or an equal balance of power. This includes access to the necessary information resources. If participants do not have equal power, they must be given opportunities to enhance their individual/organizational power through participation in the collaborative (Cox, 2006; Meadowcroft, 2004; Susskind & Secunda, 1998).

Voluntary Participation

Although all interests must be represented, parties' participation must be voluntary. Participants must be able to opt out and seek other avenues to get their needs met at any time (Crowfoot & Wondolleck, 1990; O'Leary & Bingham, 2003; Reed, 2008).

Direct Engagement

A successful collaborative process provides opportunities for participants to meet face-to-face and engage in open dialogue and deliberation (Bingham, 1986;

Crowfoot & Wondolleck, 1990; Dukes, 2004; O'Leary & Bingham, 2003). This deliberation, built on principles of civic discourse, must adapt and incorporate high-quality information, generate new insights, transform initial perspectives, and enhance participants' mutual education and understanding of both the issue and needs of the other (Dukes, 2004; Innes, 1999; Meadowcroft, 2004).

Mutual Agreement on Process

In order to get buy-in, participants in a collaborative process must agree on how decisions will be made (Bingham, 1986; Cox, 2006; Crowfoot & Wondolleck, 1990; Dukes, 2004; O'Leary & Bingham, 2003). Successful processes often involve a neutral third party to act as the **convener** or facilitator whose role it is to ensure an open, fair, and flexible process (Dukes, 2004; O'Leary & Bingham, 2003; Susskind & Secunda, 1998).

Mutual Agreement on Decisions

A hallmark of collaborative processes is the buy-in and support of all decisions that are made. Participants must have equal say as to the decisions made by the group (Bingham, 1986; Cox, 2006; Crowfoot & Wondolleck, 1990; Dukes, 2004; O'Leary & Bingham, 2003). Further, group members must take accountability for both the decision and the implementation (Dietz & Stern, 2008; Innes, 1999) We recognize that national and international laws rarely allow agencies with responsibilities for environmental policy to completely turn decision-making authority over to locally formed groups, but the credibility of both the formal decision makers and the process will be compromised if members of the collaborative group believe that their recommendations have been ignored.

Considering Culture

Collaborative Ways to Provide Opportunities for Cultural Connection

Collaborative efforts to solve environmental issues provide more than just the opportunity to develop socially legitimate policy. They offer the chance to overcome divisions of class, culture, and ideology. In her study of environmental democracy in Appalachia concerning forest politics, Taylor (2009) argues that community members were brought together in an effort to create shared stewardship of place, but in addition to integrative deliberation, the community members were able to address class and cultural differences and develop a respect for each other as they jointly addressed environmental concerns. Land issues brought them together, but the connection of cultures became the defining aspect of their collaboration.

(Continued)

(Continued)

In Cyprus, there is a long-standing division between Greek-Cypriot and Turkish-Cypriot citizens. The history of mutual exclusion, economic inequalities, and cultural differences has negatively impacted joint political projects and halted many community initiatives. Environmental projects, however, have been the exception. Agreement on various environmental issues has provided a common frame of reference where differences are put aside providing a starting point for cooperation.

In 1979, the Greek Cypriot and Turkish Cypriot mayors in the divided city of Nicosia bypassed political obstacles to reconciliation and worked together to solve one of the most pressing environmental issues: reconnecting the capital's sewage network. This initial cooperation based on an environmental inroad then grew into a partnership called the Nocosdia Master Plan that is still in effect today. More recently, the United Nations Development Programme (UNDP) hosted a series of public meetings aimed at stimulating dialogue on local and regional environmental issues around the island between Greek Cypriot and Turkish Cypriot. One meeting in particular focuses on sustainable cities and the creation of green public shared space. The result of the green-space meeting was a cultural agreement of shared harmony and respect for differences between the two cultures. This program provided a tremendous opportunity to open the space for reconciliation and rehabilitation of relationships that transcend political divisions on the island and build peace between the Greek and the Turkish Cypriots (Jarraud & Lordos, 2012).

If instituted correctly, the opportunity to jointly address environmental issues can serve as a catalyst to cooperation and improved relations between ethnic communities by providing a common sense of purpose and a process of equalization in political, economic, and cultural life (Grossman, 2005).

Benefits of a Collaborative Approach

Practitioners and scholars have identified several benefits of a collaborative problem solving approach to environmental conflict. These benefits include the following:

Development of Sound Solutions

Perhaps the number-one benefit of a collaborative process is effective decision making and the creation of sound policy. Broader, more diverse representation of interests provides a better chance that all the relevant issues will be raised, so that the substantive issues can be more effectively addressed (Reed, 2008). There is also less risk involved than associated with win-all or lose-all procedures such as litigation. Further, it promotes better and more equitable environmental decisions that are typically long-lasting and take into account the best available technical and cultural information. This increases both satisfaction and legitimacy of both the process and the decision in the eyes of all participants and the general public (Birkhoff & Lowry, 2003; Dietz & Stern, 2008; O'Leary, Nabatchi, & Bingham, 2004; Reed, 2008; Stringer, Reed, Dougill, Rokitzki, & Seely, 2007; Webler, Tuler, & Krueger, 2001).

Socially legitimate solutions are more durable and are less likely to be appealed (O'Leary et al., 2004). Several researchers refer to legitimacy as a unifying construct and justification of collaborative **engagement**. Mascarenhas and Scarce (2004) drew on the concept of legitimacy to study natural resource planning in British Columbia, Canada. They found that the most fundamental criterion for a successful public process was legitimacy.

Mutual Learning

Collaborative processes provide opportunities for deliberation and dialogue and in turn support mutual learning about environmental issues and concerns. Collaborative efforts can build understanding and resolve uncertainty by educating and fostering exchange of information and ideas among agencies, organizations, and the public (Dukes, 2004; Ravnborg & Westermann, 2002; Stringer et al., 2007). In a watershed governance case in the Blackfoot River area of Montana, participants identified a commitment to learning from each other the key to a successful collaboration (Weber, 2012).

Reduction of Transaction Costs

Collaborative approaches to environmental conflict can reduce implementation costs through the creation and use of **social capital** and more efficient use of natural and human capital (Dukes, 2004; Ostrom, 1990; Peterson, Peterson, Peterson, Allison, & Gore, 2006). Using collaborative processes in resource and environmental management can generate a means to get work done by organizing cross-boundary activities, fostering more efficient use, and mobilizing shared resources (O'Leary et al., 2004; Wondolleck & Yaffee, 2000).

Conflict Management Capacity Building

Collaboration has the potential to build individual and community capacity in such areas as conflict management, leadership, decision making, and communication (Birkhoff & Lowry, 2003; O'Leary et al., 2004; Walker, 2004). Collaborative processes increase accountability between agencies and organizations involved in environmental decision making, allowing for active citizenship and democracy (Reed, 2008). It also allows for the public to take responsibility for environmental issues. This public ownership helps to develop an environmental ethic that can strengthen a community and enhance community actions (Dietz & Stern, 2008b; Dukes et al., 2011). **Capacity building** can help agencies, organizations, and communities deal with similar or other challenges in the future (Reed, 2008; Wondolleck & Yaffee, 2000).

Strengthened Relationships and Increased Trust

Collaboration provides the opportunity for stressed relationships to be mended and weak relationships to be strengthened. The opportunity to hear from others their reasoning and interests provides commonality on which to build, creates trust, and dispels cynicism (Birkhoff & Lowry, 2003; Reed, 2008; Stringer et al., 2007). Dukes (2004) refers to these improvements as "relational by-products" of a process (p. 205). Also sustained dialogue between business, the government, and the public increases confidence in government officials and helps empower disadvantaged groups. The result is trust between both, setting a strong precedent for future collaborations (O'Leary et al., 2004; Wondolleck & Yaffee, 2000).

Are Collaborative Processes Always Appropriate?

In their literature review, Alex Conley and Ann Moote (2001) summarize the criticisms of collaborative processes. They argue that collaborative processes often include members with unequal resources such as time, money, information, and negotiation training. These power differences prohibit true collaboration. Critics of collaboration also contend that these processes may exclude urban-based environmental groups or be negotiated on an inappropriate level, such as addressing issues through local processes rather than a national dialogue. Further processes may work to delegitimize conflict and produce the lowest common denominator outcomes. Others have argued that, while collaborative processes may be appropriate, collaboration should not be confused with consensus. They warn against overuse of consensus, because the attempt to placate everyone limits opportunities for change (Peterson, Peterson, & Peterson, 2005; Peterson, Peterson, & Peterson, 2006). While there will always exist challenges to collaboration, including institutional barriers, such as lack of support, opportunity, or incentive; unequal power of participants; and conflicting political goals, in most cases, the benefits of a collaborative process outweigh the challenges. Further, most concerns can be addressed through proper planning and process design. It would be naïve, however, to assume that every environmental conflict is suited for collaboration. Before engaging in a collaborative process, many factors must be considered. A conflict must be "ripe" for collaboration (Carlson, 1999). Timing, opportunity, and institutional support must come together to create an appropriate situation for addressing a particular environmental conflict through collaborative efforts. The following chapters provide more specific guidance that should help you design and implement a collaborative process, should you determine that such a process is an appropriate way to help resolve a particular environmental conflict.

Voices From the Field

Collaboration, Even When It's Difficult

Cathy Humphrey

NEPA Training coordinator

BLM National Training Center

The project area was enormous—30 million acres of agency-administered lands in 7 states, not to mention the intermingled private, state, federal, and tribal lands. Our charge was to develop new management direction for lands managed by the Bureau of Land Management (BLM) and the U.S. Forest Service supported by a broad scientific assessment. One of its requirements was to be a multiagency strategy involving the public in an open process. To do that, we brought scientists, land managers, interest groups, and the public into a close, working partnership; worked openly with our partners; developed a common understanding of *ecosystem management*; and built trust.

Seven years in, millions of dollars spent, and with the change of administration, no decision would be signed—but not because of an inadequate collaborative approach, which was messy and exhausting and beautiful.

Because of the extensive geographic scale and complexity of issues, we tried new and different ways to involve the public and our partners. The communication strategy required frequent, early communication, sharing information as soon as we got it—often in draft form. It meant reaching out to a wide spectrum of people, often using nontraditional methods. It meant consulting and coordinating with tribal, federal, state, and county governments. It meant showing how we used their input in the EIS (Environmental Impact Statement) process and final document.

The Tribal Liaison Group developed a consultation process with each of the 22 tribes. The Eastside Ecosystem Coalition of Counties facilitated involvement of 104 county governments. The Executive Steering Committee who provided direction for the project staff comprised five federal agencies.

We began teaching the public (and each other) what is ecosystem management. We taught concepts (hydrologic system, carbon cycle) and argued definitions. We involved the public in rapidly changing discussions by inviting them to watch our science team deliberate when they met in Walla Walla. The scientists weren't used to showing their "sausage-making," the public wasn't used to such an excruciatingly slow (and boring) progress. But it bought us trust. And in time, they were satisfied with monthly updates from the science team leader.

We scheduled hundreds of meetings in dozens of locations. We went to them. They came to us. The meetings had tight agendas and flexible facilitators—if we wanted to split them into small groups, but they wanted to stay together, we let them. We respected them—when Earth First! attended a meeting dressed as woodland animals, we called on "the chipmunk in the back" during question and answer time. We listened. They began to trust us.

Communication and coordination between scientists, land managers, and the public improved. Trust was built. Relationships formed. It took the right people reaching out to the right people reaching back. We may not have signed a decision, but maybe what we got was better.

Key Terms

capacity building	dialogue	representation
collaboration	ecosystem management	social capital
consensus	engagement	transaction cost
convener	facilitator	unfunded mandate
deliberation	legitimacy	

CHAPTER 3

Environmental Law and Policy

When you finish this chapter, you should be able to summarize the historical trajectory of environmental law in Western society, particularly as applied to the United States. The chapter will identify and briefly describe the treaties, statutes, and regulations that are most likely to influence the management of environmental conflict in the United States. It also will identify and describe some of the most important environmental treaties, statutes, and regulations that influence environmental conflict in other nations. Because managing environmental conflict in the 21st century has a great deal to do with existing law and policy, this chapter provides an important reference point for future chapters that focus on conflict management itself. This chapter will not make you an expert on environmental law and policy, but it should provide you with some guidance to use when you are involved in managing specific conflicts.

Brief History of Environmental Law and Policy in Western Society

One cannot understand current conflicts over the allocation and protection of natural resources—whether water, timber, wilderness, wildlife, or rangelands—without a grasp of the changing values the public has held toward these resources over time.

The environment, especially when it can be considered to be wilderness, holds a special place in the 21st century. Wilderness also is a big business. People pay for the privilege of experiencing the wilderness, ranging from cruising to Glacier Bay, Alaska, to trekking in Nepal. As part of these experiences, people purchase lots of high-tech gadgets and gear—one can't enjoy the wilderness without all the conveniences of home. We even have created synthetic wilderness, ranging from Disneyworld's Jungle Cruise to the Rainforest Café.

This love affair with things wild, however, is quite recent. For at least 4,000 years of recorded history, wilderness was viewed with fear and repugnance—something dangerous and an affront to civilization. You may recall that Adam and Eve's punishment for breaking the rules in the Garden of Eden was banishment to the wilderness. Folk traditions in Europe reflect this harsh view of wild places and wild things. The folk tales compiled by the Brothers Grimm used the fear of wild places to discourage bad behavior and to encourage both children and adults to follow the rules and to stay out of the forest. For example, *Hansel and Gretel* found the forest to be a place full of monstrous beasts and otherworldly creatures. The "Big, Bad Wolf" in *Little Red Riding Hood* illustrates public attitudes toward individual animals. Thank goodness for the civilizing forester who saved the little girl by lopping off the wolf's head, which represented the wilderness (Nash, 2001).

Not surprisingly, European settlers brought this perspective to the New World. For example, William Bradford, the first governor in Plymouth Plantation, wrote that the forests surrounding the Pilgrim's settlement were "hideous and desolate." The Pilgrims felt both a religious and practical compulsion to civilize the wilderness (Nash, 2001).

Despite the feeling that the wilderness needed to be civilized, however, many societies have established environmental laws for the purposes of conserving natural resources. For example, in the English Standard Version of the *Bible*, we read: "If you come across a bird's nest in any tree or on the ground, with young ones or eggs and the mother sitting on the young or on the eggs, you shall not take the mother with the young" (Deuteronomy 22:6).

After successfully conquering England in 1066, William of Normandy brought the forestry tradition from continental Europe to England. He declared that all forests belonged to the king and established laws to conserve them by prohibiting activities that would alter the environment. He attempted to conserve wildlife by prohibiting hunting and fishing (other than special arrangements made for his friends and supporters). During the 16th century, the government of Henry VIII developed a full range of environmental conservation measures, including the establishment of hunting and fishing seasons and generally excluding the general public from the forest (Salzman & Thompson, 2010).

Development of Environmental Law and Policy in the United States

Partly as a reaction against European and English models of environmental conservation that reserved all natural resources for the upper classes, many of these conservation measures were tossed aside in the early years of the United States. Once the Native Americans were forced off the land and onto reservations, vast tracts of uninhabited or "virgin" lands became available for development. For example, miners were given exclusive control of any minerals they were able to dig out of the land, and whoever cut down a primeval forest owned the resulting lumber (Salzman & Thompson, 2010).

The first wave of environmental action and policy development in the United States occurred at the beginning of the 20th century and is associated with the presidency of Theodore Roosevelt (1901–1909). President Theodore Roosevelt is known as a passionate conservationist. During his administration, significant environmental law and policy was codified. For example, in 1903, Roosevelt persuaded Congress to grant him executive powers to establish federal wildlife refuges. In 1905, he persuaded Congress to create the U.S. Forest Service. The day before Roosevelt left office, he worked until midnight to reserve millions of acres of national forest as well as numerous national monuments (Hays, 1987).

Of course, these changes contributed to conflict because those who had been using the country's natural resources to make their own personal fortunes were not pleased with the interference. More relevant to current environmental conflict, however, is the conflict that has developed among those who supported the development of some sort of environmental policy. Divisions between *conservation* and *preservation* began almost immediately (Oravec, 1984).

Gifford Pinchot was the dominant personality of the conservation movement. He was the first American professionally trained as a forester (at German universities) and was the consummate Washington insider. President Theodore Roosevelt appointed Pinchot as the first Chief of the U.S. Forest Service in 1905. Pinchot opposed the wholesale exploitation of natural resources that was occurring. He also opposed the concentration of benefits gained from these resources into the hands of a few wealthy entrepreneurs. He believed that expert management would ensure their optimal use for the good of the entire nation. The key words here are *management* and *use*. Pinchot recognized that there would always be competing demands for natural resources and thus supported the strategy of multiple use. His guiding principle was *utilitarianism*, or ensuring the greatest good for the greatest number of people (Oravec, 1984).

John Muir was an early ally of Pinchot and became the dominant personality of the preservation movement. He founded the Sierra Club in 1892 to protect public lands from exploitation. He and other preservationists praised the wilderness as a source of toughness and ethical values. Indeed, he argued that many of the nation's difficulties could be attributed to *too much* civilization and the effete, corrupt urban culture. Even more important, Muir argued that wilderness had intrinsic value that was more important than any specific use. Muir had no ambivalence about pure wilderness; he was the first great public defender of wilderness for its own sake. He argued that it should be preserved both for its value to society and because it was intrinsically valuable (Oravec, 1981). The two men eventually became political opponents, primarily because of differences between the conservation and preservation perspectives.

The great political battle that pitted Pinchot against Muir centered on the Hetch Hetchy Valley in what is now Yosemite National Park. Conservationists supported damming the Tuolumne River to provide water and electricity to San Francisco. They argued that fulfilling the needs of a rapidly growing city that already had more than 400,000 inhabitants was a more valuable use of the water than the aesthetic and ethical values obtained by preserving the Hetch Hetchy Valley. Muir and his supporters denounced the dam supporters as wasteful and sinful. Although the preservationists lost the battle and the Tuolumne River was dammed, the preservationists gained many new supporters. And as a concession to preservationists, Yosemite National Park, 16 other National Parks, and 21 National Monuments were designated in 1912 (Hays, 1987).

The second wave of environmental action and policy development in the United States is associated with the presidency of Franklin D. Roosevelt (1933–1945) and his attempts to pull the country out of the Great Depression. Although some of these actions and policies were primarily intended to accomplish other political goals, they had important environmental impacts. For example, F. D. Roosevelt established the Civilian Conservation Corps (CCC) for the purpose of providing jobs for two million unemployed young men. Men who worked for the CCC were removed from crowded urban centers and sited in rural areas where they planted trees, developed parks and recreation areas, restored silted waterways, controlled soil erosion, and protected wildlife. The Soil Conservation Service (SCS) was established in 1933 as a way to help farmers cope with the Dust Bowl. The SCS oversaw a process where financially strapped farmers sold farmland that had been devastated by inappropriate cultivation to the Federal government. This produced most of today's national grasslands (Hays, 1987).

The study of ecology gained a foothold in U.S. education during this time period. For example, Aldo Leopold, whose *Sand County Almanac* has become a staple in environmental literature, was educated at the Yale School of Forestry, which Gifford Pinchot helped to establish.

The third wave of environmental action and policy development in the United States can be tied to the publication of Rachel Carson's *Silent Spring* in 1962. Carson, who was a respected scientist before she wrote *Silent Spring*, realized that attacking the chemical industry would spark controversy. She spent over 4 years researching it prior to publication of *Silent Spring*, which carefully documented the health and environmental effects of the pesticide DDT. Even prior to publication, the chemical industry mounted a high-profile attack on the book and its author, trying to dismiss Carson as a nature nut. Ironically, the vitriolic attacks caught the interest of President John F. Kennedy and Secretary of Interior Stuart L. Udall, who formed an advisory group to investigate the use and control of pesticides. This, in turn, spurred congressional studies on pesticide regulation (Waddell, 1998).

For the first time, the general public became aware of environmental problems such as air pollution, nonbiodegradable detergents in the water, oil spills, oil soaked birds, and burning rivers. Charismatic species such as the bald eagle, grizzly bears, peregrine falcon, whooping cranes, and wolves were threatened with extinction because of pollution and/or habitat loss. In 1968, Senator Gaylord Nelson of Wisconsin proposed an amendment to the U.S. Constitution that would have recognized an "inalienable right to a decent environment" and required both the federal and state governments to "guarantee" that right. More than 20 million people participated in the first Earth Day in 1970 (Hays, 1987).

During most of the 1960s and 1970s, every president declared himself to be the "environmental president." Numerous environmental protections were established during these decades (see Table 3.1). President Lyndon B. Johnson signed the *Wilderness Act* (1964), *Clean Air Act* (1965), and *Wild and Scenic Rivers Act* (1968).

Note that presidential signature is not necessarily the final step for implementation, so dates and titles may differ slightly. Stewart L. Udall, who served as Secretary of the Interior under both Presidents John F. Kennedy and Lyndon B. Johnson, was strongly influenced by Carson's book. His sustained support of irrigation projects for the arid Western states places him firmly in the conservation (rather than preservation) camp. At the same time, he recognized the importance of developing an approach to environmental conflict that makes room for multiple perspectives and combines both the formal legal system with alternative dispute resolution (ADR). In 2014, the ENewsletter for the Udall Foundation lists the foundation motto as "Civility, Integrity, Consensus."

The development of environmental law and policy continued through the 1970s. President Richard M. Nixon created the Environmental Protection Agency (EPA) in 1972. He signed the National Environmental Policy Act (1970), Water Pollution Control Act (1972), Marine Mammal Protection Act (1972), and Endangered Species Act (1973). President Gerald R. Ford signed the National Forest Management Act (1976), Federal Land Policy and Management Act (FLPMA; 1976), Fisheries Conservation and Management Act (1976), and Toxic Substances Control Act (1976). President Jimmy Carter created the Department of Energy in 1977. He signed the Fish and Wildlife Conservation Act and the Alaska National Interest Lands Conservation Act (both in 1980) and made strong administrative appointments to (both the EPA and the U.S. Department of the Interior). With the help of Cecil D. Andrus, his Secretary of the Interior, he tripled the acres in the National Wilderness System, provided for the creation or expansion of 15 National Park Service properties, and set aside additional public lands for the United States Forest Service and United States Fish and Wildlife Service. Table 3.1 summarizes important U.S. environmental legislation that occurred during this period. Many of these legislative acts will play a significant role in the environmental conflicts you attempt to resolve.

Current Environmental Law and Policy in the United States

When you are asked to assist with the management of an environmental controversy, chances are good that it will be related to some of the environmental laws listed above. It also is likely to be influenced by policies that have been developed by the agencies that are responsible for upholding the laws. Because there are literally hundreds of individual laws and policies that pertain to the environment, we cannot list all of them in this chapter. Instead, we will provide brief descriptions of a few that are most likely to influence your options for managing environmental conflicts.

Public Trust Doctrine

This doctrine dates at least to the Roman republic. The Roman Institutes of Justinian stated that the ocean and its shores, as well as running water and air, were

TABLE 3.1 Major U.S. Environmental Laws Enacted During the 20th and 21st Centuries

Migratory Bird Conservation Act	1929	Establishes a procedure for acquiring habitat for migratory birds. Funding was provided in the "Duck Stamp Act" of 1934.
Federal Aid in Wildlife Restoration Act (Pittman-Robertson)	1937	Provides federal assistance to states for the restoration, rehabilitation, and improvement of wildlife habitat. It also supports public access and education.
Federal Aid in Sport Restoration Act of 1950 (Dingell-Johnson)	1950	Provides federal assistance to states for the restoration, rehabilitation, and improvement of fish habitat. It also supports public access and education.
Atomic Energy Act	1954	Establishes a general regulatory structure for construction and use of nuclear power plants and nuclear weapons facilities. It does not permit **citizen suits** and affords limited opportunities for suits by public interest groups.
Wilderness Act	1964	Sets aside lands to be preserved in their natural condition for the use of the American people. Provides a legal definition of wilderness.
Clean Air Act	1970	Sets goals and standards for the quality and purity of air in the United States. Significantly overhauled the 1965 act. Amendments in 1990 toughened air quality standards and placed new emphasis on use of markets.
Occupational Safety and Health Act	1970	Ensures worker and workplace safety by limiting exposure to toxic chemicals, excessive noise, mechanical dangers, extreme temperatures, and lack of sanitation.
National Environmental Policy Act (NEPA)	1970	Requires that federal agencies conduct thorough assessments of the environmental impacts of all major activities undertaken or funded by the federal government. It established the President's Council on Environmental Quality.
Marine Mammal Protection Act	1972	Seeks to protect whales, dolphins, sea lions, seals, manatees, and other species of marine mammals. It has become an international model.

Clean Water Act	1972	Establishes and maintains goals and standards for U.S. water quality and purity. Significant amendments in 1987 and in 1990 focused on toxic pollutants and oil spills.
Coastal Zone Management Act	1972	Provides a partnership structure for states and the federal government to protect U.S. coastal zones from environmentally harmful development. Includes federal funding to participating states.
Endangered Species Act	1973	Protects and recovers endangered and threatened species of fish, wildlife, and plants in the United States and beyond.
Safe Drinking Water Act	1974	Establishes drinking water standards for tap water and requires rules for groundwater protection from underground injection. Amendments in 1996 added a fund to pay for water system upgrades, revised contaminant standards, and inserted right-to-know requirements.
Federal Land Policy and Management Act (FLPMA)	1976	Provides for protection of the scenic, scientific, historic, and ecologic values of federal lands and for public involvement in their management.
Fisheries Conservation and Management Act (Magnuson Stevens)	1976	Governs the management of U.S. marine fish populations and is intended to maintain and restore healthy levels of fish stocks.
Resource Conservation and Recovery Act	1976	Seeks to prevent the creation of toxic waste dumps by setting standards for the management of hazardous waste.
Toxic Substances Control Act	1976	Requires reporting, record keeping, and testing of chemical substances used in the United States. It also specifies procedures for production, importation, use, and disposal of substances, such as asbestos and lead-based paint.
Surface Mining Control and Reclamation Act	1977	Ensures that coal mining activity is conducted with sufficient protections of the public and the environment and requires restoration of abandoned mining areas.

(Continued)

TABLE 3.1 (Continued)

Comprehensive Environmental Response, Compensation, and Liability Act (CERCLA/Superfund)	1980	Requires the cleanup of sites contaminated with toxic waste. Amendments in 1986 clarified the level of cleanup required and degrees of liability. Because it is retroactive, it can be used to hold liable those responsible for disposal of hazardous wastes before 1980.
Lacey Act	1981	Centerpiece for federal regulation of commercial activities with wildlife. Provides criminal and civil penalties for violations. Completely overhauled the 1900 act. Applies to all wildlife, including those bred in captivity.
Nuclear Waste Policy Act	1982	Supports the use of geological repositories for storage and disposal of radioactive waste. It establishes procedures for evaluating and selecting sites and provides a timetable for the process.
Emergency Planning and Community Right-to-Know Act	1986	Requires companies to disclose information about toxic chemicals they release.
Marine Protection, Research, and Sanctuaries Act	1988	Establishes standards for permitting the transportation of material from the United States or by U.S. flagged vessels for ocean dumping. It also establishes permitting standards for dumping material transported from outside the United States into U.S. territorial waters.
Oil Pollution Act	1990	Streamlines federal response to oil spills by requiring oil storage facilities and vessels to prepare spill-response plans and provide for their rapid implementation. It increases polluters' liability for cleanup costs and imposes measures to prevent spills.
Pollution Prevention Act	1990	Focused attention on pollution reduction by encouraging operational changes that prevent production of hazardous substances rather than through management of pollution after it has been generated.
National Marine Sanctuaries Act	1992	Provides for designation of discrete areas of the marine environment as national marine sanctuaries to maintain ecological communities and to restore natural habitats, populations, and processes. Overhauled and replaced Marine Research and Sanctuaries Act of 1972.

Food Quality Protection Act	1996	Amended the Federal Food, Drug, and Cosmetic Act (1938) and the Federal Insecticide, Fungicide, and Rodenticide Act (1947).
Chemical Safety Information, Site Security, and Fuels Regulatory Relief Act	1999	Amends the Clean Air Act with required provisions for reporting and disseminating information, especially regarding flammable fuels.
Federal Food, Drug, and Cosmetic Act	2002	Ensures that levels of pesticide residues in food meet strict standards for public health protection. It was originally passed in 1938, amended in the Food Quality Protection Act of 1996, and completely rewritten in 2002.
Energy Policy Act	2005	Addresses United States energy production, including efficiency, tax incentives, and climate change technology. It encourages innovative approaches to multiple energy sources, including fossil fuels, hydropower, nuclear, and wind.
Energy Independence and Security Act	2007	Moves the U.S. toward greater energy independence and security by increasing the production of clean renewable fuels, increasing efficiency of products, promoting research and development of technologies to mitigate climate change, and improving the energy performance of the Federal Government.
American Clean Energy and Security Act	2009	Puts a cap on emissions and orients U.S. energy systems toward low-carbon energy production. It also requires that utility rates remain affordable and strengthens opportunities for U.S. energy companies to compete in emerging international markets.

by the "law of nature" incapable of exclusive private ownership. The codes or customs of most European countries subsequently reaffirmed this principle. Although we could have discussed the Public Trust Doctrine in the section on environmental history, we save it for this section because, even though it has a long history, it is an extremely important contemporary policy (Salzman & Thompson, 2010).

In the United States, the Northwest Ordinance of 1787 incorporated the concept, declaring that the navigable waters of the Mississippi River "shall be common highways and forever free . . . to the citizens of the United States." The most famous **public trust** case in the United States is *Illinois Central Railroad Company v. Illinois* (1882). In 1869, Illinois granted over 1,000 acres underlying Lake Michigan along the Chicago shore to the Illinois Central Railroad for harbor and commercial development. Four years later, Illinois changed its mind and sued to declare the original grant invalid. The U.S. Supreme Court ruled in its favor, holding that the grant was voidable because submerged lands are "different in character" from most other governmentally owned lands. As navigable waterways, they are of special importance to the public, and the state holds title to the underlying lands "in trust for the people" so that "they may enjoy the navigation of the waters, carry on commerce over them, and have liberty of fishing therein freed from the obstruction or interference of private parties." Although the state might convey small parcels of submerged land to private parties where it would not injure the purposes of the trust, the government could not convey an entire harbor without violating the public trust (Hays, 1987; Salzman & Thompson, 2010).

The public trust doctrine is at the core of many environmental conflicts. Although some commentators have urged courts to use it more aggressively to protect natural resources of all types, the courts have shown little interest in extending it beyond its traditional amphibious setting, the fishes and other aquatic life therein, and terrestrial wildlife that are analogous to these aquatic creatures. Critics of the public trust doctrine argue that the courts are effectively legislating. Although the legal basis for the public trust has never been clear, it remains a powerful influence in environmental decisions. The few courts to have speculated on its power have held that the trust flows from common law rather than from state or federal constitutions.

Administrative Procedure Act of 1946

This act sets out procedures that all U.S. agencies must follow when promulgating rules and adjudicating conflicts. It established the standard for judicial review when agency actions are challenged in court. Although the Administrative Procedure Act (APA) applies to more than just environmental conflict, it is important to understand APA requirements. It guides all U.S. agency rule making and adjudication. The main lines of attack against any agency actions will be procedural (did the agency follow the APA) rather than substantive. For example, the APA requires agencies to provide notice of a proposed rule in the *Federal Register*, including the agency's source of authority for issuing a proposed rule. They must include a description of the proposed rule, give notice of location and time of public hearings, and provide an opportunity to submit comments. After the final rule is issued, the agency must again publish it in the *Federal Register*. This final publication must include agency responses to submitted comments and a justification of the rule's final form. The purpose of the APA is to ensure that agency rules are well crafted and that they consider the views of affected parties. It is a rigorous process for agency action (Salzman & Thompson, 2010).

National Environmental Policy Act

The National Environmental Policy Act (NEPA) of 1969 is the first major statute of the modern era of environmental law. It does *not* seek to ensure environmental protection through technology-forcing standards or market instruments, nor does it mandate conservation of **endangered species** or wetlands. Instead, NEPA relies on information. It requires agencies to consider the environmental impacts of their proposed actions and alternatives to those actions. This approach reflects the belief that, if given sufficient information, people will make the best decisions. NEPA's influence has been far-reaching, with its progeny in the statute books of more than 19 U.S. states and over 130 of the world's nations (Hunter, Salzman, & Zaelke, 2010; Salzman & Thompson, 2010).

The fundamental goal of NEPA is to *inform* decision makers, whether they are agency personnel, elected officials, or members of the general public. A NEPA process should sensitize decision makers to environmental issues and help the agencies find feasible means of mitigating negative environmental impacts. NEPA requires that federal agencies create an **environmental impact statement** (EIS) regarding proposals for legislation and other major federal actions that will significantly affect the environment. Preparing an EIS is a considerable undertaking that can take years. The required analysis must consider both unavoidable adverse impacts and mitigation alternatives. While laying out the environmental impacts of all options, an EIS is to be agnostic and leave the formal choice to the decision maker. The document that summarizes the entire EIS is called the **Record of Decision** (ROD).

Some actions are exempt from NEPA. For example, Congress may exempt either a specific action or a category of actions. In cases of national emergency, an action may be exempted from NEPA, as may actions that occur outside the United States. And NEPA does not always require preparation of a full EIS. Agencies may obtain a categorical exclusion (CE), or they may successfully argue that the less comprehensive **environmental assessment** (EA) is sufficient in the case of minor federal involvement and insignificant impact on the environment.

NEPA also created the Council on Environmental Quality (CEQ) to oversee the NEPA process and its implementation. Perhaps surprisingly, the CEQ does not have (nor does NEPA provide for) enforcement authority. In practice, enforcement comes through citizen suits under the APA and the federal question jurisdiction. NEPA cases generally raise one of two questions: (a) Should the agency have prepared an environmental impact statement, and (b) if so, was the prepared EIS adequate? The general remedy for a NEPA violation is a remand to the agency to stay its proposed project until it prepares and considers a satisfactory EIS.

NEPA's seemingly innocuous requirement of preparing an EIS has led to more lawsuits than any other environmental statute (numbering in the thousands). From an advocacy perspective, an EIS provides a source of leverage for internal agency opposition. A study of several cases throughout the United States showed that the requirement to prepare an EIS led the Army Corps of Engineers and the Forest Service to raise environmental considerations earlier in the process (Taylor, 1984). They then revised projects to make them less damaging to the environment. An EIS also provides information that can be used to fight an agency's decision in court. From a political perspective, the EIS can be used to educate the public and to provide information that can be used to fight the decision through the legislature or voting booth. Finally, EIS requirements can delay a project (particularly if litigation results in a requirement that the EIS must be redone), allowing time to organize opposition and, in some cases, making the project so costly that it expires on its own.

The logic behind preparation of an EIS is straightforward; a better informed agency should make better decisions. However, because agencies have limited resources, they often prefer not to create a full blown EIS. One way to avoid creating an EIS is to establish that the federal action is not major. Agencies have attempted to avoid the EIS requirement by segmenting otherwise connected actions. Imagine that the Forest Service decides to build a small road into a timber harvest area but does not prepare an EIS because the road will not have significant impacts. Soon after, they approve a timber sale in the area but do not prepare an EIS because the timber harvest will not have significant effects. Some groups have argued that the road and timber sale should be considered together in a joint EIS. In response to situations such as this, the CEQ has stated that interconnected actions must be considered together, and many courts have ruled against such segmentation, stressing NEPA's purpose of encouraging agencies to consider broadly the impacts of their actions.

The courts have gone to great lengths to make clear that NEPA is a procedural, rather than a substantive, statute. Once an agency has made a decision subject to NEPA's procedural requirements, the judge may only consider whether the agency was arbitrary and capricious in failing to prepare an EIS or consider the relevant environmental issues. So long as the agency complied with the NEPA process and fully considered the EIS, the decision must stand even if the agency did not choose the environmentally preferable option.

Endangered Species Act

Congressional passage of the current Endangered Species Act (ESA) in 1973 was a nonevent. No Senator and only four House members voted against it. Most legislators thought of the ESA as protecting charismatic birds and megafauna—such as grizzly bears, bald eagles, and alligators—against hunters and poachers. Few newspapers thought that the ESA's passage was important enough even to report. Ironically, the ESA is probably the most powerful environmental law in the United States (Salzman & Thompson, 2010).

Most ESA controversies center on the question of how regulatory implementation of the ESA should balance the benefits of preserving a species against the economic costs of preservation. Cost plays only a marginal role in the direct implementation of the ESA's regulatory restrictions, however. Federal agencies, for example, cannot take any action that would jeopardize the continued existence of an endangered species or materially alter the species' **critical habitat**, no matter how much money that action will net. Private property owners cannot use their land in a way that would appreciably reduce the likelihood that the species will survive and recover, no matter how valuable the land use.

This does not mean that cost is irrelevant to ESA implementation. Congress has never provided the funds needed to ensure full recovery of most endangered species under the ESA—reflecting an implicit judgment that other budgetary items are more important. Faced with significant regulatory costs, moreover, property owners and other interest groups have tried, sometimes successfully, to undermine or weaken ESA regulation through lawsuits, congressional legislation, and political pressure. At any rate, the law itself does not provide for any explicit balancing of costs and benefits.

Two federal agencies split administrative responsibilities under the ESA. The U.S. Fish and Wildlife Service (FWS) within the Department of the Interior is responsible for protecting terrestrial and avian species and freshwater fishes. The National Marine Fisheries Service (NMFS) within the Department of Commerce takes responsibility for marine species, including anadromous fish such as salmon. Far more species fall within FWS jurisdiction, so it is the principal ESA agency.

There are two primary ways species become listed as endangered or threatened. Usually, an individual or organization petitions the FWS to list the species, or the FWS can decide to list a species on its own initiative. The FWS must determine within 90 days of receiving a listing petition whether the petition presents sufficient evidence to pursue a full review of the species' status. Then, they have 1 year to determine whether to list the species. The FWS must list a species if it finds that "natural or manmade factors" render the species endangered or threatened. They are required to use the "best scientific and commercial data available" and they cannot consider the potential economic consequences of listing the species. *Endangered* species are those "in danger of extinction throughout all or a significant portion of its range." **Threatened species** are those "likely to become an endangered species in the foreseeable future."

The FWS faces strong pressure from landowners, developers, and industry to avoid listing species. These groups have exerted political pressure by seeking administrative, congressional, or White House intervention. The FWS has a variety of legal means to avoid listing a species. The agency can conclude that it needs additional information to decide whether a species should be listed, or it can determine that a listing is *warranted* but that it is *precluded* by higher listing priorities. The FWS has sometimes tried to avoid listings by asserting that state efforts to preserve a species provide adequate protection.

One of the most contentious aspects of the ESA is the designation of critical habitat for the endangered species (Peterson, Peterson, Peterson, Allison, & Gore, 2006). Because cost is not a legitimate factor in deciding *whether* to designate critical habitat, the FWS has sometimes delayed this task by arguing that it does not have sufficient information to determine the critical habitat or that designation would be imprudent (e.g., because the designation would alert poachers and collectors where to find the endangered species and thus increase the risk to the species). This practice has put the agency on a collision course with environmental groups. Deciding *how much* and *which* habitat to designate as *critical* to a species is one of the few situations where the ESA permits the FWS to consider cost. The FWS can exclude an area from the critical habitat if the benefits of excluding the area outweigh the benefits of including it, unless the exclusion "will result in the extinction of the species concerned."

Another aspect of the ESA that sparks controversy is the prohibition on *takings*. No one is allowed to "take" an endangered species of fish or wildlife. ESA defines *take* to include actions that "harass, harm, pursue, hunt, shoot, wound, kill, trap, capture, or collect" an endangered species. It is easy to apply this prohibition to poachers taking bald eagles. Controversies erupt, however, when the take is indirect. For example, do landowners take an endangered species when they cut juniper in the critical habitat for the endangered golden-cheeked warbler, when they pave sand dunes inhabited by the endangered Delhi sands flower-loving fly, or when they pump water from an Idaho river were endangered salmon spawn?

In 1981, the FWS attempted to clarify the law by issuing a regulation stating that a take is constituted by "significant habitat modification or degradation" that kills or injures wildlife "by significantly impairing essential behavioral patterns, including breeding, feeding, or sheltering." Although the regulation may have clarified which behaviors are/are not allowable, it also has generated huge controversy, including numerous lawsuits.

Congress amended the ESA in 1982, to authorize the issuance of **incidental take** permits to mitigate Section 9's potential restrictions on the use of private property. The FWS may permit an otherwise unlawful taking of a species if the taking is merely incidental to an otherwise lawful activity (such as property development) and the permit applicant has devised an acceptable **habitat conservation plan** (HCP). To be acceptable, the HCP must (a) minimize the impact of the taking "to the maximum extent practicable," (b) ensure that the taking does not "appreciably reduce the likelihood of the survival and recovery of the species in the wild," and (c) provide evidence of adequate funding.

A number of communities have developed regional HCPs encompassing multiple property owners and, where relevant, multiple species. Regional HCPs reduce the burden on individual property owners, and they enable regions to take a more comprehensive and coherent approach to species preservation. Typically, federal, state, and local governmental officials; property owners; and environmental representatives meet over a lengthy period of time to hammer out acceptable terms for regional HCPs (Peterson & Feldpausch-Parker, 2013). Mediators and facilitators play an important role in these processes.

Citizen Suits

In practice, the implementation of both NEPA and the ESA has been strongly influenced by **citizen suits**. All federal environmental laws passed since 1970 also have contained a citizen suit provision (Salzman & Thompson, 2010). The citizen suit provision says that individuals and organizations can pursue two new categories of lawsuits not authorized by the APA. First, they can sue anyone alleged to be in violation of an environmental law, serving in effect as private attorneys general. Environmental groups commonly have used this opportunity to supplement the government's limited enforcement resources and to pursue violations that the government is ignoring. The opportunity to bring private prosecutions remains extremely important. Second, individuals or groups can sue relevant governmental officials who are failing to carry out a nondiscretionary Congressional obligation, such as the promulgation of a specific regulation. It is important to note that the purpose of citizen suits is not to provide compensation to the plaintiffs for injuries but to ensure more effective enforcement of environmental laws.

Whenever a group or individual seeks to file a citizen suit, one of the first questions the court will ask is whether the plaintiff has standing. According to the Supreme Court, an individual generally must demonstrate four facts to establish standing. The plaintiff must demonstrate that (a) an injury has occurred, (b) the injury can be traced to the action being challenged, (c) the court has a reasonable possibility of redressing the injury, and (d) the injury is directly relevant to the group or individual that is seeking standing. These conditions are intended to avoid frivolous lawsuits.

International Environmental Law and Policy

Of course, environmental law has been developing in multiple nations, as well as international contexts (Hunter, Salzman, & Zaelke, 2010; Axelrod, VanDeveer, & Downie, 2011). For example, the 1972 Stockholm Declaration of the U.N. Conference on the Human Environment stated that people have a "fundamental right to freedom, equality, and adequate conditions of life, in an environment of a quality that permits a life of dignity and wellbeing." It proclaimed a "solemn responsibility to protect and improve the environment for present and future generations." At the same time, the Stockholm Declaration (U.N. Conference on the Human Environment) also affirmed the "sovereign right" of all nations to "exploit their own resources pursuant to their own environmental policies."

The Stockholm Declaration served as an impetus for the Brundtland Commission (U.N.). The **Brundtland report** (World Commission, 1987), titled *Our Common Future,* defined *sustainable development* as "development that meets the needs of the present without compromising the ability of future generations to meet their own needs." Sustainable development provided the core message for the 1992 Earth Summit in Rio de Janeiro (United Nations Conference on Environment and Development). *Rio Declaration on Environment and Development* more or less codified the premises developed in *Our Common Future.*

More recently, the *Convention on Access to Information, Public Participation in Decision-making, and Access to Justice in Environmental Matters* (**Aarhus Convention**) was signed in Aarhus, Denmark, in 1998, and entered into force within signatory nations in 2001. Its primary purpose is to provide public access to environmental policy. In May 2013, it had been ratified by the European Union (EU) and 45 nations throughout Europe and Central Asia. The Aarhus Convention grants members of the public the right to be involved in governmental decision-making processes on matters concerning the environment. These rights are intended to apply at local, national, and transboundary levels. They are based on three principals: All citizens should have (a) access to environmental information, (b) the opportunity to participate in decision making and legislative processes leading to environmental policy, and (c) recourse via judicial procedures in cases where any entity violates environmental law or the convention's principles. The EU has begun applying the Aarhus Convention to legislation that is binding on member states, such as the **Water Framework Directive**.

The Water Framework Directive (WFD) was approved by the European Parliament in 2000. It commits all EU member states to achieve a certain quality in all water bodies (including marine waters up to 1 nautical mile from shore) by 2015. Consistent with the Aarhus Convention, it identifies steps that states must go through as they work toward the goal rather than specifying detailed limits across all EU member states and watersheds. Individual nations are responsible for working within their own legal systems to ensure that water quality improvements (when needed) are achieved in a manner consistent with the Aarhus convention principles.

Given the importance of globalization in contemporary politics, environmental laws and policies throughout the world have the potential to impact your work in environmental conflict. Even if you think you are working exclusively within the United States, you may be surprised to find that policies emanating from international bodies such as the United Nations or the World Bank influence the options available. Depending on the specific case, you may need to familiarize yourself with EU laws and policies such as those mentioned above, with the Ministry of Environmental Protection in the People's Republic of China, or with the 2008 Ecuadorian Constitution, which granted rights to nature and ecosystems. Wherever you find yourself working, we recommend that you ground your approach to environmental conflict in a basic knowledge and understanding of the region's relevant laws and policies.

Conclusion

Environmental protection has progressed from reliance on Common Law, to reliance on prescriptive regulatory commands, to reliance on market instruments and information. In comparison to other areas of the law—such as torts, property, or even corporate law—environmental law is still a very young field (~30 years). We should not be surprised that it remains remarkably dynamic and contentious, with major reforms proposed in the U.S. Congress and the European Parliament nearly every year. Although this brings challenges, it also offers opportunities for new and creative ways to manage and resolve environmental conflict.

Voices From the Field

Piedras Blancas—Salinan and Northern Chumash Consultation and Collaboration

Terry L. Joslin

Central Coast Archaeological Research Consultants

A narrow, winding two-lane road is the tenuous thread that ties the Big Sur coastline to the San Francisco Bay Area to the north and the central and south coast of California. With the rugged Santa Lucia Mountains on one side and the picturesque Pacific Ocean on the other, stunning roadside views draw international tourists to this raw, untamed beauty. Access to the region is solely dependent on maintaining the Highway 1 corridor within the Carmel to San Simeon Highway Historic District and along the Piedras Blancas roadway. The ongoing dilemma for resource conservation along this stretch of coastline is how to manage and protect sensitive resources in a dynamic environment, where construction projects are essential to the road's existence. Federal laws, including Section 106 of the National Historic Preservation Act of 1966 (as amended; 36 CFR Part 800), require cultural resource studies to be conducted prior to construction projects to evaluate their effects on historic properties, such as archaeological sites.

Integral to Section 106 studies within the Piedras Blancas study area is consultation and collaborative dialogues with Native American descendants, who once occupied these lands, to ensure they are active project participants. At the time of Spanish contact, two groups resided in the Piedras Blancas region: the Salinan and the Northern (or Obispeño) Chumash. By working with these groups and individuals, the goal is to include different perspectives on the project's potential effects on the cultural landscape and archaeological sites.

Consultation with Salinan and Northern Chumash representatives includes exchanging letters and telephone calls, providing copies of cultural resource documents to review, facilitating meetings and field reviews, and ensuring that Native American consultants are present to observe site excavations. Project participants are also invited to the laboratory to observe the processing of site materials recovered during excavations. These items include artifacts, or tools and objects crafted by skilled hands, and discarded food remains (shells, bones, and plant fragments). Daily monitoring records are available for monitors to fill out and share their thoughts with other participants.

Fundamental to understanding Native American experiences during these consultations is a holistic perspective on the management of the environment and cultural resources beyond site-specific locations. Over the course of consultation, the comments received from Salinan and Northern Chumash community members focus on the following: the respectful treatment of Native American sites, particularly human remains; the importance of keeping artifacts in local museums; the need for experienced monitors at archaeological sites during

(Continued)

(Continued)

construction activities; the importance of site preservation; and scientifically collecting as much of the materials as possible when the site cannot be preserved.

The collaboration captures multiple passions and the long-term knowledge of practitioners who are committed to understanding and protecting the lifeways of the people who have walked these lands for at least 9,000 years. Driving the pastoral roadway, vacationers are unwittingly aware of sites that are protected along the road because of careful negotiations. The case study speaks to the challenges Native Americans and archaeologists face in reconciling traditional tribal values with the science of archaeology and regulatory obligations.

Key Terms

Aarhus Convention

Brundtland report

citizen suits

critical habitat

endangered species

environmental assessment

environmental impact statement

habitat conservation plan

incidental take

public trust

Record of Decision

threatened species

Water Framework Directive

CHAPTER 4

Initiating a Process

E ach environmental conflict has its own dimensions and contextual aspects, which make it unique and complex. This means that your first step in any collaborative process is to determine if a collaborative effort is appropriate. Timing, opportunity, and institutional support must come together to create an appropriate situation for addressing a particular environmental conflict through collaborative efforts. Initiating a collaborative effort is called **convening**, and the organization that initiates a collaborative effort is called the **convener** (O'Leary, Nabatchi, & Bingham, 2004). Often, the convener for a collaborative approach to environmental conflict is a government agency, but it also could be another organization, perhaps one from the private sector or a nongovernmental organization (NGO). Most often, the convener is a local, state, or federal government agency that has regulatory power or enforcement responsibilities for an issue or decision related to natural resources (Dietz & Stern, 2008; Ramirez, 1999). On many occasions, more than one government agency is responsible for an environmental decision or project, or more than one environmental law or regulation applies. In these cases, agencies work together to convene a collaborative process, while outlining the role of each organization in a **memorandum of understanding** (MOU). For example, in a project involving the critical habitat designation of the Rio Grand Silvery Minnow, multiple agencies were involved, including the New Mexico Department of Fish and Game and the United States Army Corps of Engineers. Because both organizations were responsible for the decision, they entered into an MOU and co-led a collaborative process. Governmental agencies are not the only organizations that may convene a collaborative process. A nonprofit organization with an interest in an issue may propose a process. For example, the Greater Yellowstone Coalition (GYC) is a nonprofit organization that seeks to protect the 20 million acre ecosystem that includes Yellowstone National Park, several small towns, forests, farms, and ranches. The GYC attempts to preserve the land, water, and wildlife in this region, as well as to protect recreational and business opportunities for people. Over the years, the GYC has cooperated with numerous federal agencies to convene collaborative processes that explored ways to manage conflict over management of wildlife disease, domestic livestock, and other issues in the GYC. The processes they have convened have included a wide variety of stakeholders, including numerous federal and state agencies, as well as people from the private sector. Commercial or private entities who have a stake in an issue may also initiate a collaborative process. For example, during their relicense process with the Federal Energy Regulatory Commission (FERC), PacifiCorp convened a 15-member collaborative stakeholder team to facilitate an implementation plan that relicenses three hydroelectric projects on the Bear River in Idaho. Representatives included federal and state agencies, tribes, and recreational and environmental organizations charged with the task of providing a stakeholder-supported mitigation package to the Federal Energy Regulatory Commission.

The convener must correctly select those situations where collaboration is an appropriate strategy and structure the process to encourage mutual gain. The specific issue and dynamics of an environmental conflict will determine if engaging in a collaborative process is a sound idea (Carpenter, 1999). The convener must decide if the issue is of sufficient significance to warrant the effort and if it is ripe for collaboration. If conflict is too intense, a collaborative process might not be effective, and other means of moving forward should be considered. The convener should also consider the sociocultural, historical, legal, political, and economic contexts of the conflict (Luyet, Schlaepfer, Parlange, & Buttler, 2012; Stenseke, 2009). We will further explore these considerations in Chapter 4, where we discuss the conflict assessment process.

In relation to the social and cultural aspects of the situation, the convener should consider if the cultural dynamics of his or her organization are supportive of a collaborative effort. Government agencies, as well as other organizations have unique organizational cultures and this can either support or impede a process. Their willingness to share decision-making power and their level of respect for creative approaches to environmental problems and resource distribution must be considered (Daniels & Walker, 2001).

The culture of the local community is also a key factor in determining if a collaborative process is suitable. The success of a collaborative process is more likely if there is substantial public interest in an issue and a strong sense of commitment to place (John, 2004). For example, during the Southwestern Willow Flycatcher Habitat Designation Process, members of the community in Lake Isabella, California, who had lived in the area their whole lives, were resistant to any environmental policy that would possibly change the dynamics of their community. In protest to the habitat designation, a group of community members dressed up in bird costumes and passed out recipe books titled, *101 Ways to Eat a Southwestern Willow Flycatcher*. This strong commitment to their home became an important aspect of the meeting dynamics.

John (2004) argues that the social capacity or cultural aptitude of a community is necessary for a successful collaborative effort. Building on this idea, he argues that in communities there is often an informal network or **shadow community** of professionals who are interested in overlapping problems and have a shared understanding of complex local environmental problems. Success is more likely when local civic environmentalism includes this shadow community (John, 2004).

Related to the sociocultural dynamic is the history between the convening organization and the public. How they have interacted with different publics in the past will influence their current relationship. These histories can result in either a level of trust or distrust between them and can support or thwart a process (Siegrist, Earle, & Gutscher, 2007). For example, ranchers and real estate developers near Austin, Texas, are extremely hostile to the U.S. Fish and Wildlife Service (USFWS), and they tell horror stories about USFWS behaviors that further strengthen existing distrust. One well-known tale centers on a little old lady who died of a heart attack because the USFWS had designated her ranch as critical habitat for an endangered songbird, which meant she was no longer allowed to maintain her fences. The facts that only a small portion of the ranch had been designated as critical habitat, that the little old lady was required to alter (rather than abandon) her protocol for fence maintenance in this portion, and that she merely told a friend that she "about had a heart attack" over the issue never became part of the much-told story (Peterson & Horton, 1995).

Likewise, success is more likely when environmental professionals have worked with each other before (John, 2004). The environmental professionals in the GYC have worked across organizational lines to jointly manage numerous conflicts over the past few years. This has provided them with a solid foundation for building additional collaborations.

The legal context in which the environmental issue rests is also important to consider. Government agencies as well as other organizations are subject to rules and regulations governing how they make decisions and interact with the public. A convener should know the legal or regulatory mandates that will constrain if, or how, a collaborative effort is structured (Dietz & Stern, 2008). As discussed in Chapter 2, it is often a specific environmental law that sets forth the minimal public engagement required. However, these laws only dictate the minimal effort required and, although they govern what can and cannot be done in a process, there is oftentimes room for extended community engagement through a collaborative process. Even stakeholder consensus-based processes that are initiated by a nonprofit organization or a commercial entity may be governed by existing environmental laws. Such was the case in the PacifiCorp FERC relicensing process and the GYC processes mentioned earlier in this chapter.

It is also important to note that even if there is pending legal action between a convener and an interested party, a collaborative process can still move forward. In a transportation partnership called the Legacy Parkway Partnership, involving the design of a parkway to alleviate traffic in Northern Utah, a coalition of environmental organizations had a pending suit against the Utah Department of Transportation. The partnership resulted in a decision acceptable to all parties, but it was not until a collaborative decision had been made that the parties lifted their suit.

When stakeholders began their efforts to establish the Edwards Aquifer Recovery Implementation Plan (EARIP) in 2007 (mentioned in Chapter 2), one of the state agencies most crucial to water management in Texas was not able to participate because it was involved in a lawsuit with another organization that was participating in the RIP and the lawsuit prohibited them from interacting. Other parties moved the collaborative process forward and after the lawsuit concluded, the missing state agency joined the process. Although their late entry brought new tensions, the process continued pressing toward a mutually acceptable habitat conservation plan (HCP), which was achieved in 2013.

Pending legal action will impact a process but does not necessarily halt a process. In fact, the threat of a lawsuit can often propel those with interests in an environmental issue toward an agreement. In fact, the EARIP, which received the U.S. Department of the Interior's Partnership in Conservation Award in 2013, grew out of a lawsuit that the Sierra Club won in 1993 (Tombouctou2000, 2014). As a result of the lawsuit, the state of Texas was required to develop a plan that maintained the aquifer's spring flows and protected its endangered species by 2012. As a first step, the state established the Edwards Aquifer Authority immediately after the lawsuit. In 2007, the USFWS convened a collaborative process that grew into the EARIP. The HCP that received final approval in 2013 fulfilled the 1993 mandate, and did so in a way that involved dozens of stakeholders, ranging from large cities to environmental groups to farmers.

Environmental issues or projects never stand in isolation but respond to external political factors that influence the likelihood of a successful collaborative. For example, the U.S. Endangered Species Act (ESA) prohibits people from *taking* endangered species of fish or wildlife (Allison, 2002). Taking is defined in the ESA as "to harass, harm, pursue, hunt, shoot, wound, kill, trap, capture, or collect." As you might imagine, owners of private property worry that their property management could be limited by this broad definition. In response to these concerns, the U.S. Congress created a process to mitigate potential restrictions on private landowners whose property has been designated as critical habitat for endangered species. In many cases, this process has enabled people to develop and implement HCPs that have benefited both the endangered species and the human community (Loew, 2000). The success of these HCPs that were created to protect private property owners made them extremely popular with local governments. Because many local and state governments began embracing, supporting, and even leading these processes, some private property advocates began to fear that private property rights would be neglected. The Texas legislature responded to these concerns by passing a state law mandating that at least 33% of the members who develop the plan must own property that is either undeveloped or in agricultural use. The law also specifies additional rights for landowner members of any HCP process. The first HCP process to go forward after the new state legislation occurred in Bastrup County, Texas, where stakeholders were attempting to resolve an escalating dispute over the endangered Houston Toad (Allison, 2002). Following Texas state law, the workgroup included seven business owners, six landowners, one state agency employee, and one member of a local environmental organization. They excluded the USFWS from membership and did not include any nationally known environmental groups. Over a year after the workgroup convened, it offered the USFWS a draft plan that was rejected because it did not comply with federal law. Angry local residents gave up on the issue, claiming the failure of the process demonstrated their deeply held belief that the USFWS was unreasonable and arrogant. Eventually, the issue was turned over to a consulting company that worked with the USFWS to craft a development plan that would comply with federal law (Peterson, Peterson, Peterson, Allison, & Gore, 2006). Potential political challenges and opportunities, such as those presented in this case, must be considered before proceeding with a collaborative effort.

Finally, the economic contexts of an environmental issue must be thought through. The convener's ability to allocate sufficient resources, including both time and funding, to a collaborative process has to be weighed against the potential benefits of such a process (John, 2004). Quantifying the benefits can be difficult, but if there is not sufficient funding or support, success is unlikely.

If a preliminary analysis of the social, cultural, legal, political, and economic dynamics surrounding an environmental issue or conflict suggests a collaborative process is likely to yield a successful result, the convener should engage in a collaborative effort with clarity of purpose and commitment to process and outcomes.

Collaborative Process: General Overview

There are common dimensions of environmental conflict management (ECM) or collaborative processes that cut across different scales and types of conflicts. These dimensions call for a generic framework that can be adapted to a broad variety of environmental conflicts. Our ECM framework consists of four elements: **assessment**, **design**, **development**, and **implementation**.

Assessment

To determine what type of ECM approach is appropriate, the first step is to conduct an assessment of the conflict. The issues, key players, and potential for collaboration must be considered in light of the political climate and available science. This process is called a conflict assessment or is sometimes referred to as an issue assessment. It is a tool for generating knowledge about key players in a dispute to understand their intentions, interrelations, and interests and for assessing the influence and resources they bring to a decision making or implementation process (Dukes, Firehock, Leahy, & Anderson, 2001; Grimble, Chan, Aglionby, & Quan, 1995; Ramirez, 1999; Reed, 2008; Varasokszky & Brugha, 2000). It is an information-gathering exercise that produces recommendations regarding who has a stake in a conflict or proposed collaborative effort, the issues, potential areas of agreement and disagreement, and whether or not it makes sense to proceed and in what manner (Susskind & Thomas-Larmer, 1999).

Design

A successful approach to ECM requires innovative decision-building structures, designed with considerable attention to the incentives that they create. This step in the collaborative process involves the direct conduct of meetings, field trips, and workshops designed to promote mutual learning, innovation, constructive debate, and decision making. Design is the development of an effective process for engaging stakeholders and includes both macro- and micro-oriented approaches for creating a situation that is most likely to produce agreement on good decisions.

Development

Our preferred approach to ECM emphasizes collaboration and places significant importance on constructive and civic communication. This step in the process is characterized by using communicative and procedural skills designed to foster trust, cultivate creativity, and to enhance the decision-making process and craft solutions that produce mutual gain for all parties involved.

Implementation

In the implementation stage of ECM, it is important to understand and discuss not only how a decision will be carried out but also what challenges and opportunities may come as a result of the decision. Contingency factors that could assist or impede the future success of the process that has been designed and developed should be identified, and ways to address potential challenges should be discussed. Factors to consider include timelines, funding sources, political climates, the discovery of additional and new science, and unforeseen outside forces.

Working With a Third-Party Neutral

We strongly recommend the use of a **third-party neutral**, at least for relatively complex environmental conflicts. Convening organizations may want to serve as the third-party neutral, but there are many drawbacks to this approach. Most obvious is that each organization has a mission, which is likely to influence its agenda in any given conflict. Even if it were possible for personnel from a convening organization to isolate themselves from their employer's mission, other stakeholders are likely to remember that mission and to distrust the organization's ability to play a neutral role.

Natural resource management agencies often have extremely limited financial resources devoted to running stakeholder processes and may be tempted to save resources by playing the third-party neutral role in processes they have convened. This is rarely a good idea, because agency employees will never be perceived as neutral, no matter how hard they try. As parties with legitimate power, agencies play a key role in settling natural resource disputes and in fostering a collaborative climate especially when they are involved in the process. Turning the **facilitation** role over to a neutral third party frees the agency to honestly pursue its own goals and is advantageous to the collaborative process in general (Dietz & Stern, 2008).

Depending on the situation, the third-party neutral will function as a facilitator or mediator. The roles of facilitator and mediator are very similar, and some people use the terms interchangeably. To avoid confusion, we will differentiate between the two in this text. First, we will briefly discuss facilitation, and then we will explore **mediation** and serving as a mediator.

Facilitation

Most meetings, whether or not they are meant to respond to a conflict, could benefit from an experienced facilitator (Reed, 2008). Facilitators play a variety of roles, including (a) chairing the meeting, (b) encouraging and managing participation, (c) checking to ensure that all participants understand both content and process, (d) following up on comments, and (e) explaining the goals/objectives and expected outputs of a meeting. A good facilitator spends a significant amount of time preparing for a meeting as well as following up afterward. In addition to ensuring that all materials are properly prepared, he or she must ensure that potential meeting participants and attendees feel their needs and interests have been attended to. A facilitator should invite participants prior to the meeting, structure the discussion during the meeting, and check in with participants following the meeting (Dewulf, Francois, Paul-Wostl, & Taillieu, 2007). In addition to outstanding process skills, the best facilitators also have sufficient understanding of the scientific content to be able to follow the discussion. This does not mean, however, that the facilitator needs to be an expert in the science (Peterson, & Feldpausch-Parker, 2013). To sum up, facilitators perform a host of interrelated functions. They may guide the group process, manage meeting dynamics, organize events, monitor fiscal and budget issues, and engage in shuttle diplomacy between individual participants (Singletary et al., 2008).

Mediation

Facilitators may or may not function as mediators, depending on whether or not mediation is part of a process. Although mediations vary, when properly conducted they share the feature of having a third-party mediator who assists disputants in reaching agreement. Mediation empowers the disputants by allowing them to deal directly with neutral facilitators of their own choosing rather than with adversarial judges and lawyers who have been assigned to their case (Rieke, Sillars, & Peterson, 2012). Mediation has become a standard complement to legal systems of jurisprudence. It differs from other aspects of the legal system in how it distributes responsibility for decision making. In lawsuits and arbitration, someone else (such as a judge or an arbitrator) makes the final decision, but in mediation, the parties to the dispute retain full responsibility for decisions.

The flexibility of mediation may be the reason why some people have referred to it as the feminine face of dispute resolution (Phillips, 2001). It offers an opportunity to reframe power relationships as the parties to a dispute work together to reason through the possibilities presented by a situation. Rather than relying on power *over* their adversary, they are encouraged to envision how sharing power *with* that person may be used to craft a common enterprise that will meet everyone's needs. Participants should understand mediation as a problem-solving process where two or more people voluntarily discuss their differences and attempt to reach a joint decision. For mediation to be successful, all parties need to identify their disagreements, educate each other about their needs and interests, generate possible options, and honestly discuss the terms of any possible agreement.

Frank Dukes and his colleagues provide an excellent summary of the qualities and skills that an ethical and effective environmental mediator must develop (Dukes et al., 2001). They include (a) the ability and willingness to advocate for sustainable processes and solutions; (b) environmental literacy, or familiarity with the language and substance of environmental science and policy; (c) significant life experience; (d) commitment, integrity, and trustworthiness; (e) the ability to adopt different dispute resolution styles and behaviors; and (f) good planning and organizational capacity. If you think this seems like a lot to ask, you are correct. This is why it is a good investment for a convening organization to hire a third-party neutral.

Environmental Case Studies

Scholars in the field of environmental conflict resolution argue that case study analysis is an effective way to explore theoretical points and process steps (Dewulf, Francois, Pahl-Wostl, & Taillieu, 2007; Schon & Rein, 1994). To explore multiple management options at every stage of a collaborative process, we included six case studies that span significant breadth in terms of particular environmental conflict situations. Beginning with this chapter, each of the following chapters is dedicated to a particular aspect of environmental conflict management or step in the environmental policy development process. Each chapter includes application activities, questions, and worksheets related to the six case studies. Students will be divided into teams as they jointly explore the process of environmental conflict management. Student teams will use the same case study in each chapter and throughout the remainder of the course as they apply concepts and techniques at different stages of the collaborative process. A description of each case study along with detailed information relating to the conflict is outlined in Appendix A. Below is a general overview of each case study to aid student groups in choosing which case study they explore for the remainder of the book and course. Although the case studies are fictional (using different names for places and parties), they are based on real environmental conflicts mediated by one or both of the authors of this text.

- Case Study 1—Sandspit Watershed Committee: This case study addresses the management of salmon fishing in British Columbia, touching on issues such as endangered species, environmental justice, tourism, economic development, water quality, policy regulation, and international relations.
- Case Study 2—Woodpecker County Water Supply: This case study addresses water quality in Woodpecker County, Texas, touching on issues such as quantity, quality, use, water rights, economic development, land use planning, environmental justice, and policy regulation.
- Case Study 3—North Umpqua Hydroelectric Relicensing: This case study addresses dam relicensing in Douglas County, Oregon, touching on issues

such as energy development, endangered species, tourism, environmental justice, water flow, and policy regulation.

- Case Study 4—Cyprinus Lake Phosphorous Total Maximum Daily Load (TMDL): This case study addresses water quality assessment in rural Saline County, Georgia, and touches on issues such as development, water quality, point and non-point source pollution, agriculture, and policy regulation.
- Case Study 5—Bowcrest Mountain Ski Resort: This case study addresses ski resort development in Big Pine, North Dakota, and touches on issues such as permitting, endangered species, wildlife management, economic development, tourism, and policy regulation.
- Case Study 6—Wolf Reintroduction in the State of Minnesota: This study addresses wolf reintroduction in the state of Minnesota and touches on issues such as wildlife management, endangered species, economic development, agriculture, and environmental justice.

Case Study Application

After your team has chosen a case study, discuss as a group the sociocultural, historical, legal, political, and economic nuances of your specific case study. Based on the factors you've identified, does it make sense to proceed with a collaborative effort? Be prepared to justify your answer with sound reasoning.

Voices From the Field

Convening With the Condor Club

Matt T. Cook

Associate Librarian

California State University Channel Islands

In 2009, the County of Ventura deeded to California State University Channel Islands (CSUCI) 367 acres of underdeveloped land adjacent to the school in Camarillo, California. The university envisioned this area serving both as a classroom and a recreation area for staff, students, and faculty. Projects discussed included connecting the park and its trails to the Santa Monica Mountains Backbone Trail for hikers, a restoration study of Calleguas Creek by environmental studies students, and opening a Chumash dig site for archaeology students. The area was dubbed University Park.

However, the fact that the land was largely untouched, open, and underdeveloped made it an enticing location for Camarillo residents wishing to pursue activities not welcome in populated areas. For instance, the American Legion

(Continued)

(Continued)

routinely held a biannual turkey shoot in the area and the Camarillo Pond Rats and model boat enthusiasts used a retaining pond to host races. Perhaps the most active group was The Channel Islands Condors, a model airplane club.

The Condor Club included some 250 members in 2010 and had used their air field in University Park for 25 years prior to the university's taking over the plot. In that time, they dedicated financial and human resources to improve their area, including grading the access road, paving a runway, installing a sprinkler system, planting turf, building a concrete work area, clearing brush, and attempting to control the rodent population.

The deeding of the land to the university made them the sole body responsible for maintaining the land in a manner consistent with the university's mission. As the decision maker, the university opted to act as convener and held an open forum at the university library in February, 2012. The university used this session to note that many of the Condor Club's activities might not support some of CSUCI's desired uses. Conversely, the Condor Club explained that they were stakeholders in the process and welcomed the opportunity to address CSUCI. However, it was not clear if the initiation of this collaborative process would work due to the discrepancy between the university's vision for the park and the Condor's use.

The university recounted that between 2010 and 2012, University Park was the site of two fires, one of which was sparked by a Condor Club member's aircraft. In the summer of 2012, the office of the state fire marshal inspected University Park and found that flying planes there was not safe and issued a report stating that flying must be "discontinued until further notice due to recent fire activity at this site resulting from downed model aircraft." In August of 2012, the university informed the Condors that they were no longer able to fly, calling into question the ability for the two parties to resolve the matter collaboratively.

According to the university, the decision to close the airfield was based solely on the state fire marshal's report. "This is really a response to a report from the state fire marshal," said Ysabel Trinidad, vice president for finance and administration at CSUCI. "As a state agency, we need to comply, as we would for any kind of inspection of our facilities or grounds."

Members of the Condor Club, however, were not convinced. "My belief is, the university, rather than having an open, transparent process, has decided to use the fire marshal as a tool to uproot us from our spot out there," said Chris Spangenberg, 67, a long-time Condor and resident of Camarillo. The *Ventura County Star* editorial board added, "The discussions should involve realistic options to make it possible for the public to continue enjoying model airplanes there while the university develops its desired uses for the parkland."

The university, as convener, is committed to fostering communication between themselves and the Condor Club. On July 20th and 21st, 2013, the airfield was opened for the Condor Club and other enthusiasts for a regional competition featuring 45 pilots, the first time since August 2012. "We're thrilled they've given us permission to hold this event," said Richard Hodgson, secretary of the Channel Islands Condors. "We're actively in negotiations to get the airfield reopened, and we consider this a friendly sign from the university." Perhaps the collaborative process will yield a successful result.

Key Terms

assessment

convener

convening

design

development

facilitation

implementation

mediation

memorandum of
    understanding
    (MOU)

shadow community

third-party neutral

CHAPTER 5

Conflict Assessment

As indicated in Chapter 1, environmental policy problems are complex and specific to their social, political, and environmental contexts. Meadowcroft (2004) suggests that environmental policy problems can be distinguished by their degree of complexity and by the intensity of the associated conflict. As a conflict management professional, you need the ability to assess both the complexity and intensity of an environmental conflict. In this chapter, we will explore different approaches to **conflict assessment**. It is up to you to decide on an assessment approach that will help you to design a process that helps the parties move forward in a positive way. In their classic book, *Working Through Environmental Conflict*, Daniels and Walker (2001) remind us that successful approaches to environmental conflicts "need to be appropriate for, and responsive to, the complex, diverse, and systemic nature of those situations" (p. 154). To determine what type of approach is appropriate, the first step is to conduct an assessment of the conflict. The issues, key players, and potential for collaboration must be considered in light of the political climate and available science. This process is called a *conflict assessment* or sometimes referred to as an **issue assessment**. It is a tool for generating knowledge about key players in a dispute. This knowledge should help you understand their intentions, interrelations and interests, and it should help you determine the influence and resources each player brings to a decision-making or implementation process (Dukes, Firehock, Leahy, & Anderson, 2001; Grimble, Chan, Aglionby, & Quan, 1995; Ramirez, 1999; Reed, 2008; Varasokszky & Brugha, 2000). This information-gathering exercise should produce recommendations regarding who has a stake in a conflict or proposed collaborative effort. Susskind and Thomas-Larmer (1999) note that an effective assessment should go beyond identifying key players; it also should help you discover potential areas of agreement and disagreement, categorize central and peripheral issues, and decide whether (and how) it makes sense to proceed.

Reed et al. (2009) state that a conflict assessment

> i) defines aspects of a social and natural phenomenon affected by a decision or action; ii) identifies individuals, groups, and organizations who are affected by or can affect those parts of the phenomenon (this may include non-human and non-living entities and future generations); and iii) prioritize these individuals and groups for involvement in the decision-making process. (p. 1933)

It also helps to identify political roadblocks, develop strategies for achieving objectives, and find paths to collective agreement (Weible, 2006). Conducting a conflict assessment is essential to understanding the dynamics of the situation. If an assessment is not conducted, the convener runs the risk of leaving out a key player, missing essential elements of the situation, and wasting everyone's time by proceeding when agreement is not likely given the nature and dynamics of the issue.

Assessment Process

Who Conducts an Assessment?

The conflict assessment should be conducted by a neutral third party. A neutral third party does not have a stake in the outcome, is knowledgeable about environmental issues, and has good interviewing skills. Typically, this person is a **mediator** or **facilitator** who has been trained in communication and collaborative processes. Because the person who conducts the assessment may or may not be a mediator/facilitator, for clarity we will use the word **assessor** throughout this chapter to refer to the person who takes on this role. Having a neutral professional conduct the assessment allows those being interviewed to speak candidly about the issue without worrying about social or political repercussions. The assessor is required to keep confidential any issues or concerns requested by the interviewee. Confidentiality is necessary for those interviewed to feel comfortable and to develop trust in the assessor. The more comfortable an interviewee feels, the more honest the responses, and the better the interview will be. The conflict assessment can be conducted by an individual or team. A single interviewer can provide a more unified approach, but a team can compensate for biases and provide additional perspective (Varasokszky & Brugha, 2000). Whether the analysis is conducted by a single assessor or a team of assessors is determined by the available resources including money, personnel, and time. The nature of some conflicts also may influence the decision regarding whether a single person or a team should conduct the assessment. It is important to note that although the convener pays for the conflict assessment, that is not the same as paying for a specific outcome. For example, although the convener may want to approach the conflict in a collaborative way, the assessor may discover that collaboration is not appropriate. The assessment should be an independent analysis of the situation. This independence must be understood by the convener, the person or team conducting the assessment, and everyone who is interviewed.

Conducting an Assessment

1. Conduct background research

2. Identify key stakeholders

3. Develop an **interview instrument**

4. Contact and schedule stakeholder interviews

5. Conduct interviews

6. Synthesize findings and perform analysis

7. Assess feasibility

8. Write **conflict assessment report**

Assessment Process

A conflict assessment will vary in scope and organization depending on the issue, goals, and eventual use. However, most assessment processes contain the following steps:

1. **Conduct background research.** To understand an environmental conflict situation, the first step is to gather all documents related to the environmental situation, such as relevant news articles, press releases, published and unpublished documents, technical reports, meeting minutes, and the like. Reviewing these sources will help the assessor understand the scope of the conflict and will provide an initial sense of the issues, beyond the understanding that was shared by the convener. It can also help guide the development of questions related to the issue.

2. **Identify key stakeholders.** The second step is to identify those who have an interest in the issue. Given the complex nature of environmental conflict, there are many public and private interests with a stake in any issue. These parties, or key players, are called **stakeholders**. The term stakeholder was first recorded in 1708 as a person who holds a stake in a bet (Stanghellini, 2010). Within environmental conflict, a stakeholder is usually defined as anyone who holds an interest in something, who is affected by policy decisions, and who has the power to influence their outcome (Dietz & Stern, 2008; Freeman, 1984). In relation to environmental policy, stakeholders could be any natural resource users or managers. Stakeholders can include local, state, and/or federal government officials from multiple agencies (e.g., the Bureau of Land Management, the Forest Service, or Utah Fish and Game) or branches of government (e.g., Congress and Department of the Interior). In international disputes, conflicts can arise between governments of different countries. Stakeholders can also include a number of public interests, such as advocacy, interest or community groups, nongovernmental organizations, researchers and

scientists, technical consultants, and private interests, such as industry, commercial and other business entities, and the general public.

In the context of environmental policy decision making, it is useful to make distinctions among various stakeholders. Classification of stakeholders is a useful step in conducting an effective assessment (Stanghellini, 2010). DeLopez (2001) divides stakeholders into four categories: *key players*, those who take an active role; *context settings*, those who are highly influential but do not have interest or time to take an active role; *subject*, those who have high interest but low influence; and *crowd*, those who have little interest or influence. Mitchell, Agle, and Wood (1997) classify stakeholders in terms of urgency (of their claim), legitimacy (of their relationship), and power or influence. Using these three attributes, they identify latent (low salience), expectant (two of these attributes), or definitive (all three attributes). For example, in a conflict about running a highway through a neighborhood in the United States, stakeholders whose homes are scheduled to be demolished for the road may have the most urgent claim. Their claim may also have high legitimacy because under U.S. law, private dwellings enjoy more legal protections than a city park, or even a small business. If one of the buildings scheduled for demolition is home to a stakeholder who has served on the town council for the past 10 years, that person's power and influence may become relevant. According to Mitchell et al. (1997), our politically active stakeholder would be considered definitive and a crucial participant in any collaborative process.

Building on the ideas of influence and salience we suggest using the Overseas Development Administration (ODA, 1995) approach to categorizing stakeholders as primary, secondary, and peripheral. We define **primary stakeholders** as major players in the conflict who have direct influence on the decision-making process. Primary stakeholders can be direct, where parties interact and negotiate for themselves or for an organization, or indirect, where parties use a conflict agent (attorney, advocate, etc.) to negotiate on their behalf but retain decision-making authority. **Secondary stakeholders** are those who have vested interest in, or may be affected by, the outcome but are not necessarily involved in the collaborative process. Their interests are either already represented or beyond the scope of the policy decision. Finally, **peripheral stakeholders** are aware of the conflict but are not as likely to be directly affected by the outcome (Vella, Bowen, & Frankic, 2009).

The Edwards Aquifer Habitat Conservation Plan (HCP) that we have discussed throughout the text included all three levels of stakeholders. Primary stakeholders in this conflict included the U.S. Fish and Wildlife Service (a national-level agency that is responsible for implementing recovery plans for endangered species), the Sierra Club (an environmental organization that filed a lawsuit that served as the legal catalyst for mandating that the state of Texas implement management strategies for the aquifer that would protect the endangered species inhabiting it), and the Edwards Aquifer Authority (this state-level organization that is responsible for managing the aquifer). Secondary stakeholders included several communities that rely directly or indirectly on the aquifer for various reasons, such as its contributions to outdoor recreation or real estate development. Peripheral stakeholders include any residents of the region surrounding the Edwards Aquifer.

The convener of a process should have an initial idea of who the primary stakeholders are and can provide the mediator with a preliminary list. Secondary stakeholders are not typically interviewed unless a particular aspect of the issue has not been identified through interviews with the primary stakeholders. Additional primary stakeholders may emerge as the process continues.

3. **Develop interview instrument.** The assessment process includes interviews with stakeholders to determine their perceptions of the problem and the possibility of moving forward with a collaborative process (Carpenter, 1999). After you identify the key stakeholders, the next step is to prepare an interview protocol or list of questions to be asked of each stakeholder. The sample list below is based on suggestions by Susskind and Thomas-Larmer (1999). Note that each question is more open-ended than closed. This should allow the assessor to follow the guidance of those being interviewed when deciding where to focus the discussion. Assessors need to remember that they are learning from their interviewees and should not approach the process with too narrowly defined objectives (Varasokszky & Brugha, 2000). An assessor's list of questions might include the following:

1. What is the history of the conflict?

2. What is your role in the conflict?

3. What issues relating to this situation are important to you?

4. What other organizations or individuals have a stake in this issue?

5. What are the interests and concerns of those individuals or organizations as you understand them?

6. What is your history with the other stakeholders?

7. Have you taken any measures to address the situation?

8. Would you be willing to engage in a consensus-building process to address these issues with all interested stakeholders?

9. What is your status within your organization?

10. What additional information is needed to better understand the issue?

11. Do you have any concerns about coming to the table in a collaborative effort?

12. Do you have any logistical constraints to participating in a collaborative process?

As an assessor, you should start with these relatively generic questions, and then allow your interviewees to direct how you make the questions specific to the situation. Assessment questions should focus on understanding the substantive issues involved, the political and historical context surrounding the conflict, the perspective of the stakeholder, and their willingness to negotiate.

4. **Contact and schedule stakeholder interviews.** The next step in the assessment process is to contact the initial list of stakeholders and schedule interviews. The assessor should work with the convener to draft an introduction letter/e-mail to potential interviewees. This letter introduces the issue, introduces the process, promises confidentiality, and requests their participation in an initial interview. It is also appropriate to include a list of the general questions to be asked so the stakeholder can feel confident and prepare for the interview. After the initial letter/e-mail, the assessor then calls each stakeholder to schedule an interview. Interviews should be no longer than 30 minutes and should be conducted as soon as possible, preferably within a week after they are scheduled. Gaining access depends on how the approach is made; if stakeholders believe that their perspectives are valued and that their comments will be kept confidential they are more likely to participate. If participants are reluctant to speak with the assessor, it is a good idea to help them understand the purpose of the assessment, the independent role of the assessor, and the basics of a collaborative process so they feel more comfortable. An assessor could also point out the benefits of having their voices heard and participating in a decision-making process. If some stakeholders refuse to participate in the assessment, it is essential that the assessor accepts their refusal in a respectful manner.

Sample letter/e-mail invitation

Dear Casey Taylor,

Morgan Valley City District is interested in understanding issues surrounding the potential expansion of a parkway along Coal Creek to protect existing development from flooding and soil erosion, connect existing park and trail facilities, and provide access to natural resources along the stream in Cedar Canyon. Because it is important to the city to work directly with interested stakeholders such as yourself, we have hired Clarke Collaborative Consulting to conduct a series of confidential interviews with all affected stakeholders.

We invite you to participate in a confidential interview regarding this potential project. The purposes of stakeholder interviews will be to identify relevant stakeholders and their concerns, highlight points of agreement and disagreement, and assess the willingness of stakeholders to participate in a consensus-building process. We are hopeful that this is a first step to jointly addressing the above issue.

If you agree to an interview we will be sensitive to your busy schedule and keep the interview to 30 minutes or less. Clarke Collaborative Consulting will be contacting you shortly to arrange a meeting time.

Thank you in advance for your consideration,

Eric Winslow

Community Development Director

Morgan Valley City District

5. **Conduct interviews.** Interviews with stakeholders should be conducted in person and located at a place that is convenient for them. Interviews often take place in the stakeholder's office or a neutral place such as a coffee shop or community library. In-person interviews help to build rapport between the assessor and the stakeholder. They can also provide the assessor with nonverbal cues to supplement understanding of what is said. If the interviews cannot be conducted in person, they may be conducted by telephone, but many nonverbal cues will be lost. A third approach is to solicit e-mail responses, where still more non-verbal cues are lost. Still, the reality of some environmental conflicts may necessitate acceptance of e-mail responses from some stakeholders. Whatever media are used, the assessor should strive to obtain answers to all questions from each stakeholder.

Interviews can be conducted by an individual or a two person team (Hjortso, Christensen, & Tarp, 2005). The advantage of a team is that one person asks the questions, while the other takes notes. This frees the person asking questions to focus on the answers given by the stakeholder and to craft appropriate follow-up questions.

While some practitioners believe audio recording the interviews is inappropriate because it does not allow the interviewee to speak candidly (Varasokszky & Brugha, 2000), we have found that the advantages of recording an interview outweigh the disadvantages. The comfort level of the stakeholder depends on a number of factors, many of which can be controlled by the interviewer. Recording an interview frees the assessors to focus on what is being said. It also allows them to go back to parts of the conversation and listen again for important information. Note that it is not appropriate to record without the permission of the interviewee. All stakeholders must give permission for being recorded. If the interviews are not recorded then the person taking notes should capture main ideas and specific important quotes.

When asking questions, it is important to adhere to the protocol and ask each interviewee the same set of questions. It is appropriate to ask follow-up questions based on their responses and the interviewer should always provide them an opportunity to add any further comments. The interviewer should strike a good balance between standardization of the interviews and allowing the interviewee to guide the discussion, candidly expressing his or her thoughts about an issue (Susskind & Thomas-Larmer, 1999). At the end of the interview, the assessor should ask each stakeholder for names of others who should be interviewed (Luyet, Schlaepfer, Parlange, & Buttler, 2012). This is called *snowball sampling* (Singleton & Straits, 1999). To guard against sample bias, the assessor should specifically ask for the names of those who hold opposing viewpoints. This process of eliciting, comparing and contrasting different perceptions, and asking for nominations is repeated until no new information or categories are forthcoming is described as reaching saturation of data (Ravnborg & Westermann, 2000). It enables the assessor to determine when he or she has achieved sufficient understanding of the issue to move forward to the next step.

6. **Synthesize findings and perform analysis.** Once the appropriate stakeholders have been interviewed, the information gathered must be analyzed. Issues must be better defined, stakeholders and their relationships with each other must be

categorized, areas of agreement and disagreement must be mapped, and the feasibility of moving forward with a collaborative process must be assessed. Several different frameworks may be used for this step. In this chapter, we build primarily on Daniels and Walker's (2001) **progress triangle**, incorporating approaches drawn from others and our own experience, to outline an approach to analyzing the results of your assessment research. Daniels and Walker's (2001) progress triangle organizes the basic dimensions of all environmental conflicts: substance, relational, and procedural, and highlights the important relationships between these dimensions.

This visual representation identifies three basic dimensions of all environmental conflicts and highlights the relationships between these dimensions. The substance dimension refers to the tangible and symbolic issues, sources of tension, complexity, information needs, meanings and interpretations, and opportunities for mutual gain. The relational dimension focuses on the stakeholders, their relational histories, incentives, positions, and interests; level of trust; sources of power; knowledge and skill; and their status. Finally, the procedural dimension focuses on the logistics of a process. It answers questions about decision space, resources (e.g., time & money), jurisdiction, timing, procedural history, procedural alternatives, and procedural preferences (Walker, Daniels, & Emborg, 2008).

Substance Issue Identification

The first step is to define and break apart the primary issue and secondary issues. This definition includes a report of the history, complexity, scope, and magnitude of the conflict (Dukes et al., 2001; Susskind & Thomas-Larmer, 1999). It also includes distinguishing between issues that are tangible, such as fish passage through a dam, and those that are primarily symbolic such as the cultural significance of fish to a Native American tribe. Questions to guide this portion of the analysis might include the following:

1. What are the issues important to this situation? Are they complex? Technical?

2. Do the issues vary among the parties?

3. Which of these issues are tangible and which are primarily symbolic?

4. What are the likely sources of tension over these issues (facts, values, interests, jurisdiction, person/parties, history, and culture)?

5. Are there differences in how the major parties understand the situation, define the issues, and prioritize the issues?

6. What are the parties' interests and concerns about these issues?

7. What policies or actions have been tried in the past to deal with this situation?

8. What are the key information needs (e.g., data) or information gaps that should be addressed as part of the process?

9. Is information accessible and understandable?

10. Is the issue sufficient to warrant a collaborative effort?

Once these questions are considered, the assessor will have a better understanding of the substance of the conflict. Describing the issues and their complexity is not enough, however. The issues and their relation to each other must then be mapped so as to further understand the dynamics and opportunities for solutions. *Cognitive maps* are representations of the network of concepts people use to form arguments or to make sense of a situation. Individual maps can be synthesized and merged to show clusters of related concepts or areas of agreement or disagreement. These areas of agreement or disagreement must be charted, overlapping or divergent interests must be documented, and opportunities for mutual gain must be noted (Hjortso et al., 2005; Susskind & Thomas-Larmer, 1999; Varasokszky & Brugha, 2000).

Relational-Stakeholder Analysis

The next step entails better understanding and analyzing the stakeholders. Stakeholders must be categorized, and their relationship to each other and the convener must be evaluated. Questions that guide the categorization of stakeholders as suggested by Daniels and Walker (2001) and Dietz and Stern (2008) might include the following:

1. Who are the primary stakeholders and/or their spokespersons?

2. What are the values, interests, and cultural views of each stakeholder?

3. What are the positions and interests of each stakeholder?

4. Are there fundamental values at stake for any of the stakeholders?

5. Also are there issues of face and respect that need to be taken into account?

6. Do any parties have unique status (e.g., Indian tribes)?

7. To what degree can stakeholders act for the organizations they represent?

8. Do relevant decision-making authorities support the effort?

9. Is appropriate representation available for all interests and issues?

10. Who are the secondary stakeholders? Do they bring additional concerns?

11. Who are the peripheral stakeholders?

12. What does the scale of the issue imply for the range of affected stakeholders?

Stakeholders can be divided according to their position related to each identified issue. To fully understand the interests of each stakeholder, the assessor should move beyond basic categorization to explore how the issues impact stakeholders' sense of self or identity (Clarke, 2008; Rothman, 1997). Challenges to a stakeholder's identity can impede the collaborative process from moving forward. For example, in a conflict surrounding the storing of nuclear waste on their reservation, the Goshute Native American tribe was deeply offended by the efforts of local government officials to stop the process and considered their actions a direct insult to tribal culture and identity. This led to the tribe's refusal to engage in a collaborative process with local leaders and agency members (Clarke, 2002).

The next step is to analyze the relationship among the stakeholders. Their differences in ability, worldviews, and interests as well as their history must be taken into account (Dietz & Stern, 2008). Questions to ask include the following:

1. What are the historic relationships among the primary stakeholders?

2. Have stakeholders worked together in the past? Have there been coalitions formed?

3. What are the significant differences in values, interests, cultural views, and perspectives among the parties? And how does this affect their relationship?

Social network theory seeks to understand actor's behaviors by analyzing the types of relationships they experience and the structure of those relationships (Reed et al., 2009; Rowley, 1997). This matters to an assessor because it helps in understanding the interdependent nature of stakeholders and the web of relationships within which they are embedded (Susskind & Cruikshank, 1987). The history of cooperation or competition (Freeman, 1984; Savage, Nix, Whitehead, & Blair, 1991) among stakeholders can also shed light on the potential success of a collaborative process.

A collaborative process offers the ability to build trust over time but understanding the level of trust at the onset of a process is critical. Trust also includes the belief that stakeholders will negotiate in good faith. Questions to ask might include the following:

1. What is the degree of trust among the stakeholders? How might it be improved?

2. Is there trust that the convening organization will proceed in good faith?

3. Are the scientists viewed as partisan or objective?

4. Are there indications that some participants are likely to proceed insincerely or to breach the rules of the process?

Trust is important when considering if a situation is appropriate for a collaborative process. A successful negotiation requires that parties hold, or be able to achieve, a minimal level of trust among themselves (Dietz & Stern, 2008; O'Leary, Durant, Fiorino, & Weiland, 1999). Government agencies or other organizations with low trust are unlikely to have the level of confidence among participants that is required for a collaborative process to have success (Carlson, 1999).

In addition to trust, power or power differences among stakeholders directly influence their ability to negotiate and the potential for agreement among participants. We follow Boulding (1989) in defining *power* as the ability to get what you want or to influence a decision or decision-making process. It can come in many forms such as personal credibility and reputation, political clout, funding, access, education, communication style, culture, and so on (Dukes et al., 2001). The advocacy coalition framework assumes that the most useful unit of analysis for conducting a stakeholder analysis is the policy subsystem and focuses on access or ability to mobilize resources such as social capital, public opinion, access to information, and the like (Weible, 2006). Drawing from the advocacy coalition framework, the following questions related to power could be asked in relation to all stakeholders in a process:

1. What power resources do the primary stakeholders have?

2. Do parties have the power, resources, and capacity to work through the conflict collaboratively? Can capacity be improved?

3. Are there substantial disparities across participant groups in their power to influence the process?

4. Are there disparities in the attributes of individual stakeholders that may affect their level of influence or power? For instance, levels of education, social capital, financial, technical, or other resources that may influence participation?

Power can also manifest itself as knowledge of an issue or process. Knowledge mapping involves identifying areas of power and those relations which would work well together.

Whichever approach to power the assessor emphasizes, it is important to learn as much as possible about the power differentials between stakeholders. If the power differential is too high it will negatively impact certain stakeholders and skew the negotiations. Further, those who don't feel they have enough power or influence through a process may seek to increase their power through other strategies, such as community organizing, media outreach, referendums and initiatives, lobbying, and litigation (Elias, 2012; O'Leary et al., 1999).

Finally, stakeholders' willingness to participate in a collaborative process must be considered. If one or more primary stakeholder is not willing to come to the table, the collaboration will be negatively impacted, if not completely impeded from moving forward. Understanding their incentives to participate becomes important, because it may enable the mediator to persuade a reluctant stakeholder that their needs could be better met through a collaborative process. The following questions could help an assessor learn about stakeholder interest in collaboration:

1. Are stakeholders willing to collaborate? To what extent? Can those opposed to collaboration be persuaded to try?

2. What are the primary stakeholders' alternatives to collaboration?

3. Are there any stakeholders who have an incentive to be conflictual, or to impede progress?

Conflict professionals agree that required conditions for a collaborative process include a strong desire to solve the dispute and the willingness to enter into formal agreement should settlement be reached (Susskind & Secunda, 1998).

Procedure-Logistical Consideration

After you have identified the issues and analyzed the stakeholders and their relationships to each other, the next step is to consider the logistics or procedural dimensions of a collaborative process. Understanding the logistical details of a potential process is necessary and critical as the procedural dimension answers questions about decision space, resources (e.g., time & money), jurisdiction, timing, procedural history, procedural alternatives, and procedural preferences (Carlson, 1999; Carpenter, 1999; Dukes et al., 2001; Susskind & Thomas-Larmer, 1999). To assess the procedural feasibility, the following questions should be considered:

1. At what stage is the conflict? Does the situation seem ripe for constructive action?

2. Is there appropriate legal protection (laws and regulations) to compel fair negotiations?

3. Is a collaborative process mandated?

4. Are there drivers (incentives) for all stakeholders that can provide sufficient leverage to compel fair negotiations?

5. If not collaboration, what are the alternative methods or venues the primary stakeholders may use to pursue their goals (e.g., litigation or lobbying)?

6. Are there legal restrictions on any stakeholder's participation?

7. Are there negative attitudes toward collaboration? From whom?

8. Is sufficient time available (and allocated) to address the key issues? Are there deadlines? Can a collaborative process be conducted before the deadline?

Procedural constraints may influence the scope of authority a collaborative process may have. For example, in a NEPA process the agency with decision authority cannot legally relinquish its decision-making power. However, a collaborative process can move forward and make agreed upon recommendations to the agency. The limitations of any decision space must be disclosed at the beginning of the process (Carpenter, 1999). Additional procedural questions to ask include the following:

1. Is implementation of any agreement likely?

2. What is the decision space for the parties? What can stakeholders contribute to the policy decision?

3. What is the potential for a collaborative agreement to be trumped (blocked or overturned) by a decision authority outside the process?

4. Is a potential decision likely to be precedent setting?

Understanding the procedural constraints will help determine the potential and nature of a collaborative process.

7. **Assess feasibility.** Answering the above questions related to substance of issues, relations of stakeholders, and procedural opportunities can help determine if moving forward with a collaborative process is feasible. If the dynamics are such that agreement is unlikely, then moving forward with a collaborative process is not in the best interest of the convener or stakeholders. In relation to the substance of the conflict, if issues are too complex or technical, if they are framed as a deeply rooted moral issue, or if there are few areas of potential agreement and no obvious areas to work on, then moving forward may be too much of a risk (O'Leary & Bingham, 2003). If there are deeply entrenched and polarized positions, irreconcilable differences, a contentious history, mistrust, hostility, low incentive, lack of support, and/or huge power imbalances among stakeholders then consensus is unlikely (Clarke, 1999, 2002). In relation to procedural constraints, if one or more key stakeholders refuse to participate, if there are unrealistic deadlines, no funding, or no legislative pressure to engage in a consensus-based process, then moving forward with a collaborative process is not the best course of action (Susskind & Thomas-Larmer, 1999). If relational, procedural, and substantial factors can be improved to increase collaborative potential, there may still be the possibility of moving forward, but it is the job of the assessor to give a realistic appraisal of the likelihood a collaborative process will yield positive results. If agreement is not feasible, the assessor should make known in a report that moving forward with a collaborative process is not a reasonable alternative.

8. **Write a conflict assessment report.** After analyzing the nuances of the conflict situation and assessing the feasibility of moving forward with a collaborative effort, the next step is to document the findings and provide a recommendation to the convener in a conflict assessment report.

When writing the report, the assessor must present issues in a synthesized, neutral, and confidential manner. It is important not to jeopardize your neutrality or share specific information a stakeholder may want to keep confidential (Carlson, 1999). For example, when presenting issues, an accurate description of the nuances of each issue organized by stakeholder category such as government, special interest group, or commercial interest can outline concerns without attributing them to a specific stakeholder. The purpose of the assessment report is to set forth a range of ideas, not to polarize the conflict in any way.

The structure of the report should be constructed and organized efficiently. The specific order and level of detail will be determined by the nuances of the environmental conflict but as a general guideline, a conflict assessment report should include the following sections: (a) executive summary (for longer reports), (b) introduction (to the report), (c) background information (of the conflict), (d) findings and analysis, and (e) recommendation. Organizing the report in such a manner will provide clarity and support the assessor's recommendation.

Report Outline

Conflict assessment report

    1) Executive summary

    2) Introduction (to the report)

    3) Background information

        History of conflict and introduction to issue

    4) Findings and analysis issues

        Stakeholders

        Areas & level of agreement / disagreement

        Opportunities and challenges

    5) Recommendation

        Level of engagement

In the report, the analysis of each dimension (substance, relational, and procedural) should be clearly articulated, as well as the areas of agreement and disagreement. Challenges and opportunities should also be clearly defined. It is often a good idea to organize information visually by a matrix or Venn diagram (ODA, 1995; Reed, 2008). For example, stakeholders identified by categories such as government, nonprofit organization, interest groups, and/or commercial interests could be placed on a matrix according to their relative interest and influence on a given issue. Another possibility is mapping the issues according to levels of agreement or disagreement, outlining opportunities for mutual gain. Finally, the assessor's recommendation as to whether or not a collaborative process is feasible should be noted and the suggested level of effort or engagement outlined. This may also include basic suggestions for public or community outreach to engage peripheral stakeholders and the general public.

In addition to the convener, a copy of the conflict assessment report should be given to each primary stakeholder interviewed. With its detailed analysis of the issues, it provides the parties with an impartial map of the underlying conflicts that will need to be addressed. Seeing their own interests represented in a neutral manner can be validating to stakeholders and can help widen their perspective regarding possible options for addressing differences.

If the assessment yields a positive recommendation to commence with a collaborative process, the convener then decides to initiate a process and works with the mediator to design a process that will help meet project goals and engage stakeholders and the public. The next chapter (Chapter 6) outlines the guiding principles, strategies, and mechanisms for engaging stakeholders and the general public in environmental policy development.

Considering Culture

Using Cultural Dimensions to Improve Assessment

The *dimensions of culture* is a framework for cross-cultural communication, introduced by Hofstede in 1984. Hofstede originally proposed four dimensions along which cultural values could be analyzed: individualism/collectivism, uncertainty/avoidance, power/distance (strength of social hierarchy), and masculinity/femininity (task orientation versus person orientation). He later added two more dimensions: long-term orientation versus short-term orientation and indulgence versus self-restraint (Hofstede, 1984, 2001). Building on Hofstede, Lebaron and Pillay (2006) argue that the dimensions of culture can be viewed as guiding lights displayed on a continuum to help decode cultural ways of making meaning during conflict resolution processes. The following cultural dimensions are especially useful in assessing environmental conflict.

Individualism/Collectivism

Cultures with more individualistic perspectives value self-reliance, autonomy, and independence where individuals are accountable for their own choices. Identity comes from individual efforts toward personal growth, and competition is encouraged. Cultures with a more collectivistic view value cooperation, group harmony, and cohesion. Groups hold primary responsibility for decisions. Identity comes from interdependence within the group and is directly related to the reputation of the group. For example, the collaborative potential of a conflict over forest management in Sikkim, India, needs to be assessed within the collectivist cultural context of the region. Residents may be hesitant to engage in a process they fear could endanger the fragile harmony they have crafted over many generations.

Low-Power Difference/High-Power Difference

The cultural dimension of power difference highlights the degree of deference and acceptance of unequal power between people. High-power distance cultures accept that some people are superior to others because of their social status, which is often based on gender, race, age, formal education, or family lineage. Hierarchical structures are accepted and the special privileges awarded to those with more power are not questioned. This often leads to acceptance of an autocratic decision-making process. In low-power distance cultures, status and authority are less permanent. Additionally, although differences in achievement and status may be recognized, these differences do not translate into decision-making

(Continued)

(Continued)

authority. In these cultures, equality and shared power are supported as part of the desired democratic decision-making process. Conflicts over forest management in Sikkim, for example, have developed within a relatively high-power distance culture, where family lineage is recognized as fundamental to a person's decision-making status. Residents are accustomed to granting authority to people with certain family names, rather than to those with other family names.

When assessing collaborative potential, it is important to consider how these dimensions of culture interact rather than thinking about them in isolation. In the example given above, villagers may express disapproval for illegal forest harvesting by their fellow residents in a private interview, but be unwilling to express their displeasure in a group setting because they fear the resulting exchange could damage group harmony. They may accept a hierarchic decision structure, but only so long as the decision makers have demonstrated that they are acting in the best interests of the community. In this case, collaborative potential is strengthened to the degree that community members with high social status have used their authority to support policies that seem to improve conditions throughout the community. On the other hand, collaborative potential is weakened to the degree that those with high social status have used their authority to support policies that seem to favor the interests of some individuals over others.

Case Study Application

Questions/Worksheets and Activities:

Referring to your chosen case study in Appendix A, conduct a conflict assessment and write a report of your analysis. The following steps will help guide you in your analysis:

1. History of Conflict—Discuss as a group the history of the conflict. What primary and secondary sources are available? How has the conflict been framed in the past? As a group, begin your assessment report by writing a background information section including the history of the conflict and a brief introduction to the issues.

2. Identify Key Stakeholders—List the stakeholders. An initial list of stakeholders is provided for you in Appendix A. Categorize your stakeholder list according to their type (government agency, interest group, industry, etc.) and their relationship to the issue: primary, secondary, and peripheral. Building on this list, identify additional key stakeholders and their potential concerns making sure all potential interests are represented.

3. Develop an Interview Instrument—Guided by the history of the conflict and your initial understanding of the issue, develop an interview instrument or list of questions to be asked of each stakeholder. Be sure to develop open-ended questions that will engage the participants and provide insight into the conflict.

4. Contact and Schedule Stakeholder Interviews—Your next step is to write an introductory e-mail/letter inviting stakeholders to participate in an interview. This letter should identify the issue, explain the assessment process, and invite the stakeholder to participate.

5. Conduct the Stakeholder Interview—Because your case study is fictional, you will not conduct an interview with an outside stakeholder, but practice your interviewing skills by conducting a role-play with members of your group, where one individual is the interviewer and another the interested stakeholder.

6. Synthesize Findings and Perform Analysis—Using Daniels & Walker's (2001) progress triangle explained in this chapter, conduct an analysis of the substance, relational, and procedural elements of the issue. Using the suggested questions (or additional ones developed by your group) discuss as a team each aspect of the conflict: issues, relationship, procedures, and how they relate to each other. Continue your analysis by synthesizing your findings.

7. Assess Feasibility—Based on your discussion, write your recommendation regarding the potential for collaboration. This should include justifications based on your analysis.

8. Write a Conflict Assessment Report—Document your analysis and recommendation by providing a full detail assessment report (see outline above).

Voices From the Field

The Grand/Neosho River Committee (GNRC)

James Triplet

Professor of Biology

Pittsburg State University

In the spring of 1993, the Kansas Oklahoma Flood Control Alliance (KOFCA), whose membership consisted primarily of landowners immediately upstream, downstream, and those along the shoreline of the Grand Lake O' Cherokees, were concerned with management of water levels in the lake. Failure to release water through the flood gates in an attempt to use all of the water for hydropower generation would create a backwater effect upstream when the lake was full, inundating valuable properties and marinas on the lake when the water went into the flood pool, washing out downstream riparian owners, threatening the integrity of the dam and forcing an opening of the flood gates. KOFCA had approached the flood control managers, the U.S. Army Corps of Engineers (USACE) and the reservoir operators, the Grand River Dam Authority (GRDA), but had been summarily dismissed by both, with GRDA commenting they would run the system the way GRDA wanted and KOFCA did not have enough political clout to do anything about it. As a result, KOFCA filed a lawsuit against the USACE and GRDA. In an

(Continued)

(Continued)

effort to avoid the litigation, congressional leaders in Kansas (Senator Nancy Kassebaum and Senator Bob Dole) and Oklahoma (Senator David Boren, Senator Don Nickles, and Representative Mike Synaur) organized an interstate committee to review the issues and make a recommendation. The GNRC consisted of 40 congressional appointees from Kansas, Missouri, and Oklahoma with the USACE and GRDA assigned as ex-officio technical support.

While there was no funding set aside for the committee, congressional staffers initially took turns helping with clerical work and postage, but the committee took that over as it developed, with most agency and industry representatives contributing to the costs. The USACE mostly provided technical presentations and facility tours, while the GRDA helped with meeting logistics and meals, mostly lunches. At the outset, there was a high level of animosity between several members of KOFCA and GRDA as a result of the dismissive treatment by the GRDA Board and the Executive Director. In fact, some members of KOFCA refused to be in the same room with members of GRDA and refused to accept any meals. Over time, that was defused and people could sit and visit amicably. The focus of GRDA's members at the time was hydropower production, and they believed their position was the only one of merit. One of the industry representatives pulled out of the committee when it became clear this was going to be a democratic process and his group would be unable to run roughshod over the proceedings.

Initial meetings were set aside to hear from the stakeholders and identify the issues, which expanded beyond flood control (above and below) to include recreation, water quality/supply, navigation, hydropower, upstream erosion, and wildlife. Subcommittees were formed to address each of these issues, with the charge to develop their position relative to water level management in the system. The full committee met monthly for nearly 3 years and reached a consensus on a water level management plan (guide curve) that gave some recognition to the concerns of the stakeholders. The recommendation in the final report was approved by the Federal Energy Regulatory Commission (FERC) and adopted by the USACE and GRDA in 1996. The Oklahoma Department of Wildlife Conservation (ODWC) quit participating in the final stages of deliberation as their concerns about being able to meet one of their goals was not gaining traction in the process. After the final report was sent to FERC, ODWC attempted to do an end run to get FERC to disapprove the recommendation, but FERC sided with the committee. That guide curve has withstood numerous efforts to change it and is still in use today.

Key Terms

assessor	mediator	relational-stakeholder analysis
conflict assessment	peripheral stakeholder	
conflict assessment report	primary stakeholder	secondary stakeholder
facilitator	procedure-logistical consideration	stakeholder
interview instrument	progress triangle	substance issue identification
issue assessment		

CHAPTER 6

Design:
Stakeholder Process

After you have assessed the potential for a collaborative approach to the conflict, the next step is to design a process that will help you meet your project goals. To accomplish this, your process must engage stakeholders and the public in joint efforts to develop sound environmental policy decisions. This step is most likely to be successful if approached with an innovative mindset. As a process designer, you must build structures that provide a broad variety of incentives for stakeholder participation. It involves planning and designing meetings, field trips and workshops, open houses, and other activities intended to promote mutual learning, innovation, constructive debate, and decision making. At the same time, you need to keep an eye on the bigger picture, so participants don't get trapped in the details. Ideally, your design will help all participants negotiate between the broad system-level questions and their individual concerns.

Managing environmental conflict also requires that you look beyond the process to the interconnected biophysical and sociopolitical systems that have given rise to the dispute. As we noted in the first chapter, one of the characteristics of environmental conflicts is that they encompass both natural and social systems. You do not want to design and facilitate a process that leads to more positive interpersonal relations between stakeholders but encourages development of poor environmental decisions. This is a real possibility and one you must guard against. Of course, your emphasis should be on the process, and there is considerable evidence that when it comes to environmental management, "the quality of a decision is strongly dependent on the quality of the process that leads to it" (Reed, 2008, p. 2421). Although you cannot guarantee positive results, you can certainly offer a reasonable likelihood that a well-designed collaborative process will contribute to good environmental decisions.

This chapter outlines who designs a process, provides guiding principles for the development of a thorough process, outlines the steps in the design process, and develops a stakeholder plan. The chapter concludes with information on how to develop a stakeholder plan and direction to apply the concepts to your chosen case study introduced in Chapter 4.

Who Designs the Process?

The neutral third party, either the person who conducted the conflict assessment or a member of that person's team, is typically the one who designs the collaborative and community engagement process. Having firsthand knowledge of the issues and concerns of the stakeholders enables that person to design a process that addresses those concerns and provides opportunities for primary, secondary, and peripheral stakeholder input. It is important, however, to get buy-in and project ownership by having the process ratified and approved by the participants.

In Chapter 5, we discussed the need to distinguish between different stakeholders, and we suggested labeling them as primary, secondary, and peripheral. When designing a community engagement process, it is necessary to consider these different groups and how a convener might best engage them in a policy development or decision-making process. Throughout this book, we distinguish between **stakeholder engagement**, which engages primary stakeholders directly in environmental policy decision making, and **public involvement**, which involves secondary and peripheral stakeholders, what many people describe as the general public. This chapter outlines the principles and offers specific steps that should guide a stakeholder engagement process, and the following chapter focuses on a public involvement process and ways to involve secondary/peripheral stakeholders, or the general public.

Guiding Principles of Design

Susan Senecah (2004) offered the metaphor of a *trinity of voice* as a guiding principle in designing policy development processes. Senecah's trinity addresses the need for all stakeholders to have a meaningful role in determining the political future of their communities and offers a guide for engaging communities in socially legitimate policy development. Voice, argues Senecah, is comprised of three critical elements; **access, standing**, and **influence**. Access, the first element, begins with ensuring the availability of information to all potential stakeholders. Generally, this can be accomplished by providing opportunities for education and learning. Standing, the second element, refers to civic legitimacy. Senecah is not referring to the legal meaning of standing that we explained in Chapter 3. Rather, she is referring to the trust and mutual respect that emerge when all potential stakeholders have the opportunity to actively participate in decision-making processes. Finally, influence refers to authentic ability to make a difference. While this does not necessarily mean the final decision will be what we would have chosen, it does mean that our choices will be given serious consideration (Senecah, 2004). The trinity of voice (TOV) is a useful framework when designing collaborative processes so stakeholders and the general public are encouraged to provide input and provide citizens with the ability to be empowered.

Access

Access to information and every aspect of the process are at the core of stakeholder engagement and public involvement in environmental decisions (Blackstock, Waylen, Dunglinson, & Marshall, 2012; Cox, 2006; Depoe & Delicath, 2004; Dietz & Stern, 2008; Ozerol & Newig, 2008; Webler, 1995). Information must be honest, timely (early and often in the process), and communicated with good-faith intentions. The process of decision making and plans for how information will be used must also be transparent or, in other words, must be clearly communicated. Transparency is a hallmark of good stakeholder engagement and public involvement (Arnstein, 1969; Blackstock et al., 2012; Dietz & Stern, 2008; Johnson & Dagg, 2003; Lockwood, 2010; Ozerol & Newig, 2008; Rauschmayer, Berghofer, Omann, & Zikos, 2009; Rauschmayer & Wittmer, 2006; Reed, 2008; Webler, Tuler, & Krueger, 2001).

Access also refers to appropriate support such as resources and includes education (Leventhal, 2006) and capacity building so stakeholders have the technical capability to engage effectively (Blackstock, Kelly, & Horsey, 2007; Burger, Harris, Harper, & Gochfeld, 2010; Carlson, 1999; Chase, Decker, & Lauber, 2004; Daniels & Walker, 2001; Ramirez, 1999; Tippett, Handley, & Ravetz, 2007; Wondolleck & Yaffee, 2000). Dietz and Stern (2008) describe capacity building as

> 1) becoming better informed and more skilled at effective participation; 2) becoming better able to engage the best available scientific knowledge and information about diverse values, interests, and concerns; and 3) developing a more widely shared understanding of the issues and decision challenges and a reservoir of communication and mediation skills and mutual trust. (p. 2)

While access alone is not enough, it forms the basis for voice and is critical to any policy development process.

Standing

Standing, or civic legitimacy, involves respect and the authentic consideration of stakeholders' perspectives. It requires the fair inclusion of diverse individuals in the decision-making process and is the basis for environmental justice. An appropriate collaborative process must offer social, cultural, and political legitimacy to a sufficiently wide range of knowledge and experience relating to the conflict being considered (Blackstock et al., 2007; Carpenter, 1999; Gunton, Day, & Williams, 2003; Lockwood, 2010; Ostrom, Burger, Field, Norgaard, & Policansky, 1999; Rauschmayer & Wittmer, 2006; Stringer, Reed, Dougill, Rokitzki, & Seely, 2007; Webler, 1995). A legitimate process is one that both observers and participants believe is fair (Dietz & Stern, 2008). Without ensuring standing for at least those who would be considered primary stakeholders, there is little possibility that a collaborative process will be accepted as legitimate.

Influence

Access and standing are mutually dependent on each other, and both are necessary to achieve influence. Influence does not mean that all participants get exactly what they want. Rather, it refers to the respectful consideration of the concerns and ideas of all participants and awareness that all parties have the potential to help determine the outcome of a policy decision (Chase et al., 2004; Dietz & Stern, 2008; Parkins & Mitchell, 2005; Rauschmayer et al., 2009; Rauschmayer & Wittmer, 2006; Senecah, 2004; Stringer et al., 2007; Tippett et al., 2007; Walker, Senecah, & Daniels, 2006).

Voice Leads to Trust

When all interested stakeholders have access, standing, and influence in policy and program development, greater trust is established, which is the foundation for socially legitimate policy development and effective programming (Beierle & Cayford, 2002; Bingham, 2006; Parkins & Mitchell, 2005; Senecah, 2004). Just as in the assessment phase outlined in Chapter 4, when designing collaborative processes, it is important to consider the level of trust between the convening organization and the different stakeholders. Participants have histories with each other and with the organization responsible for convening the process and making environmental policy decisions. Those histories provide both challenges and opportunities for how best to manage the conflict.

Depending on the historical and institutional context, a designer will encounter mutual trust that provides support for the process, or distrust that thwarts the process (Siegrist, Earle, & Gutscher, 2007). If the convener is an organization with low public credibility and trust, a designer is unlikely to find the level of confidence among participants that is required to enable a process to succeed (Carlson, 1999; Dietz & Stern, 2008).

In their research on trust in government agencies, Beierle and Cayford (2002) identified five indicators of preexisting trust in government agencies: (1) the reputation of the agency with the public, (2) the reputation of the agency with primary stakeholders, (3) a history of withheld information, (4) a history of unacceptable management, and (5) a history of ignoring management problems. Numbers 3, 4, and 5 on their list identify specific actions that can either build or destroy trust. You may have noticed that these actions are similar to the components of voice identified by Senecah (2004). Bierle and Cayford's (2002) indicators suggest that trust is cultivated by the open sharing of correct information (access), involvement in decision making (standing) and responsiveness when problems are identified (influence).

How the process is designed and conducted can further strengthen existing relationships, provide voice for the community, and build trust. The number of meetings, their formal structure, how they are conducted, the timing and location, and other logistical details all communicate the relative power status of participants and the intentions of the convener.

For example, in a Bureau of Land Management (BLM) resource management plan (RMP) for Moab, Utah, the designation of wilderness was controversial. In order to give members of the community voice while respecting the role of BLM agency members, the meetings were designed in a workshop format with different stations representing various related interests, such as grazing, off-road vehicle use, and so on. This allowed community members to give direct input about the issues that were important to them while not allowing grandstanding and showboating in a large group setting. The burden is on the process designer to understand power dynamics and design a process that provides voice for stakeholders and motivates participants to work within a given process (Dietz & Stern, 2008).

Design Process

Develop Project Goals

With the TOV as a guiding principle, the convener and the designer should develop the specific goals of the project (Susskind & Thomas-Larmer, 1999; Wondolleck, Manring, & Crowfoot, 1990). Project goals will determine the level of engagement and types of activities in the design process. For example, suppose a creek flowing through Pittsburgh, Pennsylvania, has repeatedly failed to meet the water quality standards mandated by the EPA for its designated use. The Pennsylvania Department of Environmental Protection, which is mandated to ensure water quality standards throughout the state, will be the convening organization. If the department hires you to develop a public process, you need to know what their goal is. If they simply want to clean up the water sufficiently to meet federal pollution requirements, you will want to minimize the resources spent engaging stakeholders in coming up with new ideas. Instead, your process should focus on ensuring that all primary stakeholders have access to relevant information, that they have an opportunity to share their opinions related to the technological approach proposed, and that the state agency listens and responds to all relevant suggestions offered by stakeholders. A solid information sharing process may be sufficient.

On the other hand, even assuming the same environmental conditions, the social situation could generate a very different project goal. If the state's Game Commission determined that the creek could provide habitat for a popular sport fish and Pittsburgh's planners were interested in developing additional outdoor recreation opportunities to enhance residents' quality of life, the conflict suddenly becomes more complicated. Perhaps multiple agencies will serve as co-conveners. Some of the primary stakeholders are likely to seek more than the minimum federal requirements for water quality, perhaps even changing the creek's designated use to *fishable/swimmable*. As a conflict professional, you will need to work carefully with the convening organization/s to determine clear project goals. Based on these goals, you probably will need to design a process that engages stakeholders in actually coming up with management options that have not previously been considered. You will probably want to design a process that engages primary stakeholders more deeply than in the previous example, ideally moving to the level of collaboration.

Building on Luyet, Schlaepfer, Parlange, and Buttler (2012) and others, we suggest distinguishing four levels of engagement. The first level is **information sharing**. This refers to providing one-way transfer of information and data about a project to stakeholders and the general public. The next level of engagement is **consultation**. This refers to presenting the project to stakeholders and the public and then collecting their suggestions and input to influence decision making. Information exchange is a two-way process in a consultation process. The third level of engagement is **collaboration**. This refers to presenting the project to stakeholders and then soliciting their direct involvement in the decision-making process. In a collaborative process, stakeholder engagement is iterative and interactive. The fourth level is **empowerment**. This refers to complete delegation of decision making over project development and implementation to stakeholders.

To illustrate the different levels of engagement, we provide examples of each. An example from India demonstrates information sharing as engagement. Villagers living along the forest edges of East Sikkim, India, for example, have been told that entering the forest is prohibited and they may no longer use forest products. The villagers are not familiar with the national laws that have led to their expulsion from the forest and have no idea why they have been banned from using forest products. They are angry with the foresters and the central government they represent. Although they are fearful of the harsh penalties for entering the forest, they do not necessarily follow the law. Instead, they time their forays into the forest to match the frequent absence of the foresters, hoping they will not be caught. Both broad cultural patterns and specific historical events identified in the conflict assessment have made it clear that villagers are not willing to sit together in a meeting with the foresters. Additionally, the foresters have no decision authority on this topic; they are simply enforcers. Some of the villagers have expressed an interest in learning what the law is, but written materials will not be useful because most of the villagers do not read. As a first step, the facilitator worked with the forest agency to write a relatively short and simple summary of the forest law. Then, with the permission of the agency, she attended village gatherings, where she requested an opportunity to read the summary. Some of the gatherings have followed up by inviting foresters to attend the village gathering, for the purpose of answering questions about the law.

An example of consultation can be found in Florida with the Florida Department of Transportation. One of the issues limiting real estate development in the Florida Keys is human safety during hurricane evacuations. In order to allow more residential development, the state of Florida needed to expand the transportation corridor. Florida Department of Transportation (FDOT) determined that the most effective way to do this was to widen the highway running from the mainland. At the same time, the Florida Keys provide critical habitat for a host of endangered species.

Widening the highway would destroy some of that habitat and would likely result in more deaths as wildlife crossed the highway, traveling from one part of their habitat to another. Faced with this dilemma, FDOT came up with a plan to elevate part of the highway and put in underpasses for the wildlife. They also asked the county government to purchase vacant lots that could be used to mitigate acreage loss. Facilitators guided meetings where FDOT presented their plan to local residents, relevant federal agencies, other state agencies, and the county. They then incorporated feedback from these stakeholders into the final plan for expanding the highway.

In a collaborative effort to develop on-farm and system water conservation measures to deliver 103,000 acre feet of water annually to San Diego Water Authority, the Imperial Valley Irrigation District created a technical advisor team with the charge of developing an incentive package to engage farmers to implement water conservation measures. Farmers in the area were directly involved in the development of incentives and the final decision implemented by the Imperial Valley Irrigation District.

An example of sea turtles in El Salvador highlights an empowered level of engagement. Hawksbill sea turtles are highly endangered in the eastern Pacific Ocean, yet their eggs continue to be an important subsistence resource for impoverished coastal residents in El Salvador. The three principal hawksbill nesting sites in El Salvador represent the largest known hawksbill nesting aggregation in the eastern Pacific Ocean. When turtles lay these eggs, local residents collect and sell them. International conservation groups have attempted to stop the sale of turtle eggs by pressuring the Salvadoran government to make it illegal to collect, sell, and buy eggs. Although the new law has ignited small bursts of violent protests, its contributions to conservation have been limited; the central government simply lacks the resources for enforcement. Recognizing that support from local residents is required for turtle conservation to succeed, several of these organizations provided financial support for developing a process to involve local residents. A conflict assessment suggested that, although local residents deeply distrusted the central government, they recognized that sea turtles could be important to future development in the region. Further, they were willing to work hard at something they believed would contribute to both turtle conservation and community development. Facilitators designed a process that encouraged local residents to envision, plan, and then implement a turtle conservation program that fit well with local culture. The result was an annual sea turtle festival that now involves many local residents, as well as other Salvadorans who had not previously thought of themselves as conservationists.

Choose Process Approach

Because collaborative processes can be applied in so many different contexts, there are numerous possibilities that could be used in any situation. Although there are numerous tool kits, best practices, and individual techniques, you will need to sift carefully through them to determine which are appropriate for a particular conflict. As a designer, you will need to customize your approach to fit the unique circumstance of each situation. This customization process should be guided by your consideration of dimensions such as the objectives, type of participants, and desired level of engagement (Reed, 2008).

Collaborative processes have been labeled in many different ways throughout the literature, indicating different purposes or levels of decision-making power. Some are official names, such as a technical advisory committee (TAC) whose charge it is to advise on technical aspects of a given project. Other names, such as *joint fact-finding process*, are coined by various authors or conflict professionals. An explanation of each approach is provided below as well as outlined in Figure 6.1.

Policy Dialogue Process

In a **policy dialogue process**, representatives of groups with divergent views or interests are assembled to generate discussion and improve communication and mutual understanding as they seek to exchange information and build consensus recommendations between the public, private, and civic sectors. For example, in the Utah Lake Total Maximum Daily Load (TMDL) process, community members, farmers, and developers in the Provo Valley were brought together to discuss point source pollution and amount of pollutants allowable in a fresh water stream. While the decision concerning the TMDL remained with the Department of Environmental Quality, the perspectives of stakeholders were valued and helped shape the final decision.

Technical Advisory Committee (TAC)

Technical advisory committees are groups made up of technical experts, environmental advocates, and other interested stakeholders that a government agency brings together to discuss particulars about a specific project. For example, the Los Angeles County Transportation Commission has developed a TAC to provide technical assistance to Metro by reviewing and evaluating the various transportation proposals and alternatives within Los Angeles County.

Citizen's Advisory Committee

A **citizen's advisory committee** (CAC) is similar to a TAC but composed of individuals chosen to reflect different segments of the community and is focused on soliciting input from diverse interests in a community, who may or may not have technical expertise about a specific project. The committee provides recommendations to the sponsoring authority on issues. For example, CACs have been convened to advise the Department of Energy (DOE) about the concerns of citizens living near temporary nuclear waste storage sites. Although they do not have the authority to make decisions, they are able to identify potential issues that the DOE may not realize are important to a community.

Monitoring Committees

This type of committee seeks to engage interested and affected stakeholders, public agencies, and scientific and technical experts in a variety of roles, such as determining target outcomes, defining criteria and indicators to monitor those outcomes, determining the appropriate system for monitoring, participating in data gathering and analysis, and interpreting data over time. For example, the Rhode Island Coastal Resources Management Council, in partnership with The University of Rhode Island, the Coastal Resources Center, Minerals Management Service, the U.S. Army Corps of Engineers, other state agencies, industry, nonprofit groups, and stakeholders, employs spatial planning techniques to regulate appropriate uses through its statewide zoned waters and through a series of place-based special area management plans developed by the group.

Natural Resource Partnerships

Informal working groups organized around regions with natural recourse concerns such as the use of rangelands, forests and water resources, or protection of wildlife, watersheds, and the like are often called **natural resource partnerships**. Organized in 1992, the Applegate Partnership in northern California is one of the earliest models of natural resource collaboration. After years of conflict among ranchers, government, loggers, and environmentalists, the BLM initiated conversations with community interests.

> The Applegate Partnership is a community-based project involving industry, conservation groups, natural resource agencies, and residents cooperating to encourage and facilitate the use of natural resource principles that promote ecosystem health and diversity. Through community involvement and education, the partnership supports the management of all lands within the watershed in a manner that sustains natural resources and that will, in turn, contribute to economic and community stability within the Applegate Valley. (Wondolleck & Yaffee, 2000, pp. 140–141)

What makes natural resource partnerships unique is that they are long term and ongoing.

Community-Based Collaboration

A **community-based collaboration** involves individuals and representatives of affected groups, businesses, or other agencies in addressing a specific or short-term problem in the local community. The collaborative groups often operate by consensus (although not always) as they identify goals and issues of concern, form sub-working groups to investigate alternatives, and seek support for solutions. They are voluntary associations and operate without legal sanction or regulatory power. Community-based collaborations are different in that they tend to focus on specific, local problems that involve a shorter time frame. Residents who live in a small village and along the banks of Lake Tämnarån in Sweden became concerned that their lake was shrinking and the water quality was suffering. They formed a voluntary association for the purpose of trying to identify causes for the problem and then to explore options for correcting it. The association has no formal decision-making authority, but it presents recommendations to both the local village council and regional natural resource agency.

Environmental Mediation/Conciliation

This process involves efforts by a third party to improve the relationship between two or more disputants in an environmental conflict. The third party works with the disputants to correct misunderstandings and generally improve communication between them. In the early 1990s, the California Regional Water Quality Board, Los Angeles Region, began to identify sources of groundwater contamination in the Azusa/Baldwin Park area. Azusa Pipe and Tube Bending was named as a potential responsible party and a suit was filed by the Environmental Protection Agency against them in the late 1990s. Representatives from Azusa Pipe and Tube Bending did not believe the evidence was conclusive and the legal conflict between the two continued until the summer of 2006, when the issue was settled through a mediation process. Through mediation, they were able to come to an agreement on the nature, cause, and cleanup of the groundwater contamination.

Negotiated Rule Making

Negotiated rule making became official after Congress passed the Negotiated Rulemaking Act of 1990. The convener (usually a government agency) develops a proposed rule by using a neutral facilitator and a negotiating committee composed of representatives of all interests that the rule is likely to affect. Negotiated rule making is intended to be a consensus-based process. When properly conducted, it can lead to better, more acceptable rules—rules that account for the concerns of all potential stakeholders. It is especially useful when the convening organization itself has responsibilities that seem to conflict. For example, the U.S. National Park Service (NPS) used negotiated rule making to help work through the issue of off-road vehicle use at Cape Hatteras Seashore. Given that the NPS is equally responsible for preserving natural resources and supporting their enjoyment by the public, it was important for them to respond to the demands of multiple user groups, including those who opposed any limit on vehicle use on the beach and those who opposed any use of vehicles on the beach.

Joint Fact Finding

Joint fact finding is a process to address scientific or technical issues or needs within a collaborative process. Members of the process pool relevant information or identify information needs, solicit data from an agreed upon source, and jointly craft the objectives and standards to evaluate and apply the data. The piping plover is an endangered shorebird that inhabits coastal areas of the United States from North Carolina to Texas. When the U.S. Fish and Wildlife Service was faced with the need to balance their legal responsibility to work toward recovery of the piping plover and public demands for continued access to National Park Service lands, they engaged conflict professionals to organize joint fact-finding forums to provide information to citizens about the piping plover and to provide citizen feedback regarding concerns and questions.

Within any process there may be other activities designed to assist participants with information gathering or decision making.

Training

Increasing the knowledge base of participants in conflict management, communication, or law is an excellent way to level the playing field if there exists different collaborative capacity or knowledge about an issue (Carlson, 1999; Daniels & Walker, 2001; Leventhal, 2006; Ramirez, 1999; Susskind & Thomas-Larmer, 1999; Wondolleck & Yaffee, 2000). When the U.S. Fish and Wildlife Service convened a group of stakeholders to initiate the Edwards Aquifer Recovery Implementation Program in Texas, the facilitator designed the process to begin with formal training in collaborative learning techniques. During the ensuing months, stakeholder meetings also included short minitrainings, and these trainings were always linked back to the full training. Eventually, long-time participants took over the training role from the professional facilitator. In Cyprus, Greece, the Greek and Turkish communities on the island were unable to resolve common environmental problems regarding development and use of natural resources. In the *Cyprus Future Together* project, Greek and Turkish Cypriot stakeholders were offered training and were provided with the skills and capacities necessary to lead planning exercises in both communities focused on issues of sustainable development and cultural heritage preservation. This not only helped stakeholders understand the issues but provided a pathway for later collaborations that resulted in breaking down barriers between the different cultures (Jarraud & Lordos, 2012).

Group Modeling/Game Exercises/Workshops

Workshops wherein the community members are able to interact or exchange ideas and develop a common language and basis for understanding are very useful in a decision-making process (Dewulf, Francois, Paul-Wostl, & Taillieu, 2007). Gaming workshops have become common to develop a conceptual framework to support policy development and construct *meaningful play*. Games can be used in various phases of development from research to policy choice scenario testing (Bots & Daalen, 2007; Krolikowska et al., 2007). For example, Bots and van Daalen (2007) used role-playing and an investment game to prioritize options and reach consensus with community members on large transportation projects in the Netherlands. Anderson (2004) used role-playing laboratory experiments to investigate different economic institutions and options for trading fishing allowance systems in Rhode

Island. Participatory modeling can also enhance the stakeholder's knowledge and understanding of a system and its dynamics and help to identify and clarify the impact of solutions to a given problem (Elias, 2008, 2012; Voinov & Bousquet, 2010).

Field Trips

Field trips are an excellent opportunity for stakeholders in a process to better understand the context for the decisions they must make (Susskind & Thomas-Larmer, 1999). Field trips can also strengthen their relationships. For example, in the Juneau Alaska Airport Expansion Project, a stakeholder collaborative group with representatives from the city of Juneau, federal and state agencies, and local environmental groups went on a number of field trips to assess potential wetland mitigation sites, helping to contextualize the options and work together to solve differences regarding alternative development and mitigation packages. In a San Antonio conflict over how to manage urban watersheds, stakeholders had difficulty understanding how they were connected with others who lived and worked along the waterway. One challenge was to help those who were familiar with the upstream waterway to understand what happened to the water as it moved downstream. We encouraged them to organize field trips to visit downstream sites, including a small farm that produced flowers and vegetables for the local market. Along with high-lighting the importance of the downstream portions of the waterway, the farmer, who spoke rarely in meetings, was the focus of everyone's attention, and he became a much more vocal participant during future meetings.

Whichever collaborative process or types of activities are chosen, the convener must proceed with clarity of purpose, agency commitment, adequate capacity and resource, timeliness in relation to decisions, and a commitment to learning (Dietz & Stern, 2008; Weber, 2012).

Consider Logistics

With goals and a chosen process in mind, the next step is to consider the management and specifics of a stakeholder engagement or public involvement process. A diagnosis of constraints or opportunities will determine the direction the process will take. Logistics such as applicable regulatory laws, project deadlines, staff, facilities, and budget as well as the amount, length, and timing of meetings must be considered (Carpenter, 1999; Daniels & Walker, 2001; Dietz & Stern, 2008; Lockwood, 2010; Luyet et al., 2012; Manring, Nelson, & Wondolleck, 1990; Rauschmayer et al., 2009; Rauschmayer & Wittmer, 2006; Straus, 1999; Susskind & Thomas-Larmer, 1999). Questions to consider during the design phase include the following:

Type of Process and Roles of Participants

1. What type of process does the situation call for?
2. What is the role of the convener?
3. What are the roles of stakeholders?

FIGURE 6.1 Process Approaches at a Glance	
Policy dialogue process	Representatives of groups with divergent views or interests are assembled to generate discussion and improve communication and mutual understanding as they seek to exchange information and build consensus recommendations between the public, private, and civic sectors.
Technical advisory committee (TAC)	Made up of technical experts, environmental advocates, and other interested stakeholders that a government agency brings together to discuss particulars about a specific project.
Citizen's advisory committee	A citizen's advisory committee is similar to a TAC but composed of individuals chosen to reflect different segments of the community and focused on soliciting input from diverse interests in a community, who may or may not have technical expertise about a specific project.
Monitoring committees	Interested and affected stakeholders, as well as public agencies and scientific and technical experts in a variety of roles, such as determining target outcomes, defining criteria and indicators to monitor those outcomes, determining the appropriate system for monitoring, participating in data gathering and analysis, and interpreting data over time.
Natural resource partnerships	Informal working groups organized around regions with natural recourse concerns, such as the use of rangelands, forests and water resources, or protection of wildlife, watersheds, and the like.
Community-based collaboration	Voluntary individuals and representatives of affected groups, businesses, or other agencies in addressing a specific or short-term problem in the local community. Operate without legal sanction or regulatory power.
Environmental mediation/ conciliation	Involves efforts by a third party to improve the relationship between two or more disputants in an environmental conflict.
Negotiated rule making	The convener develops a proposed rule by using a neutral facilitator and a negotiating committee composed of representatives of all interests that the rule is likely to affect.
Joint fact finding	Members pool relevant information or identify information needs, solicit data from an agreed upon source, and jointly craft the objectives and standards to evaluate and apply the data.
Training, group modeling/game exercises/workshops, and field trips	Techniques to further engage stakeholders, providing opportunities to contextualize project options and opportunities

Laws and **Decision Space**

1. What laws and regulations apply?

2. What is the time frame in which a decision must be made?

3. What are the key decision points in a process?

Structure and Participation

1. Which and how will primary stakeholders be invited?

2. How will the process be structured?

3. How will the process be managed and monitored?

4. How often should the stakeholders meet and for how long each time?

5. Where should meetings be held?

6. What other activities are appropriate and needed (trainings, field trips, modeling, and/or joint fact finding)?

Making Decisions and Gathering Information

1. Are there constraints on how decisions can be made?

2. How will information be gathered, stored, and disseminated?

3. What kinds of technical experts/information or research are needed?

4. What kinds of training do stakeholders or the public need?

5. What, if any, outreach to the larger public is needed?

Budgetary Considerations

1. What will the project cost? And what is the available budget?

When designing a collaborative process, it is important to be flexible and open to changes should the situation demand (Blackstock et al., 2007; Straus, 1999; Stringer et al., 2007). For example, if during a collaborative it is decided that new information or data is needed, a fact-finding process may be integrated. In addition, the process should be structured to take into account dynamics learned during the assessment process. As indicated earlier, trust is a key component of any collaborative effort. To increase trust or strengthen relationships between stakeholders, the process should be designed for opportunities to interact. Small-group discussions, meals, field trips, or other occasions for social interaction allow for informal conversation and relationships to be built naturally (Armstrong & Stedman, 2013; Carpenter, 1999; Dietz & Stern, 2008). In a rapid seasonal in-migration conflict between permanent residents and newcomers purchasing a second home in upper New York State, the key to addressing intracommunity tensions was creating opportunities for social interaction and dialogue between the two groups. Once relationships began to form, members of the community more easily discussed their differences and jointly created guidelines for living in their community (Armstrong & Stedman, 2013).

Considering Culture

Designing a Two-Tier Stakeholder Process With Culture in Mind

When designing a stakeholder engagement process, culture must be considered and opportunities to address cultural interest must be included. In Canada, a specifically unique collaborative process used a two-tier model for a planning process in British Columbia's Great Bear Rainforest. One of the challenges in this area is accommodating the interests of two, often opposing, groups: the First Nations, who have special legal and cultural rights, and non-First Nation stakeholders. Previous collaborative planning had not adequately engaged the First Nations leading to distrust between local tribes and the provincial government. As a sovereign entity, First Nations have specific governmental standing and require government-to-government negotiation, so engaging them is of particular importance (Clarke, 2002).

In the Great Bear Rainforest planning process, the first tier of the planning model consisted of negotiations between all stakeholders (resource agencies, industries, conservationists, and government), including First Nations. The first-tier planners then submitted recommendations to a second-tier, *government-to-government* negotiation composed of only the First Nations and the provincial government. The decision from the second tier was then ratified by the provincial government, which retained final decision-making authority. This two-tier approach provided inclusiveness and a respect for the unique position of First Nations in Canada. The process was evaluated by all stakeholders and received high marks as an inclusive, effective process that represented multiple interests and produced high-quality information for sound decision making (Cullen, McGee, Gunton, & Day, 2010).

Developing a Stakeholder Plan

The stakeholder engagement design should be documented in a report called the **project design document**. This document justifies and outlines the project outreach goals, identifies the collaborative process and activities for the stakeholder engagement process, provides a timeline of activities, and proposes a project outreach budget. It is important to note that this is a preliminary document. Activities, schedules, and budget may be impacted by outside constraints. Remember, when designing a collaborative process, it is important to be flexible and open to changes should the situation demand (Blackstock et al., 2007; Straus, 1999; Stringer et al., 2007). The details of the design plan are certainly important, but the overall goal of the project should guide the planning as the designer considers if the activity planned will support the process of decision making (Daniels & Walker, 2001). Further, it is important to get the buy-in of primary stakeholders. They may have suggestions for stakeholder engagement and a flexible plan will allow for iterations and changes.

FIGURE 6.2 Visual Project Timeline

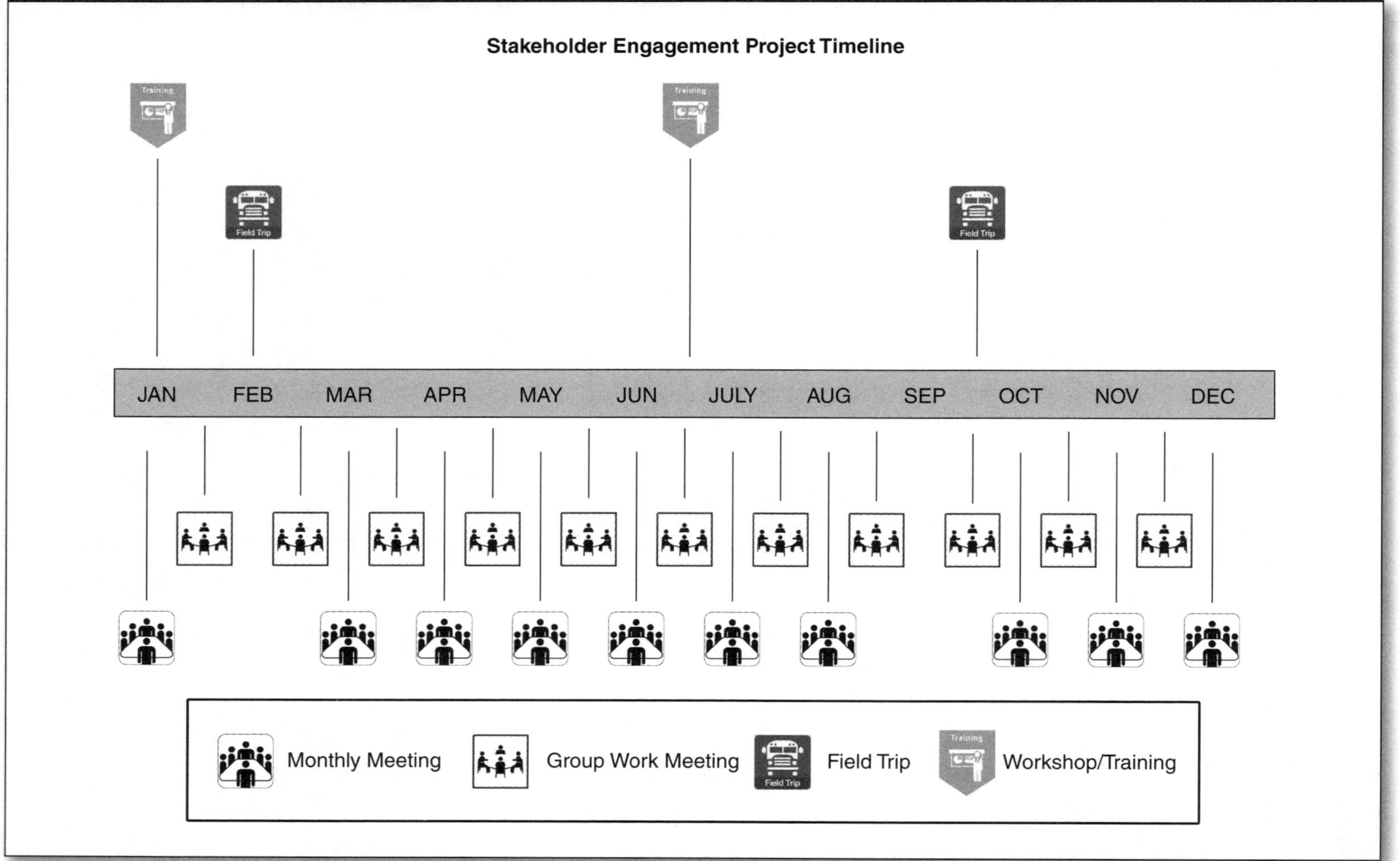

Stakeholder Engagement Project Timeline

The project timeline for activities may be dictated by the governing regulatory law or the specifics of the project. When developing the timeline, it is important to indicate key decision points in the process or how the process relates to other related regulatory processes. Straus (1999) suggests a graphic road map or a visual representation of the flow of face-to-face meetings and other activities indicated by a symbol. Visual representation outlining the flow of the process provides a powerful medium to communicate information clearly, educate stakeholders on the process, build support for an outreach effort, and act as a scheduler and reminder (Straus, 1999).

Project budgets will vary depending on the type and number of meetings or activities. When developing the project budget, specific costs must be broken down such as staff, materials, training, and travel. Estimating the number of hours the facilitator will work in preparation and execution of stakeholder activities, as well as the costs of meeting materials, outreach materials, printing, facilities reservation, food, and travel for field trips can be difficult. However, paying careful attention to the details of an activity and planning ahead can alleviate the risk of going over budget.

The project design document can be organized as appropriate to each specific project; however, as a general guideline the document should include the following: (a) introduction; (b) overview of the project, conflict, or situation; (c) outreach goals for engaging stakeholders; (d) suggested timeline; and (e) a budget. Below is a sample outline for developing the project design document.

1. Introduction

    1.1 Brief overview of project, conflict, or situation

2. Stakeholder Engagement

    2.1 Outreach goals for stakeholder engagement

    2.2 Process design strategies and mechanisms

3. Public Involvement (introduced in next chapter)

    3.1 Outreach goals for public involvement

    3.2 Process design strategies and mechanisms

4. Project Timeline

    4.1 Narrative

    4.2 Visual timeline

5. Project Budget

    5.1 Narrative

    5.2 Total budget

The goal of stakeholder engagement should always be to "improve the quality, legitimacy, and capacity of environmental assessments and decisions" (Dietz & Stern,

2008, p. 1). Designing a decision-making process built on the practical theory of trinity of voice, in which design structures, mechanisms, and strategies are meant to provide access, standing, and influence for stakeholders and the general public, ensures the quality, legitimacy, and capacity of both the process and decision.

Case Study Application

Referring to your case study, design a collaborative process to address the issues. You will develop as a group a project design document including the following elements. Be sure to justify your design choices, relating them to your outreach goals while keeping the practical theory of trinity of voice in mind.

1. Introduction
   1.1 Brief overview of project, conflict, or situation

2. Stakeholder Engagement
   2.1 Outreach goals for stakeholder engagement
   2.2 Process design strategies and mechanisms

3. Public Involvement (introduced in next chapter)
   3.1 Outreach goals for public involvement
   3.2 Process design strategies and mechanisms

4. Project Timeline
   4.1 Narrative
   4.2 Visual timeline

5. Project Budget
   5.1 Narrative
   5.2 Total budget

Voices From the Field

Parks and People: Whose Needs Count? The Case of Limpopo National Park, Mozambique

Nícia Givá

Environmental Communication, Department of Urban and Rural Development, Swedish University of Agricultural Sciences, Uppsala

Faculty of Agronomy and Forest Engineering, Eduardo Mondlane University, Maputo, Mozambique

Limpopo National Park (LNP) was established in 2001 in Southern Mozambique, as part of a visionary project of creating the Great Limpopo Transfrontier Park

(GLTP). The GLTP integrates three national parks: LNP in Mozambique, the Kruger National Park in South Africa and Gonarezhou National Park in Zimbabwe. LNP occupies an area of 11.233 km², 20.9% of which is allocated to the buffer zone, and is home for around 28,000 people distributed in 44 villages along the Limpopo and Elephants Rivers. Being dependent on an agricultural livelihood, the harsh conditions of erratic and scarce rainfall place the people at a disadvantage when interfaced with conservation and tourism objectives. Cyclical droughts and crop raiding by elephants are two interconnected factors that increase the LNP communities' exposure to food insecurity. In addition, these communities feel marginalized as none of the promised benefits (such as livelihood diversification, job creation, roads, and market infrastructures) are being delivered by the park authorities; instead their livelihoods are made worse as the coping strategies already adopted toward food security become incompatible with those against crop raiding, creating tension between communities and the National Park authorities.

Systemic Action Research has been the chosen methodological approach and this allows for creation of spaces for engagement of multiple actors, in this case including LNP's communities, park authorities, and other interest groups. Through facilitated dialogue, they explore diverse range of dilemmas plaguing the relations among actors and between them and nature, as well as explore alternatives for coexistence in the future.

Iterative workshops conducted at different levels have been the main method of choice, incorporating several participatory tools and techniques for information gathering and intervention. Some of the processes used and outcomes reached in the first of the workshops are elaborated here. All relevant actors were convened for 2 days in the town outside the park gate, including 10 members of park staff, five representatives of one community, and eight others from the local government, NGOs, and researchers. The design of the workshop enabled sharing of different understandings and worldviews among actors of the present situation and exploring of areas requiring concerted action for transformational change.

The technique of photo language was used at the outset to introduce participants, as well as to set the expectations among them regarding the workshop. Similarly, the timeline technique was applied toward constructing a shared understanding of the history of the settlements and the park. Then the rich picture of the people's livelihood systems and its dynamics in relation to the park and climate variability was also presented to stimulate dialogue and the opportunity to communicate people's concerns and differences. The main outcomes of the workshop outlined above that required action in the subsequent iteration of the action research cycle were (a) the need for improving communication between communities and the park, (b) the need to revise the management plan toward more participatory ways, and (c) a mechanism for clear and effective allocation of benefits to communities through the 20% revenue already established by law. Secondary outcomes from the workshop included the acknowledgment by all involved actors, especially the park staff and government authorities, of the importance of dialogue and sharing of perspectives and the openness created through the workshop process between all interest groups toward future interaction.

Key Terms

access

citizen's advisory
committee (CAC)

collaboration

community-based
collaboration

consultation

decision space

empowerment

influence

information sharing

joint fact finding

Mediation/Conciliation

natural resource
partnerships

negotiated rule making

policy dialogue process

Project Design
Document

public involvement

stakeholder engagement

standing

technical advisory
committee (TAC)

CHAPTER 7

Design:
Public Involvement Process

Public Involvement: Designing for the Larger Public

To create socially legitimate environmental policy it is necessary to get the buy-in of the larger community, including secondary and peripheral stakeholders and create a sense of ownership over policy development in their community. The world commission on environment and development (WCED) calls for **public participation** by *all* concerned citizens and sets forth the need for broad public participation in decision making (Johnson & Dagg, 2003). Effective environmental management and policy development must include enhanced public involvement (Dukes, 2004). This chapter focuses on ways to engage and provide opportunities for the public to give input on environmental policy. Traditional approaches such as public meetings, hearings, and comment forums will be outlined along with new, creative approaches such as van wraps, fair booths, and coffee chats. The use of new and social media to engage publics will also be discussed.

Public participation, as defined by Cox (2009), is "the ability of individual citizens and groups to influence environmental decisions about the environment" (84). It includes any organized process or mechanisms intentionally instituted, organized, or adopted by government agencies to engage the public in administrative decision making, environmental assessment, planning, management, monitoring, and evaluation (Beierle & Cayford, 2002; Dietz & Stern, 2008).

Arnstein's (1969) ladder of participation describes a continuum of increasing stakeholder involvement from passive dissemination of information to active engagement. Other versions of a similar ladder have been proposed by other researchers and scholars. One of the most cited is Bigg's (1989) who described the level of engagement as a relationship that can be contractual, consultative, collaborative, and collegiate. Farrington (1998) simplified this to a three-distinction ladder in which consultative, functional, or empowering described the level of engagement. Lawrence (2006) built on this, adding transformative participation as an alternative top rung. The ladder metaphor implies that higher rungs are preferred over lower rungs. However, different levels of engagement are most likely to be appropriate in different contexts and to achieve different goals. For this reason, others have suggested a *wheel of participation* is an appropriate metaphor (Davidson, 1998).

Public involvement was traditionally characterized by the managerial model in which government was entrusted to identify and pursue the common good. It was a *decide-announce-defend* approach. According to Beirle and Cayford (2002), "A fundamental challenge for administrative governance is reconciling the need for expertise in managing administrative programs with the transparency and participatory demand by a democratic system" (p. 3). Throughout the managerial era, the main justification for public involvement was accountability, to ensure that government agencies were acting in the public interest. That idea shifted to the belief that public involvement is necessary to develop real substance in policy in addition to keeping government agencies accountable. Reed (2008) provides an excellent overview of the history of public participation from awareness in the late 1960s, incorporating local perspectives in data collection and planning in the 1970s, development of techniques that recognize local knowledge in the 1980s, increasing use of public participation as the norm in the 1990s, and disillusionment over its limits and failings in the early 2000s. This disillusion is explained by Depoe and Delicath (2004) as they outline five primary shortcomings of traditional models of public participation:

1. Typically operates on technocratic models of rationality, in which policy makers, administrative officials, and experts see their role as educating and persuading the public as to the legitimacy of their decisions.

2. Often occurs too late in the decision-making process, sometimes even after decisions have been made.

3. Follows an adversarial trajectory.

4. Lacks adequate mechanisms and forums for informed dialogue among stakeholders.

5. Lacks adequate provisions to ensure that input gained through public participation makes a real input on outcomes. (pp. 2–3)

Depoe and Delicath (2004) also argue that what is needed is a public involvement process in which people have a say in the decision that affects them and one where there is early and ongoing participation. This, they say, "is the hallmark of sound public policy" (p. 3). This emphasis has also been referred to by others as "deliberative democracy… [which] advocates a shift from general calls for increased public participation in environmental policymaking to more focused efforts to extend deliberative democratic engagement" (Meadowcroft, 2004, p. 183). The goals for public involvement should be to not only incorporate public value into decision making, but to engage the public, deliberatively improving the quality of the decision while producing greater trust and institutional credibility (Beierle &

Cayford, 2002; Johnson & Dagg, 2003). Engagement of the greater public for environmental decisions has increased significantly over the past decade.

The International Association for Public Participation (IAP2), a worldwide organization providing direction and support for different communities and organizations engaged in public involvement, identify seven core values for the practice of public participation. These values include the following:

1. Public participation is based on the belief that those who are affected by a decision have a right to be involved in the decision-making process.

2. Public participation includes the promise that the public's contribution will influence the decision.

3. Public participation promotes sustainable decisions by recognizing and communicating the needs and interests of all participants, including decision makers.

4. Public participation seeks out and facilitates the involvement of those potentially affected by or interested in a decision.

5. Public participation seeks input from participants in designing how they participate.

6. Public participation provides participants with the information they need to participate in a meaningful way.

7. Public participation communicates to participants how their input affected the decision.

These core values shape much of the discussion and practice of current public engagement.

Types of Public Involvement Activities or Mechanisms

Considering engagement of the general public, Dietz and Stern (2008) distinguish between bounded and unbounded processes. Bounded processes are where representation is based on identified organized parties or specific stakeholder interests. Bounded processes are useful for coordinating deliberation to define an issue for assessment or policy, determine information needed for action, or to identify ways in which stakeholders are affected by an issue or potential decision. For example, a process considering the removal of a dam in a community would seek to understand the impact of the removal on the local community and tourism businesses in the area. *Unbounded processes*, as defined by Dietz and Stern (2008), are more open to any interested individual. They can be formal (**public hearings**, open houses) but are unbounded because participants are self-selected. For example, an open house to gather input on the development of a resource management plan that may be attended by the general public would be considered unbounded.

When deciding the level of public involvement or engagement, it is important to remember that public involvement mechanisms that involve participants in more intensive ways have a greater degree of what Beierle and Cayford (2002) call capacity. In other words, the more experience or opportunity to understand the details of a project there is, the greater the public's capacity to help solve problems and become an asset to the project or proposal.

Engaging the general public can also be distinguished by the four levels of engagement introduced in Chapter 6: information sharing, consultation, collaboration, and empowerment (see Table 7.1 below). Mechanisms that help provide one-way transfer of information and data about a project to the general public include things like newsletters and reports, leaflets, displays or exhibits, informational hotlines, and project websites (Johnson & Dagg, 2003). These mechanisms are particularly useful on large-scale or multi-issued projects, such as a resource management plan for Bureau of Land Management land covering a large area with multiple interests such as grazing, tourism, and wilderness designation. More formal approaches such as presentations or open houses also provide a venue for information sharing. When the Texas Parks and Wildlife Department is considering making changes in areas such as facilities maintenance, hunting seasons, or regulations for animal trapping, they begin with an open house. This gives the agency an opportunity to learn who is interested in the issue and gives stakeholders an opportunity to obtain basic information. Depending on responses to the open house, the agency can then determine how extensive its public involvement process should be.

Finally, an effective way to share information with the general public is to offer training on the specific laws that govern a process or provide data gathering training (Carlson, 1999; Daniels & Walker, 2001; Ramirez, 1999; Susskind & Thomas-Larmer, 1999; Walker, Daniels, & Emborg, 2008; Wondolleck & Yaffee, 2000). For example, in a project involving the construction of a controversial overpass in Kaysville, Utah, a NEPA training workshop for stakeholders and interested members of the public was offered so they could better understand their role and opportunities in the public comment process.

Mechanisms of consultation where the focus is to gather input from the public to influence decision making or collaboration, wherein members of the public are directly involved in the decision making, include an interactive website, project hotline, public opinion polls, surveys or questionnaires, interviews, and focus groups. For the Moab Utah resource management plan led by the Bureau of Land Management, participants could leave comments on a project website, call a hotline, or attend a series of public meetings designed to gain insight into the concerns of the community. Project activities, such as public hearings or meetings (as required by NEPA), field trips, **listening sessions**, visioning or scenario workshops, conceptual gaming exercises, modeling or mapping activities, or design **charrettes**, in which professionals work with members of the community to produce design options for a specific site, are also excellent mechanisms to gather input from the general public (Beierle & Cayford, 2002; Bots & van Daalen, 2007; Daniels & Walker, 2001; Dewulf, Francois, Paul-Wostl, & Taillieu, 2007; Dietz & Stern, 2008; Elias, 2008, 2012; Hjortso, Christensen, & Tarp, 2005; Johnson & Dagg, 2003; Luyet,

Schlaepfer, Parlange, & Buttler, 2012; Vella, Bowen, & Frankic, 2009; Voinov & Bousquet, 2010; Wondolleck & Yaffee, 2000).

In Cyprus, Greece, the United Nations Development Programme (UNDP) hosted environmental cafés aimed at stimulating public dialogue on local and regional environmental issues between the Greek Cypriot and Turkish Cypriot. These meetings were held all over the island and took place in cafés, bars, restaurants, and theaters and brought together politically divided Greek and Turkish Cypriots living on the island as they discussed environmental issues that impacted both cultures (Jarraud & Lordos, 2012). Pocewicz and Nielsen-Pincus (2013) provide another example of creative consultation as they illustrate the value of using a mapping activity to engage with stakeholders and develop policy. Using mapping and GIS technology, they engaged with citizens in Wyoming to understand resident development needs and potential areas for oil and gas development (Pocewicz & Nielsen-Pincus, 2013).

The final level of engagement is empowerment, which is typically associated with primary stakeholder processes and not often employed with the general public. However, any of the strategies outlined in the consultative or collaborative level could act to empower the community if the decision making is turned over to the community, as in the case with a citizen jury.

Engaging the public also offers an opportunity to be inventive; some projects call for design creativity. Reed (2008) discusses work in Botswana in the villages with their kgotlas, or council meetings, where participatory mapping was conducted with participants drawing in the sand before maps were transferred to paper and

TABLE 7.1 Public Involvement Techniques

Participation Technique	Information Sharing	Consultation	Collaboration	Empowerment
Newsletter/leaflets	X			
Reports	X			
Presentations/open houses	X	X		
Public hearings/listening sessions	X	X		
Project website/hotline	X	X		
Questionnaires and surveys	X	X		
Interviews and focus groups	X	X		

(Continued)

TABLE 7.1 (Continued)

Participation Technique	Information Sharing	Consultation	Collaboration	Empowerment
Training	X	X		
Field trips	X	X	X	
Gaming exercises/scenario	X	X	X	
Workshops/charrettes environmental cafés	X	X	X	X
GPS/modeling/mapping	X	X	X	X
Citizen jury	X	X	X	X
Social media	X	X	X	

checked by vehicle with a GPS. Another example of creative design is provided by the BLM resource management plan process highlighted above. To reach those citizens that might have an interest in the management plan but had not taken the initiative to visit the website or attend a public meeting, BLM representatives visited trailheads, asking for hikers to take a few minutes and share their perspectives. Further the BLM sponsored booths at county fairs in the area where they handed out information about the process and invited people to leave comments. Creative approaches should always have a purpose if they are to be successful.

Considering Culture

Creating Opportunities for Cultural Storytelling

Three types of environmental conflict-related phenomena are particularly salient for their impact on the culture of a community. These include (a) intensive protracted violence or widespread violence regarding an environmental issue, (b) displacement or the forced movement of people, and (c) the merging of different cultural groups in a congested space (LeBaron & Pillay, 2006). Thus, an environmental issue related to one or more of these phenomena, such as the removal of a people for the development of a dam, impacts not only the material living space but the culture of a people as well. In such cases, an environmental conflict becomes extremely difficult to negotiate if culture is not considered and respected. LeBaron and Pillay (2006) argue that in order to address cultural conflict in a community, the stories of community members must be shared and understood. Creative engagement of the cultural stories of a community can alleviate tension and bring together disparate groups in conflict. Listening to narratives and acknowledging their significance can shed light on environmental attitudes, beliefs, and behaviors, focus the key issues of the conflict, and give insight into how to address community concerns (Clarke, 2008; Lejano, Ingram, & Ingram, 2013; Lewicki, Gray, & Elliot, 2003; Winslade & Monk, 2000).

Designing a public involvement process that allows for the telling of such stories can provide a pathway to the creation of a social network that can facilitate collaborative decision making and respect cultural values. The Nauck Community Heritage Project in Arlington County, Virginia, provides such an example. As part of a project to revitalize Nauck, a historically black neighborhood, the Department of Community Planning, Housing, and Development and the Folklore and Public Art sections of the Cultural Affairs Division partnered in a creative community engagement process. Staff members contacted community leaders from local churches and organizations and worked with them to involve local residents in a storytelling project. The cultural stories of members of the community were compiled and combined to create a local oral history that inspired the designer and redevelopers of the Nauck Town Square Project and the Nauck Village Center.

Use of Social Media

Social media are revolutionizing how publics interact with organizations. Social media employs mobile and web-based technologies to create highly interactive platforms where individuals and communities share, create, and modify content (Kietzmann, Hermkens, Mccarthy, & Silvestre, 2011). Recent reports suggest people use social media more frequently than an organization's social web page and it has surpassed e-mail as the most popular online activity. There are over one billion active users of social media worldwide (Men & Tsai, 2013). There are numerous social media platforms ranging from personal profiles such as Facebook or LinkedIn to conversational chains such as Twitter or Google+. According to the Pew Internet Project, as of February 2012, 69% of the United States online adults are active on social networks (Bryer, 2013). Twitter has more than 145 million users and they send an average of 90 million tweets per day (Kietzmann et al., 2011). This number is increasing rapidly as social media continues to gain popularity.

Social media offers unprecedented opportunities for organizations to reach publics as they allow for an organization to connect with publics on a more personal level (Bryer, 2013; Bryer & Zavattaro, 2011; Hand & Ching, 2011; Lester & Hutchins, 2012; Meijer, 2012; Men & Tsai, 2013; Osterrieder, 2013). Social media allows people to become informed about policy issues in their community, create social capital, and engage in civic activities in a more intimate way than other avenues (de Zuniga, 2012). There are different levels of engagement depending on the level of interaction an organization seeks with its stakeholders, from information dissemination or sharing to input gathering to interactive collaboration between an established project group (Kietzmann et al., 2011). Organizations or collaborative processes can communicate with their larger constituents via a number of other platforms as well.

Bryer (2013) suggests that organizations should use social media to develop trust between an organization and the community and develop supported policy and programs. In Bryer's study of how social media tools are used by local governments about environmental issues, specifically transportation projects, he argues that social media allows an organization to reach those citizens that perhaps are not as active in environmental policy development as others and engage them in authentic ways. It provides opportunities to strategically create connections with intended audiences. In his study of 55 environmental transportation projects across the United States, Bryer (2013) identified the best practices of those who reached citizens in purposeful and meaningful ways. Citing a specific case study of the Metropolitan Transit Authority (MTA) in Los Angeles, Bryer highlights the strategies taken that he believes led to a successful campaign. These include regular updates, responsiveness to inquiry, and a policy of encouraging free expression while discouraging inappropriate behavior. These strategies, argues Bryer, resulted in increased participation, levels of trust, and support for programs.

Using social media can be low cost for both an organization and the community. This will allow organizations to interact with a wider audience. It can also reduce other costs associated with meetings, such as setup and the like. In using social media, organizations should understand its potential but also be aware of the limitations. It allows information to be spread very quickly, allowing agencies to cost-effectively solicit participants at events or gather input on a project. However, misinformation can be spread just as easily. Users of social media for public involvement projects must keep on top of the information shared to ensure that it is accurate, purposeful, and timely (Bryer, 2013; Lester & Hutchins, 2012; Osterrieder, 2013).

Organizations or public involvement representatives must resist the temptation to use a social media tool just for the sake of it. With the popularity of social media and the easy access to various tools, it is too easy to be creative without being strategic. Decisions must be well thought out and be driven by established process goals (Bryer & Zavattaro, 2011; Dempsey et al., 2011; Hand & Ching, 2011; Kietzmann et al., 2011; Osterrieder, 2013; de Zuniga, 2012). The level of interaction chosen must be well thought out so public input objectives are met (Bryer, 2013) and solid *communicative bridges* with the public are formed (Lester & Hutchins, 2012, p. 849). Further, use of social media must adhere to organizational policies. In some organizational cultures, rules and procedures may inhibit implementation of social media. Those engaged in social media related to a policy development project must find out the rules and regulations of the organizations in the collaborative.

Considering Culture

Creating Convergence Through Culture

When designing public involvement processes, it is important to be aware of cultures and those impacted by a project. A project can unite or divide a community, and understanding local cultures can help put environmental issues in context. The people of Mehuin in southern Chile succeeded in stopping the construction of a pipeline that would have dumped industrial waste from the largest pulp mill under construction in South America into Maiquillahue Bay. The committee that led the opposition to the project was successful because they connected the pipeline's threat with local cultural meanings. Thus residents could make sense of the danger in the context of their culture and be motivated to defend the bay. The committee integrated local practical knowledge, religious views, and scientific concepts in a way that was consistent to various views of the Mehuin fishermen, small business owners, and citizens including Catholics and Pentecostals. The pipeline became known as fatific, ducto fatidico, the fatal pipeline or pipeline of doom. This notion of death took on a religious underpinning as *No al Ducto; si a la Vida (No to the pipeline, yes to life)* became a familiar saying. One of the community leaders organized a *Cross of May* (a Chilean Catholic celebration), which had been celebrated for years. Community members went from house to house singing for their cause. Despite differences among the various stakeholders, they believed the implications of the pipeline and came together to fight the project. Participants believe it was because they were able to explain the implications in terms of religion and culture—something all stakeholders connected with (Skewes & Guerra, 2004).

Developing a Public Involvement Plan

The project design document introduced in Chapter 6 should be modified to include public involvement design. As it does with the stakeholder process, this document justifies and outlines the project outreach goals, identifies the activities for public involvement process, including a timeline of activities, and proposes a project outreach budget. It is not necessary to develop a new timeline or budget. Public involvement activities and their cost should be incorporated into the timeline and costs should be calculated within the same budget. Again, it is important to remember activities, schedules, and budget may be impacted by outside constraints. When designing a collaborative process and a public involvement process, it is important to be flexible and open to changes should the situation demand (Blackstock, Kelly, & Horsey, 2007; Straus, 1999; Stringer, Reed, Dougill, Rokitzki, & Seely, 2007).

As a reminder, the project design document can be organized as appropriate to each specific project, however, as a general guideline the document should include the following items: (a) introduction; (b) overview of the project, conflict, or situation; (c) outreach goals for engaging stakeholders and the public; (d) suggested timeline; and (e) a budget. Below is a sample outline for developing the project design document, including both the stakeholder process and the public involvement process.

1. Introduction

    1.1 Brief overview of project, conflict, or situation

2. Stakeholder Engagement

   2.1 Outreach goals for stakeholder engagement

   2.2 Process design strategies and mechanisms

3. Public Involvement

   3.1 Outreach goals for public involvement

   3.2   Process design strategies and mechanisms

4. Project Timeline

   4.1 Narrative

   4.2 Visual timeline

5. Project Budget

   5.1 Narrative

   5.2 Total budget

Conclusion

Many scholars have written on the benefits of extended public involvement (e.g., Dietz & Stern; Beierle & Cayford). Engaging with the public in authentic and meaningful ways (a) increases the quality of decisions through added information and innovative ideas, (b) increases community goodwill and agency reputation, and (c) holds the government and the community accountable for environmental decisions (Lockwood, 2010; Parkins & Mitchell, 2005; Rauschmayer, Berghofer, Omann, & Zikos, 2009; Rauschmayer & Wittmer, 2006). As with a stakeholder engagement process, the convener or agency responsible for the environmental decision must consider many factors when designing a public involvement process. The goals and objectives of the project, the level of engagement, and types of activities must be considered in light of the opportunities, constraints, and logistics of their specific situation (Beierle & Cayford, 2002; Reed, 2008).

Case Study Application

Referring again to your case study, design a public involvement process to engage the larger public. Modify the project design document you developed previously in Chapter 6. Be sure to justify your design choices relating them to your outreach and public involvement goals.

1. Introduction

   1.1 Brief overview of project, conflict, or situation

2. Stakeholder Engagement

    2.1 Outreach goals for stakeholder engagement

    2.2 Process design strategies and mechanisms

3. Public Involvement

    3.1 Outreach goals for public involvement

    3.2 Process design strategies and mechanisms

4. Project Timeline

    4.1 Narrative

    4.2 Visual timeline

5. Project Budget

    5.1 Narrative

    5.2 Total budget

Voices From the Field

Successful Public Involvement on a Limited Budget Through Online Media

Bryant J. Kuechle

Senior Project Manager

The Langdon Group

The Tri-Cities of Richland, Pasco, and Kennewick is the fourth largest metropolitan area in Washington State with over 253,000 people. At the confluence of the Columbia and Snake Rivers, these communities are linked by three major bridges. With a growing population, congestion on the bridges in 2010 was increasing, prompting the funding of a regional study among the local agencies and the legislature to look at all reasonable alternatives for a new Columbia River crossing in the area.

As a member of a team, including H. W. Lochner Engineers and J-U-B Engineers, the Langdon Group was hired to manage the public involvement process. This posed the significant challenge of reaching and effectively engaging four distinct communities (including the City of West Richland) to guide a process of determining two to three potential crossing locations for further study, from an initial list of 10. The geographically diverse region coupled with a limited budget helped determine that online media would play a key role in the process.

In April 2010, our team launched a project website, Twitter page, Constant Contact E-Newsletter, and online survey to provide the community with up-to-date

(Continued)

(Continued)

information and receive valuable public input. Our strategy was to use the local media and existing stakeholder e-mail databases as a means to drive the public to the website. The plan worked: In response to exceptional media coverage, the website generated over 1,100 survey responses and 300 written comments were received. At the May 20, 2010, steering committee meeting, this input helped refine the initial 10 crossing alternatives to four.

In August 2010, a second survey was launched, and due to media coverage responding to the news release, nearly 700 members of the public provided online input. The carefully crafted surveys provided valuable demographic and driving habit information to help determine where people in the region were going, when, and why. Survey data ultimately revealed three preferred crossing locations, approved by the steering committee for further study.

Throughout the course of the project, members of the Tri-Cities print, radio, and television media followed the project through regular Twitter messages and Constant Contact E-Newsletter updates. The Twitter and E-Newsletter campaigns proved so successful that news outlets in Seattle, Tacoma, and Spokane provided media coverage of an October public meeting. Some traditional public involvement techniques were utilized (a public open house and an information booth at the County Fair), but the comments gathered through those processes were minimal compared to the input gathered via the online tools. Some public comments received praised the approach as the most effective way of reaching this diverse community.

Key Terms

charrettes

Project Design Document

public hearings/ listening sessions

public involvement

public participation

social media

CHAPTER 8

Working With Key Stakeholders

Once a collaborative process has been designed and the convener and mediator have agreed on the level of engagement, types of activities, and direction of the process, the next step is for the convener to invite the stakeholders to come to the table and join the collaborative process. The initial invitation should be a formal letter or e-mail invitation to the primary stakeholders outlining preliminary goals of the collaborative process, expectations and roles of the stakeholders, and an estimated schedule. These elements will be modified as the process begins and stakeholders have the opportunity to give input on the design and structure of the process, but an initial overview will give the stakeholders a shared understanding of the requirements for effective participation such as investment of time and effort, financial costs, types of representation, and the like (Dukes, Firehock, Leahy, & Anderson, 2001). The mediator can draft the initial invitation letter, but it is important that the invitation come from the convener rather than the mediator. This will help begin to develop the trust necessary for the collaborative to move forward in a productive manner.

Before stakeholders commit to a process, they must compare the costs and benefits of participating and decide if it is the most effective way to achieve their organizational goals (Daniels & Walker, 2001; Nelson, Manring, Crowfoot, & Wondolleck, 1990). They must decide if the effort is consistent with the goals of their organization, the power relations are sufficiently balanced, there is financial and structural support from their organization, and if they have sufficient expertise (technical knowledge, negotiation skill, and political skill) to participate effectively (Susskind & Cruikshank, 1987). If they decide to participate, they must engage in a collaborative process with clarity of purpose and commitment (Daniels & Walker, 2001).

Group Charter: Goals, Roles, and Rules

Once stakeholders have committed to the process and before negotiations begin, it is critical to jointly create a **group charter** or memorandum of understanding (**MOU**) that outlines the goals of the process, the **representation** and specific roles of all participants, how the collaborative group will interact, and how decisions will be made and implemented (Berardo & Gerlak, 2012; Dukes et al., 2001; Susskind & Thomas-Larmer, 1999; Wondolleck, Manring, & Crowfoot, 1990). We refer to this as establishing the *goals, roles, and rules* of a collaborative process. As with the communication assessment report and the project design document discussed in Chapter 5, the group charter or MOU is a written document and should be constructed and organized efficiently. The specific order and level of detail will be determined by the nuances of the issue or project. Because the charter is intended to guide participants, it is a good idea to include it in the report in the section of the design document that outlines the timeline or project schedule including key decision-making points and deadlines (Dukes et al., 2001).

It is very important to involve the stakeholders in the development of the group charter or MOU (Depoe, John, & Elsenbeer, 2004). Dukes et al. (2001) outline a process for building a group charter with stakeholders: (a) establish the need for shared expectations, (b) educate participants on the process through illustrations and examples of other MOUs, (c) begin with a vision of the desired outcomes for the group and then develop specific ground rules that will allow you to reach those outcomes, (d) promote full participation by all group members, (e) be accountable by honoring the agreements you have made, and (f) evaluate and revise ground rules as needed. However the ground rules are established, the key is to directly involve participants in every step of the process. Involving all stakeholders in the creation of a group charter also allows the stakeholders to see how others communicate and gives them the opportunity to begin establishing trust and building patterns of agreement. In addition, it creates shared accountability for both the process and outcome (Carpenter, 1999; Susskind, van der Wansem, & Ciccarelli, 2000).

Goals

Jointly establishing the goals of the collaborative is the first step in the development of a group charter or MOU. What is the purpose of coming together and what deliverables (policy decision) does the group hope to achieve? How will the agenda be set? Or, in other words, in what order will the collaborative address the issues (Susskind & Thomas-Larmer, 1999; Wondolleck & Yaffee, 2000)? Stakeholders will already have a good idea from their involvement in the conflict assessment and from the initial invitation, but it is important that they take ownership and discuss as a group their shared practical purpose for creating the collaborative process. This step also includes indicating milestones for assessing progress (Dukes et al., 2001). For example, in the U.S. the Clean Water Act (see Chapter 3) mandates that the public should be involved when deciding how to bring a stream into compliance with clean water standards. This is called a total maximum daily load (TMDL) process and often leads to conflicts between stakeholders. When we facilitated the public involvement component of a TMDL process in San Antonio, we began the first stakeholder meeting with exercises designed to help participants determine what they wanted to gain from the process, both as individuals and as a group. Although they initially were impatient with the idea of waiting to start *solving the problems* that had led to the TMDL in the first place, participants quickly realized that they would work together more effectively if they had clearly established goals. As part of these exercises, they broke their larger goals into individual objectives and assigned dates to each. Although the group did not always achieve their objectives by the assigned dates, this process gave them clear milestones for measuring progress. This was especially helpful for preventing discouragement because members could quickly identify progress and share that information with others.

Roles

After the goals of the collaborative have been established, the next task in creating the group charter is to outline the roles and responsibilities of the members of the group, including the convener and facilitator (Dukes et al., 2001; Stringer, Reed, Dougill, Rokitzki, & Seely, 2007; Susskind & Thomas-Larmer, 1999; Susskind et al., 2000). The list of participants and their affiliations is included in this section. Participants must clearly understand their purpose and level of decision making (Dukes et al., 2001; Innes & Booher, 2010; Susskind, Camacho, & Schenk, 2012) or what Daniels and Walker (2001) term "decision space." Are stakeholders providing recommendations or are they responsible for the decision and implementation of the policy initiatives? This must be clearly understood by all participants. If this is not clearly stated, it can cause conflict and mistrust later in the process. If stakeholders are under the impression they have full decision-making authority, and then the decision-authority agency makes a different decision, the relationship and reputation of the agency will be impaired. For example, if a group of stakeholders is involved in a conflict regarding development on land that has been formally designated as critical habitat for endangered species, it is up to the facilitator to ensure that the group realizes the U.S. Fish and Wildlife Service (FWS) is the legally designated decision-making authority. Although the group may not find it easy to work with the FWS, the process will be much more effective if they do so. Otherwise, they risk offering a solution that will not receive serious consideration, and the process will simply increase hostility between the stakeholders and the agency.

Clear defining of participant roles and responsibilities is especially useful if there are multiple agencies with decision-making authority involved in the collaborative process. For example, a controversial process regarding expansion of the state highway through the Florida Keys must meet with the approval of federal agencies including the Occupational Safety and Health Administration (OSHA) and the FWS. It also must satisfy the Florida Department of Transportation (FDOT) and Monroe County. The differing missions of these agencies sometimes conflict with each other, which makes it especially important to clarify roles and responsibilities.

Ground Rules

How members of the collaborative will interact and the procedure for decision making, communicating with outside members, and handling conflict must all be clearly articulated in the MOU. The specifics of each rule will depend on the nature of the conflict or project. However, we suggest the following rules for any collaborative process.

Representation and Attendance

All interests must be represented in a collaborative process. Further, it is best to have the organization's decision maker at the table—one who has the authority to speak for the organization or their constituents. Those at the table must be willing and able to make agreements as the collaborative moves forward. When representing their organization, stakeholders are responsible for communicating progress or decisions back to their constituents to gain buy-in and support. Information must be clear, simple, and timely (Carlson, 1999). Decisions must not conflict with their organization's objectives or values. Because gaining organizational support is critical to the success of any policy development process, the mediator must allow time between meetings or key decision points in the process for stakeholders to consult with their organizations or constituents. It may be necessary to arrange for briefings or additional meetings with a stakeholder's organization.

All key stakeholders (especially decision makers) should be present at all meetings, but even when someone has to miss a meeting, the group process needs to continue moving forward. Because environmental negotiations often occur over a lengthy period of time, participants may move on or need to be replaced. The group needs to take responsibility for deciding how to manage transitions or turnovers (Dewulf, Francois, Paul-Wostl, & Taillieu, 2007; Dukes et al., 2001; Wondolleck & Yaffee, 2000). For example, the group could require that there is overlap between changing members or that the new member be introduced in a particular formal manner. It may be necessary for the mediator to meet separately with the new member to review the process thus far.

Use of Working Groups

How **working groups**, task forces, or subcommittees will be used must also be clearly articulated in the charter or MOU (Dukes et al., 2001; Susskind & Thomas-Larmer, 1999). Often these subcommittees or working groups are created to conduct background work, initial authoring of solutions and documents, and writing that is too tedious to do as a huge group. Do these smaller groups have decision authority? How will information be circulated back to the group? These types of questions must be asked as the entire group determines the role of a working group. It is also necessary to tease out how documents will be circulated, used, and reviewed and how new information will be accessed, gathered, or stored (Dukes et al., 2001; Susskind & Thomas-Larmer, 1999). Will the group use a joint fact-finding process? Is new gained information confidential? Should it be published? Who should author any publication? All of these types of questions need to be answered before negotiations begin so group members understand expectations and requirements.

Confidentiality

Participants in a collaborative process must decide to what extent the process is public or private (Dukes et al., 2001; Susskind & Thomas-Larmer, 1999). This includes how and when the collaborative will communicate with the general public or political officials (Wondolleck & Yaffee, 2000). For example, the Agricultural Wildlife Co-existence Committee was a self-organized collaborative that brought together agriculturalists and environmentalists to come up with a way to restore the endangered aplomado falcon to its historic range in the Rio Grande Valley of Texas while continuing commercial production of cotton in the same region. The group maintained absolute confidentiality throughout its deliberations, citing this as a basic requirement of their success (Peterson, 1997). In many cases the process is related to a regulatory or legislative process, and this will limit the confidentiality that participants are allowed.

Communicating With the Media

It is especially important for collaborative groups dealing with environmental conflicts to positively and strategically engage the media. As we mentioned in the first chapter, environmental conflict includes a complex overlay of science and technology. For North American and European audiences print and broadcast media remain the main source of general scientific information (Eurobarometer, 2007; National Science Board, 2008), with the Internet providing the main source for scientific information on specific topics (Segev & Baram-Tsabari, 2012; Taneja, Webster, Malthouse, & Ksiazek, 2012). This means that media relations will be crucial to how the public perceives any environmental conflict. Assessing the political climate the collaborative operates within and how the media affect that climate is critical to the potential success of any collaborative process (O'Leary, Durant, Fiorino, & Weiland, 1999). In fact, before the process begins, it is a good idea for the mediator and convener to conduct a media assessment and design a strategy for handling the press (Kunde, 1999). Questions to consider include the following:

1. Is media coverage desirable for this situation?

2. Are the media likely to be interested in covering this process?

3. What ground rules will be developed to guide interactions with the media?

4. What media outlets should be contacted, and who should contact them?

How the collaborative participants will interact with the media should be included in the ground rules. Statements about who will speak with the press, who is responsible for writing press releases, and when to engage with the press should be articulated clearly and understood by all participants (Dukes et al., 2001; Kunde, 1999; O'Leary et al., 1999; Susskind & Thomas-Larmer, 1999; Susskind et al., 2000; Wondolleck et al., 1990).

It is often useful to designate a single spokesperson to work with the media. This provides the media with a point of contact and provides the collaborative with a single voice representing a unified process and focused message. This spokesperson must have expertise in environmental issues, must understand media relations, and must be willing to put in the time and effort to cultivate and maintain a good rapport with the media. They must also be able to communicate complex information to the media in an easily understandable manner. The media liaison may be the convener, who is ultimately responsible for the decision of the process, but it can also be the mediator or another member of the collaborative. The media liaison should use media coverage as an opportunity to enhance the public's understanding of the group's purpose, present information in an accessible way, and respond directly and quickly to misperceptions. It is this person's responsibility to help journalists understand the process and the purpose of the collaborative effort so that coverage is appropriately focused.

Media liaisons need to understand the business and political challenges faced by contemporary media, especially as they relate to science and technology. For a brief summary, we recommend a report published annually by the Pew Research Center (PEW Research Center, 2014). Although this report focuses on U.S. media, the same trends are relevant in European contexts (Eurobarometer, 2007). Reporters need access to information and decision makers in order to ensure quality sourcing and legitimacy for their stories. Their job is to catch the attention of their readers with pithy headlines and interesting information in their first paragraph. Complex environmental issues are not easily boiled down to sound bites or 800-word articles. Understanding the needs of reporters can help media liaisons to think strategically, planning some quotations that will help frame the story in terms that highlight the purpose of the collaborative or the process of decision making. It is a good idea to think about how the themes of the collaborative can translate into headlines or news stories. One way to do this is to personalize the message so that media audiences can recognize why the issue matters to them (Kunde, 1999; O'Leary et al., 1999).

The Internet has changed the media landscape in many ways, and media liaisons need to understand how traditional media intersect with *social media*, or "internet-based applications that build on . . . Web 2.0 and that allow the creation and exchange of User Generated Content" (Kaplan & Haenlein, 2010, p. 61). The opportunities and challenges that social media offer to those involved in environmental conflict have been the subject of extensive communication research (Carvalho, 2012; Endres, Sprain, & Peterson, 2009; Hopke, 2012). From the perspective of this book, social media are especially important because they provide opportunities for key stakeholders to communicate directly with the larger community, without necessarily relying on traditional sources such as newspapers and television (Endres et al. 2009). This does not, however, mean that traditional media relations are unimportant. It simply means that those who serve as media liaisons have more opportunities for sharing their story.

Decision-Making Process

What procedures will be used to reach a final decision should be clarified before the group begins to discuss the substance of the issues (Dukes et al., 2001; Susskind & Thomas-Larmer, 1999; Susskind et al., 2000; Wondolleck & Yaffee, 2000). Will decisions be made by majority voting or consensus? What is the group's definition of consensus? McKearnan and Fairman (1999) define consensus as agreement from all parties. Dukes et al. (2001) define consensus as an agreement that meets everyone's key interests in ways better than they could expect from another process, or a decision that everyone can live with (Dukes et al., 2001). For example, the ground rules for the Resource Coordination Committee, North Umpqua Hydroelectric Project Settlement Agreement defined consensus as approval of a substantive decision through a formal polling process in terms of agreement along a continuum. Committee members indicated the degree of their agreement with language from the first six columns (see Figure 8.1). The column to the far right of the continuum was not acceptable for consensus. Any of the six columns to the left were considered agreement by consensus.

It is important to remember that although agreement is the desire of a collaborative process, members of a process should not sacrifice a good agreement for a desire to agree. In other words, although consensus is desired, what is more important is an agreement that addresses the issue and meets the goals of each of the stakeholders. Renn (2004) argues that rather than seek consensus, participatory processes should adopt a shared adversity principle—one that recognizes that trade-offs are inherent in any process. A more deliberative approach focuses on

FIGURE 8.1 Consensus Polling

Endorse	Endorse with minor points of contention	Agree with reservations	Abstain	Stand Aside	Formal disagreement but will go with the majority	**Block**
"I like it"	"Basically, I like it"	"I can live with it"	"I have no opinion"	"I don't like this, but I don't want to hold up the group"	"I want my disagreement to be noted in writing, but I will support the decision"	"I veto this proposal"

Source: PacificCorp North Umpqua Hydroelectric Project Settlement Agreement, FERC No. 1927-008: Settlement Agreement: Protection, Mitigation, and Enhancement Measures, retrieved from http://www.pacificorp.com/content/dam/pacificorp/doc/Energy_Sources/Hydro/Hydro_Licensing/North_Umpqua_River/2001_2002_Annual_Report.pdf

communication and argumentation rather than negotiation, and explores the diversity of positions and assumptions.

Handling Conflict

Strategies for handling disagreement and ensuring implementation of an agreement must be understood by all participants and articulated clearly in the group charter (Susskind et al., 2000). The level of formality of the conflict resolution process will be determined by the type of conflict, as well as its legal boundaries, but typically, it involves cooperating in good faith, providing a formal notice, and a willingness to discuss concerns before bringing in a third party.

When a conflict involves multiple parties, multiple jurisdictions, and a long history of hostility between participants, it is especially valuable to formalize the process for handling disputes. The Edwards Aquifer Recovery Implementation Program (EARIP) that was discussed in previous chapters illustrates this sort of challenge. When parties first came together in the fledgling EARIP, they brought a history of hostility and mutual mistrust. Between 2007 and 2014 they developed a multispecies habitat conservation plan (HCP) that was approved by the FWS in 2013 (Edwards Aquifer Recovery Implementation Program [EARIP] Steering Committee, 2014). In 2013, the group also received the U.S. Department of Interior's (DOI) prestigious Partners in Conservation award for demonstrating "exemplary natural resource conservation efforts through public-private partnerships" (U.S. Fish and Wildlife Service, 2014). One key to the group's success was their commitment to developing a comprehensive approach to handling conflicts as they arose. They established a subcommittee to draft rules for how to proceed when consensus could not be achieved. For the first six months, these draft rules were developed by movement back and forth between the subcommittee and the larger stakeholder group. Although they have made most decisions by consensus, the group eventually established a rule that allows decisions supported by a super majority of 75% of the steering committee members in cases when consensus cannot be achieved (EARIP Steering Committee, 2014). Agreements such as these can provide any group with a road map for moving forward through conflicts that arise. Developing them together can become a focal point of commonality and an example of success for the group.

Process Management

The mediator is not responsible for the development of content, but they are responsible for the decision-making process. The various types of processes were discussed in Chapter 6. However, whichever process is chosen, the mediator must plan the details, including how often and for how long meetings should go. This may be dictated by the type of process (e.g., NEPA process or Technical Advisory Committee) or goal of the collaborative. This must be agreed upon by all participants so schedules can be planned and accommodated and individual preparations can be completed.

Meeting Management and Preparation

In the previous design chapter, we outlined a number of design choices to work with stakeholders in a policy development process. Whichever process is chosen, there will be many meetings held with all stakeholders involved. Face-to-face meetings are the building blocks of any consensus-based process as they provide an avenue for direct contact and rich communication (Dewulf et al., 2007; Straus, 1999; Weick, 1995). Carefully managed opportunities for discussion can strengthen relationships between members and provide a forum for decision making. In addition to providing the opportunity to discuss the issues and interests of participants, meetings have important symbolic or ritual elements that help strengthen a sense of collective identity and culture building between group members (Islam & Zyphur, 2009). Well-managed meetings are critical to any successful collaboration (Wondolleck & Yaffee, 2000). Conversely, poorly run meetings cause anger, distrust, and frustration among members of the collaborative. In this section we discuss how to prepare and implement successful meetings to make the most of stakeholders' time and efforts.

Plan With a Purpose

Group meetings should not be held unless there is a clear purpose and goal the collaborative group would like to achieve. This goal should be clearly outlined on the meeting agenda. Experts in meeting management assert that an agenda is paramount for meeting success. The participants need a road map to move them along and to keep them accountable (Carlozzi, 1999; Haynes, 2006; Leach, Rogelberg, Warr, & Burnfield, 2009; Malouff, Calic, McGrory, Murrell, & Schutte, 2012). Without an agenda, meetings are unprepared and unprofessional. The agenda should be well structured and communicate the meeting goals, important information and timelines, and responsibilities of attendees (Lee, 2008). At the beginning of a collaborative process, it is useful to create a binder for each member of the group with important information related to the project and a place to file meeting agendas, related data, and the like. Each member can then bring their binder to each meeting and be assured all relevant information is easily accessible. It is also a good idea to send the agenda in advance of the meeting so participants can prepare their individual roles (Haynes, 2006; Malouff et al., 2012).

Using a clever acronym outlines an easy to remember approach to meeting design (Lee, 2008).

R.A.R.A:

Rolls

Agenda

Records

Actions

Consider Logistics and Supplies

The space in which any negotiation takes place is very important. It is the responsibility of the mediator to schedule facilities and arrange for a neutral space. It is a good idea to provide refreshments such as coffee, snacks, or chocolate. And on some occasions, it is a good idea to provide lunch during daylong meetings. The complex nature of environmental conflict calls for longer meetings to address issues adequately. Breaking for lunch can sometimes give the group a needed break; however, it can also create a situation where the group loses momentum. It is a good idea to ask group members if they prefer to break for lunch or have lunch provided and work through lunch. Considering logistics also includes providing facilitation tools such as markers or flipcharts or other brainstorming supplies as well as providing an overhead projector and screen for collaborative decision making.

Send a Reminder

The agenda should be sent to participants in plenty of time for them to prepare their part of the meeting. Sending an additional follow-up e-mail is also a good idea to remind group members of the meeting and their responsibilities and to prompt preparation (Lee, 2008).

Meeting Implementation

Arrive Early & Set Up

The mediator should arrive in plenty of time to set up the room in a neutral and collaborative setting (usually in a circle or horseshoe) and be ready to greet participants as they arrive (Henkel, 2007; Malouff et al., 2012). Arriving early allows you to troubleshoot any technical difficulties or make any last minute arrangements. Setting a tone of professionalism and organization is the key to a successful process.

Set Meeting Ground Rules

In their study of successful meeting management, Malouff et al. (2012) collected data from 60 organizational meetings involving a total of 401 people. They found common characteristics that contribute to meeting productivity and satisfaction. The most common characteristic was having and adhering to meeting ground rules. Ground rules are guidelines of behavior or communication that will be accepted or encouraged during meetings and negotiations. The group charter, discussed earlier in this chapter, will outline behavioral rules and responsibilities. Ground rules are different in that they focus on behavior during meetings. It is important to dedicate time to developing meeting ground rules with the group so all will have knowledge and ownership of the ground rules (Dukes et al., 2001). Common meeting ground rules include the following:

- Meeting management
  - Meetings begin and end on time
  - No phones or e-mail during discussions
  - Anyone can call a break at any time

- Communication
  - Come prepared for meetings
  - One person speaks at a time (no side conversations)
  - Everyone receives equal time to speak
  - Speak only for yourself or your organization unless given permission from another
  - Value and respect others and diverse view points and do not attack anyone

- Focus
  - Emphasize situation rather than people
  - Look for ways to achieve mutual gain
  - Focus on present or future, not past, events

Ground rules will differ between processes but it is critical to adhere to ground rules in every meeting so healthy patterns of communication can be formed from the onset of interaction.

Encourage Dialogue

So many meetings are marked by discussion or debate that does little to move the group toward a decision. One of the mediator's main goals is to facilitate the group's best thinking through the encouragement of healthy dialogue. Dialogue differs from discussion in that the goals of dialogue are to (a) open new ground fostered by a desire to learn and discover; (b) foster open, honest, and nonjudgmental communication; (c) create shared understandings and discoveries of *both* agreement and disagreement; and to (d) see tremendous worth in collective wisdom of the participants (Anderson, Baxter, & Cissna, 2004). In creating opportunities for dialogue, the mediator creates the necessary space for listening (Lloyd, 2009). The mediator should remain positive, draw everyone out with good question asking, and focus on possibilities and potentials, not problems or pitfalls.

Considering Culture

Building and Sustaining Relationships

The single most important aspect to consider when mediating or negotiating conflict across cultures is the building of strong relationships. Relationship building should be the central focus of any conflict resolution process, especially

(Continued)

(Continued)

environmental conflict, which so often touches on or is driven by cultural differences (Huang & Bedford, 2009; Reed, 2008).

In their effort to integrate indigenous ecological knowledge and science in the management of the Wet Tropics World Heritage Area, a cultural landscape in Australia, Cullen-Unsworth, Hill, Butler, and Wallace (2012) used a cooperative research joint learning approach to develop linked cultural and biophysical indicators of ecosystem conditions. The authors identified relationship building as one of the most important determinants of success. Once relationships had been built and trust was developed, the convergence of indigenous culture and contemporary natural resource management helped to enhance social-ecological system resilience and sustainability. This would not have been possible had efforts to build relationships been incorporated into the collaborative process.

Relationship building takes a significant investment of time and does not follow a linear path but is "organic, evolving, and dynamic" (LeBaron & Pillay, 2006, p. 6). Working with stakeholders requires a process that allows for relationships to be continually built and strengthened. In their book *Conflict Across Cultures: A Unique Experience of Bridging Difference*, LeBaron and Pillay (2006) provide process suggestions to help build and sustain relationships among culturally diverse participants:

- *Balance voices*—Adopt communication norms that honor individual stories and collective learning.
- *Monitor process*—Ensure that process, relationship, and outcomes are met over time.
- *Value yin and yang*—Balance emphasis on achievement and exploration, being and doing, creativity and standardization, leadership and team collaboration, uncertainty and closure.
- *Monitor core assumptions*—Engage in ongoing dialogue about assumptions informing collaborative work, especially hidden or private agendas.
- *Expand cultural fluency*—Encourage each other to anticipate, express, and navigate differences with a spirit of inquiry.
- *Deepen collaboration*—Involve group members in ongoing attention to process dynamics, relationships, roles, and outcomes.
- *Cultivate flexibility*—Attend to tensions between assimilation and diversity.
- *Use sparks and scraps*—Use moments of uncertainty, tension, and *ah ha* as cues for reflection and dialogue.
- *Invite reflection*—Foster honest reflection on processes, relationships, and outcomes.

A process that fosters a "spirit of inquiry about differences" (p. 6) can help build relationships across cultures and create a place for creative deliberation—the kind of creativity needed to address complex environmental conflict.

Use Single-Text Method

Because of the complexity of environmental conflict, scholars and practitioners recommend using the single-text approach. This approach involves introducing a working document early on in the process, which becomes the focal point for identifying areas of agreement and disagreement, decision points, data, and decisions made by the group (Carpenter, 1999; McCreary, Gamman, & Brooks, 2001; Susskind et al., 2012; Susskind et al., 2000). The **single-text method** guards against missing critical information or losing edits and changes if a document is passed between group members. The original text is usually developed by the convener, mediator, recorder, or group member with specific technical expertise, but all participants help in the crafting and development of subsequent drafts and the final document.

Record Meeting Developments and Decisions

It is the responsibility of the facilitator (or a member of the facilitation team) to record meeting minutes. This is an accurate account of group decisions, plans, tasks, and assigned responsibilities. The sequential record and main points of the discussion should be recorded and, if necessary, who made particular contributions to the discussion. Having someone record important details frees the participants to focus on issues rather than recording their own notes or relying on individual memory or interests. In addition to the meeting notes, it is also a good idea to visually record group memory through a graphic representation of the development of the meeting on a flipchart or other means (Dukes et al., 2001). In visually recording group memory, a record of the meeting is continually displayed for the group, tracking how decisions were made and providing a physical focus for attention and a useful reference for meeting minutes. Mistakes can be more easily shown and corrected so the process of decision making is not slowed. This also gives participants a sense of being heard and guarantees as much as possible that participants share a common understanding of what is happening (Haynes, 2006; Henkel, 2007; Malouff et al., 2012).

Manage Meeting Dynamics

One of the key characteristics of a mediator's job is to manage the dynamics of meetings. It is the responsibility of the mediator to pay attention to the undercurrent and address any tension or conflict between all parties. Different parties in environmental negotiations have varying degrees of power and access to resources. This can create a power imbalance and make negotiation difficult (Folger, Pool, & Stutman, 1997; O'Leary & Bingham, 2003). Power can be manifested in a number of ways such as personality, negotiation style, organizational authority or reputation, expertise or standing, access to resources, and so on. (Dietz & Stern, 2008; Dukes et al., 2001; Gray, 2003). In order to be successful, parties involved in a collaborative process or negotiation must have a parity of power. If power is uneven, the negotiations will be skewed and it will be difficult to negotiate (Dukes et al., 2001; Nelson et al., 1990; Reed, 2008). Parties must perceive interdependence on each other in order to move forward (O'Leary, 1995; O'Leary et al., 1999). The burden is on the mediator to understand the balance of power and influence in a situation and to design a process that recognizes participant interdependency and motivates participants to work with each other (Brewer & Ley, 2012; Dietz & Stern,

2008; Reed, 2008). This can be done by giving equal time to each participant to discuss their concerns, providing opportunities to share vital information (e.g., presentations by each organization), and building relationships (e.g., field trips, project storytelling processes), and creating opportunities for dialogue within smaller work groups (Dietz & Stern, 2008).

Lack of trust is another common characteristic of environmental policy processes that can manifest itself in meeting dynamics (Harris & Lyon, 2013; Susskind et al., 2012). One way to build trust, as suggested by Wondolleck and Yaffee (2000), is to create a situation in which people are given the opportunity to be honest, respectful, and fair. "Trust is a byproduct of responsible behavior—that is, a pattern of actions that demonstrates over a period of time, through difficult and testing circumstances, that group members are responsible" (Dukes et al., 2001, p. 38). Providing opportunities for participants to build trust during meetings can create healthy communication patterns and is the key to a successful process.

Typical meeting challenges and suggestions for addressing those challenges include the following:

One or more participants dominating conversation

- Invite others to comment on topic
- Suggest a process such as small group work or a round robin to give all participants a turn
- Metacommunicate means to talk about the act of communicating. Or in other words, name it and call them out in a polite respectful manner. "We've heard a lot from Jim today, before he weighs in, does anybody else have any ideas?"

Disagreement or high conflict between a few of the participants

- Maintain a physical presence by walking in between the participants
- Remind participants about the agreed upon ground rules
- Suggest a structured process to address the conflict, such as a separate meeting

Participants can't get past history

- Coach individually between meetings to address concerns
- Intervene and name it. Naming the elephant in the room takes the power away from the situation and places it in the group's control.

Technical experts give a presentation that is too complex and full of jargon

- Coach experts beforehand
- Ask clarifying questions
- Reframe in a more understandable manner

Participants don't feel that progress is being made

- Be positive and focus on what has already been accomplished
- Demonstrate by visual map how far the group has come
- Use sign posting at intervals or at the end of each meeting

Meetings are long and energy is low

- Acknowledge low energy and suggest having breaks more often
- Interweave activities such as small group work or field trips in between long decision-making meetings

Participants coming late or slipping out before the meeting is over

- Politely remind members of the attendance policy and ground rules
- Always begin meetings on time to create respect for everyone's time
- Speak with participants between meetings to troubleshoot tardiness

One of the participants threatens to leave the group

- Respectfully discuss the benefits of staying

Different interpretations of what has happened during a meeting

- Refer to the meeting minutes or decision documentation
- Discuss openly the different interpretations

Meeting Follow-Up

Document Decisions

After the meeting, the recorder and the mediator must review the notes for accuracy, and then provide a copy to each of the participants. Outlined in these notes should be decisions made, assignments given with deadlines, and required preparation for the next meeting (Dukes et al., 2001; Lee, 2008). If notes were recorded visually on a flipchart as well, it is often a good idea to take a picture of the flipcharts to make sure nothing is missed. Notes should be distributed quickly while the meeting is fresh in the minds of participants. This will give them the needed time to do the tasks that they are assigned before the next meeting.

Plan Next Meeting and Follow-Up With Participants

The mediator should plan the scaffolding of the next meeting while work items and dynamics are still in mind. If the date has not been set, this should be discussed and agreed upon before the end of the meeting. The mediator is also responsible for following up with participants to ensure that tasks will be completed and information will be gathered.

Proper meeting planning and implementation is the key to any successful policy development process. Being organized and properly managing meeting details and dynamics will ensure a good meeting, one in which results are achieved, the planned process used, and relationships between participants are built.

Collaborative processes are challenging, but having a strong MOU between participants and structuring highly effective meetings can allow participants to put their energy toward creating possible solutions that meet the needs of all parties and move the policy development process along.

Case Study Application

Referring to your chosen case study from Appendix A, develop a group charter or memorandum of understanding (MOU) including the goals, roles, and rules of the project. This will be your guide as you begin negotiating decisions; make it thorough and complete, including all the elements described above.

Voices From the Field

The Importance of Developing Trust in a Collaborative Process: Lake Ontario Ordnance Works

Sean Kelly, PhD

Professor of Political Science

California State University Channel Islands

Located near the shore of Lake Ontario in Niagara County, New York, in the town of Lewiston, the Lake Ontario Ordnance Works (LOOW) is an environmental legacy of World War II and the U.S.–Soviet Union Cold War.

The LOOW was commissioned to produce and store TNT for the war effort. Due to the overproduction of explosives it was decommissioned in July 1943. Still owners of the large site in a then-remote area, the U.S. government designated it as a site for disposal of nuclear material from the Manhattan Project aimed at developing the world's first nuclear weapon. Nuclear material transferred to what was named the Niagara Falls Storage Site (NFSS) was used to experiment with means for coping with nuclear waste. Among those efforts was an experiment to incinerate nuclear waste, which simply served to scatter the waste across the property.

As the Cold War with the Soviet Union began to ease, the government turned its attention to the remediation of former defense sites. In the 1980s, the Department of Energy (DOE) was responsible for nuclear waste material. The DOE developed a *temporary* solution for the material that involved constructing a large pit and moving all radioactive material—including soil, buildings, and the bulldozer that moved the material—from the site into the pit. The NFSS was covered with a cap of heavy clay and soil and remains there today as an unmarked monument to America's development of nuclear weapons.

But the problems at the LOOW did not stop there. The local community was concerned that the DOE remediation failed to remove all of the nuclear material, they were unhappy that a permanent solution for the radiological waste was nowhere in sight and that the problem of chemical contamination from TNT production remained. Add to this that presumably unused portions of the property were sold to private land holders and local municipalities; one of the parcels became the site of a K–12 school complex.

Lewiston, New York, is just a few miles from the infamous and iconic Love Canal site, located in the city of Niagara Falls. Government action and inaction in response to Love Canal casts a long shadow in the minds of residents. Many local residents feel they have reason to be skeptical of government claims.

In the 1980s, Congress assigned responsibility for chemical waste to the Department of Defense (DOD) and the U.S. Army Corps of Engineers (USACE) through the Defense Environmental Restoration Program for Formerly Used Defense Sites (DERP-FUDS) program. In the 1990s, Congress passed responsibility for radiological waste to the USACE in the form of the Formerly Utilized Sites Remedial Action Program (FUSRAP).

Because the LOOW site contained both chemical and radiological waste, its remediation is complicated by the *alphabet soup* of USACE programs. The USACE sought repeatedly to incorporate the community into a transparent decision-making process using the Restoration Advisory Board (RAB) composed of local stakeholders and USACE representatives. These efforts repeatedly collapsed. Failure was due in part to the failure of the public to understand the overlapping jurisdictions within the USACE. The public also misunderstood the resource limitations of the USACE. The RAB also failed under the weight of community distrust stoked by a few vocal activists—citing past government failures—some of whom sought to undermine the RAB process from the inside.

Further Reading

Jenks, A. (2007). Model city USA: The environmental cost of victory in World War II and the Cold War. *Environmental History 12*(3), 552–577.

Key Terms

group charter	Process Management	working groups
memorandum of understanding (MOU)	representation	
	single-text method	

CHAPTER 9

Policy Development

Working with stakeholders in a policy development decision-making process requires participants to work as a team engaged in critical analysis of environmental issues and solutions. This chapter outlines how to move participants through a decision-making process, including preparing to negotiate; defining group goals; providing opportunities for education, information exchange, and joint fact finding; brainstorming and development of possible options; establishing common **criteria** and applying criteria to options; negotiating prepared packages; and ratifying agreements. After reading this chapter, you will understand policy development and how to guide participants through a decision-making process.

Decision-Making Model

Foundational to the field of alternative dispute resolution is the process of **interest-based negotiation**, sometimes referred to as integrative bargaining or distributive negotiation. Interest-based negotiation is based on the principles of interactive group decision making, wherein parties identify the problem, search for alternative solutions, and make a decision as a group (Leventhal, 2006; Walton & McKersie, 1965). The most clearly articulated and well-cited explanation of interest-based negotiation is Roger Fisher and William Ury's *Getting to Yes: Negotiating Agreement Without Giving In*, originally published in 1981 with additional republications in 1991 and 2011. In their work, they outline the difference between soft bargaining and hard bargaining, arguing that neither approach maximizes the **interests** of participants, leading to dissatisfaction with the outcome or impasse and continued conflict.

Soft bargaining assumes the participants in the negotiation are friends and the goal is agreement. Because the focus is on the relationship rather than the issue, participants yield easily to pressure and make concessions to cultivate the relationship, leading to weak agreements characterized by one-sided losses. Hard bargaining treats participants as adversaries where the goal is victory. Because the focus is on winning, participants dig into their bottom line, make threats, and demand concessions as a condition of the relationship resulting in either a stalemate or one-sided gains. As an alternative to both of these approaches, Fisher and Ury (2011) offer **principled bargaining** or interest-based negotiation. In this approach, participants are neither friends nor enemies but problem solvers focused on reaching a wise outcome efficiently and effectively. They do this, argue Fisher and Ury, by separating the people from the problem, exploring the interests of the other, and developing mutually acceptable options which meet a mutually defined set of standards. These concepts or techniques are woven into many problem-solving approaches taken by scholars and practitioners in the field of environmental conflict resolution.

We outline an approach based on Fisher and Ury's (1981) principled bargaining, or interest-based negotiation, and patterned after traditional problem-solving approaches taken by others in the field of environmental conflict resolution (Carpenter, 1999; Maser & Pollio, 2012; Susskind & Cruikshank, 1987). We provide a step-by-step method beginning with negotiation preparation and ending with **ratification** of stakeholder agreement.

Negotiation Preparation

There are a number of tasks each stakeholder or party should take before coming to the table in a collaborative process. These tasks will prepare them for their role in the process and make negotiations run smoothly. Before the first meeting, stakeholders should have a good comprehension of the issue at hand, understand their (or their organization's) position on the issue, know the sources of resources or power, and be aware of alternative options should the negotiation not succeed.

Understand the Issue

Each stakeholder will have been provided with a copy of the assessment by the mediator, which outlines the history and context of the issues. This document should be well-read, along with any additional information about the issue. Participants should also develop a set of questions they hope will be answered during the process (Leventhal, 2006; McKearnan & Fairman, 1999) and put thought into what they want to get out of the process.

Focus on Interests, Not Positions

Fisher & Ury (2011) distinguish between **positions** and interests as a critical aspect of any negotiation. They define *positions* as the bottom line, or preferred outcomes insisted by group members. They are the *what* of the participant or what the participant wants. *Interests*, however, are the needs or reasons behind the stated position(s). Interests are the *why* of the participant speaking more so to the underlying needs of the participant. For example, the participants in a public policy decision-making process may initially take opposing positions on an issue relating to a landfill in their community. Citizen Group A insists on having a landfill.

Citizen Group B is strictly opposed to the idea. Viewing the situation from a positional perspective, there is no room for negotiation. Either one side will win and the other will lose or the parties will remain at an impasse. However, the interests behind those positions may not necessarily be mutually exclusive. Citizen Group A wants a landfill because it will bring economic development and jobs. Citizen Group B does not want a landfill because they are nervous about maintaining a safe and healthy environment for the community.

When participants are negotiating, they will be more successful if they focus on interests rather than positions (Beckenstein, Long, Arnold, & Gladwin, 1996; Sagrin & Crowder, 2007). In their analysis of a decade-long transportation conflict in New Zealand, Elias, Jackson, and Cavana (2004) argue that when participants were willing to focus on the interests of the other parties rather than the positions, they were able to come to an agreement. In the landfill example above, a focus on interests opens up possibilities and allows for the opportunity to develop options that meet both the interest of Citizen Group A and Citizen Group B.

This part of the negotiation preparation asks participants to understand and distinguish between positions and interests of themselves and the other participants. It is critical to understand your organization's concerns and objectives with the issue at hand. What are your positions and interests? What are you hoping to accomplish in the process? Realizing that each side has multiple interests, it is necessary to give thought to what is driving the other party's positions. What are the potential positions and interests of the other participants? Thought given to positions and interests before negotiations begin better prepares participants for their seat at the table (Manring, Nelson, & Wondolleck, 1990; McKearnan & Fairman, 1999). It is in the interests of participants that common ground and creative workable solutions can be found. Therefore, it is important to understand not only the position of your organization and the other stakeholders but the interests as well.

Activity

Positions Versus Interests

What are the positions versus possible interests in the following comments?

Native American tribal representative—"We have our own way of coexisting with the animals. Even for those who work at a regular job, trapping with their family is a big thing for them, their way of keeping connected to the land. We will own and control all trap lines within our traditional lands. This is nonnegotiable for us."

Government wildlife manager—"No! Trap lines are a public resource that must operate for the good of all. Trap lines must be used to develop their economic potential, and you do not run them that way now."

Non-native trapper—"Why should anyone get special treatment? I don't care if they have treaty rights. Without the same rules for everyone, these guys are going to trap out all the wildlife of this region."

Understand Your Best Alternative to a Negotiated Agreement (BATNA)

Perhaps one of the most important steps in preparing for a negotiation is to determine your **BATNA** (Fisher & Ury, 2011). BATNA is your best option should a negotiation not take place, or fail to meet your needs. BATNA is directly related to stakeholder's incentives to participate (Daniels & Walker, 2001) and directly influences their dedication to the negotiation and their behavior in the process (Bingham, 1986; Innes & Booher, 2010; Keough & Blahna, 2005; Susskind, Camacho, & Schenk, 2012). O'Leary (1995) uses the term *motivation* to describe the importance of incentives to negotiate. She argues that without incentive to negotiate, the conflicting parties may believe they have more to gain by staying in the conflict (or seeking other avenues) than by reaching consensus.

If a stakeholder feels their BATNA is strong, their motivation to negotiate is weak. No group will choose to be a part of a negotiation if what it can obtain away from the bargaining table is better than it is likely going to get by negotiating. If a stakeholder's BATNA is weak, their incentive to negotiate will be strong (Van Kleef, De Dreu, Pietroni, & Manstead, 2006). Negotiations will be influenced by the parties' expectations concerning the policy or decision that will be implemented if they fail to reach an agreement. Stakeholders may believe that another strategy, such as a lawsuit, will better meet their interests (Carpenter, 1999). If this is the case, their motivation to negotiate is lacking. A stakeholder's BATNA then becomes the standard against which any proposed agreement should be measured or what Bruce (2006) terms your "bargaining lens" (p. 278).

Whatever the level of your BATNA, strong or weak, it is strategic and necessary to try to continually improve your BATNA, or the options you can take outside of a negotiation. This will, in turn, improve your negotiation power (Nelson, Manring, Crowfoot, & Wondolleck, 1990; Van Kleef et al., 2006). Efforts to strengthen your BATNA should not be viewed as disingenuous or an attempt to undermine the collaborative process. Efforts to achieve objectives through litigation, lobbying, or media attention outside a participatory process that is not meeting a party's needs may be seen from an agency perspective as insincerity. However, those are legitimate political activities and are quite different from misrepresenting interests and intentions within a particular process (Dietz & Stern, 2008, p. 213). Knowing your BATNA and working to improve it places you in a strong and honest negotiation position, as any agreement made will be well thought out and strongly supported (Daniels & Walker, 2001; McKearnan & Fairman, 1999).

Understand Sources of Power

Power is the ability to get what you want or to influence events. It is the ability to impose on a situation and influence the outcome (Bascharach & Lawler, 1981; Boulding, 1989; Ramirez, 1999). Power can come in many forms. It could be economic power and resources; cultural or political power or standing in relation to a situation; or personal power such as expertise, education, information, presence, or communication style and competency (Dietz & Stern, 2008; Falkner, 2008; Gray, 2003; Nelson et al., 1990; Reed, 2008; Van Kleef et al., 2006).

In collaborative situations, such as environmental policy processes, organizational power plays a significant role. How an organization or agency representative behaves in a negotiation is often dictated by the organizational culture and power structures. The first general resource is the perceived expertise of the organization or agency. Perceived expertise is defined and influenced by the nature of the mission or the purpose originally given to the agency or organization, the type of leadership, and the public image of an agency (Falkner, 2008). For example, the Corps of Engineers, established by Congress more than 200 years ago, has played an integral part in the development of the United States. They have a reputation of proficiency, and their participation within a collaborative group would include that historical authority. The second source of power for an organization is its political or constituency support. This is directly influenced by the size and makeup of the constituency. For example, the Bureau of Reclamation (BOR), established in 1902 and whose charge it is to provide water to its constituents, has a lot of power in a negotiation given the tenuous nature of water supply in the United States. To be most successful in a negotiation, collaborative members should understand the level of their organizational power and resources and work to increase that power (Nelson et al., 1990; Reed, 2008).

Power is often viewed as a resource for individual gain but the interdependent nature of collaboration views power differently. In his book *Three Faces of Power*, economist Kenneth E. Boulding's (1989) central message is that integrative power—which includes the power of collaboration—is the most influential and significant form of power, surpassing both threat and economic power. Power is shared and dependent on interaction, so the power of an individual or organization is based on the dependence of others in a given context. Therefore, power is seen as relational (Boulding, 1989; Daniels & Walker, 2001; Folger, Poole, & Stutman, 1997; O'Leary, 1995). If power

is unequal in a collaboration, it is difficult to negotiate. Parties must have a parity of power and perceive interdependence on each other. This will enable them to move forward with shared and balanced power (Daniels & Walker, 2001; O'Leary, 1995; O'Leary, Durant, Fiorino, & Weiland, 1999). Realizing the power you bring to the table and the potential of relational power gained during the negotiation will better prepare you to participate in a negotiation.

Problem Definition

After individual stakeholder preparation of negotiation, the next step is to jointly define the problem and set parameters as to what will be part of the discussion. Scholars and practitioners of conflict resolution processes strongly identify joint-problem definitions as a critical first priority (Carpenter, 1999; Maser & Pollio, 2012; Moore, 1996; Susskind & Cruikshank, 1987; Westley, Miller, & Lacy, 2003; Wondolleck & Yaffee, 2000). Research on environmental conflicts has shown that the way in which an issue is defined or framed sets the tone for the rest of the process and has a huge effect on the solutions that are produced (Rieman, Hessburg, Luce, & Dare, 2010; Schon & Rein, 1994; Stringer, Reed, Dougill, Rokitzki, & Seely, 2007; Wondolleck & Yaffee, 2000). Further, it is directly linked to its collaborative success or failure (Gray, 2004; Gray, Peterson, Putnam, & Bryan, 2003; Lewicki, Gray, & Elliot, 2003). Often, environmental problems are intractable because parties focus more time on solving the problem instead of carefully identifying and jointly defining the problem (Asah, Bengston, Wendt, & Nelson, 2012). For example, in a study of an interdisciplinary network on human impacts on ecosystems, Westley et al. (2003) found that a major problem between participants was not opposing viewpoints but a lack of clear problem definitions of the issue. If participants do not develop a shared definition or framing of the problem, conflicts are more likely to be left unresolved (Webb & Raffaelli, 2008; Wiersema, 2008). Parties must jointly develop a common frame so they can reach a collaborative solution.

After a common frame and understanding of an issue has been developed, the next step is what Crowfoot and Wondolleck (1990) call "bounding the issues." Parties need to draw boundaries around an issue by including or excluding certain issue elements (Dewulf, Francois, Pahl-Wostl, & Taillieu, 2007; Manring et al., 1990; Ramirez, 1999). This includes understanding the group's decision space, or what aspects of the issue the group has the authority to make decisions about (Daniels & Walker, 2001; Manring et al., 1990)

When defining the issue, it is necessary to define it as a goal and not a problem or challenge. In Rutherford County, North Carolina, a grassroots organization called Concerned Citizens for Rutherford County (CCRC) came together to fight a megachip company moving into their rural county. In meetings they took a hostile approach and were not successful. Having lost the battle to keep the chip mill out of their county, they decided to rethink their temporal reactive framework and apply it to something more proactive. They redefined themselves as not against projects, but for alternative, more ecologically sustainable forestry initiatives. They were successful and have enjoyed a decade of impressive educational programs and initiatives to change regional planning policy to include community forestry with long-term holistic economic development strategies (Taylor, 2009). To further illustrate, in a project with the Imperial Valley irrigation district, the goal was to develop on-farm and system water conservation measures to deliver 103,000 acre feet of water annually to the San Diego Authority through creating incentive packages to engage farmers' to implement water conservation measures, rather than to limit farmer's water use in the Imperial Valley District. Defining the issue positively and as a goal gives participants something to work toward rather than an obstacle to overcome (Locke & Latham, 2006; Susskind & Cruikshank, 1987).

To increase the chance of success, goals must be clear with concrete and measurable objectives (Doremus et al., 2011; Rieman et al., 2010; Susskind et al., 2012; Tear et al., 2005; Williams, Szaro, & Shapiro, 2009). They should be visionary and general so they can adapt and respond to changes and new information but precise and specific so they can be measured and assessed. Further, when defining goals and measurable objectives it is critical to refrain from reducing the issue to a limited set of dimensions so as to minimize important aspects that speak to the parties' needs and interests (Bjornberg, 2009; Bruce, Lyall, Tait, & Williams, 2004). Equally critical is to depersonalize the issue from any one participant or organization (Fisher & Ury, 2011; Maxwell & Brown, 2000). Finally, the goal must not be so narrowly defined that it is linked to an already determined solution excluding other possible solutions. During a NEPA process the Utah Department of Transportation (UDOT) was sued by a number of nonprofit environmental organizations because they too narrowly defined their purpose statement and did not properly follow the NEPA process. The need for the project was to alleviate traffic in northern Utah, but UDOT's purpose statement was to develop a legacy highway. A purpose statement this narrowly defined does not allow for the development and consideration of multiple alternatives, such as carpooling, widening the existing freeway, and so on.

Education and Information Gathering

After the problem has been defined and the parameters of the goals and objectives have been set, the next step is to create opportunities for participants to exchange relevant perspectives and information regarding the dispute. This phase gives participants the opportunity to tell their story, hear how others view a problem, and learn how the issue affects others (Carpenter, 1999). Further, decision-making studies have found that processes tend to lead to better decisions when members share or pool relevant information. Thus, the opportunity for collaborative members to share information and educate others is highly valuable and paramount to a successful process. Mutual education and information sharing must be part of the negotiation process (Chase, Decker, & Lauber, 2004; Daniels & Walker, 2001; Dewulf et al., 2007; Lynam, De Jong, Sheil, Kusumanto, & Evans, 2007; Malouff, Calic, McGrory, Murrell, & Schutte, 2012; McCreary, Gamman, & Brooks, 2001; Postmes, Spears, & Cihangir, 2001; Ravnborg & Westermann, 2000; Reed, 2008; Rofougaran & Karl, 2005; Walker, Senecah, & Daniels, 2006; Walker, 2004; Walker, Daniels, & Emborg, 2008; Williamson & Fung, 2004; Yukl, 2010). This can take the form of group or individual presentations, field trips, or a facilitated dialogue of perspectives and knowledge central to the issue at hand.

After participants have shared and pooled relevant information, the participants should then identify information gaps or areas where additional information is needed. Information gaps are inherent in environmental policy development because, as discussed in Chapter 1, issues are complex, technical, and situated within high scientific and technical uncertainty (Dukes, Firehock, Leahy, & Anderson, 2001). Answers to policy problems often require complex scientific and multidisciplinary data (Keough & Blahna, 2005), but data may not be current, may not be comprehensive in scale and scope, and may not be considered acceptable or reliable by all parties. The question of good science is one of the biggest challenges faced by those in a collaborative process. Participants must decide the quality of information and how it will be applied, and the role of science must be clearly identified and be clearly understood by all participants to promote a transparent process (Saarman et al., 2013). We suggest the following standards when using science in collaborative processes: (a) use the best available science, (b) tailor objectives to the issue at hand, (c) ensure transparency of decision-relevant information and analysis, (d) pay attention to both facts and values and incorporate both local and traditional knowledge, (e) include independent review of official analysis or collaborative effort, and (f) allow reconsiderations of past conclusions on the basis of new information (Dietz & Stern, 2008; Tear et al., 2005; Yearly, 2000).

If data is incomplete, this step may involve the production and dissemination of new scientific knowledge (Berardo & Gerlak, 2012). Questions to guide the development of new data include the following:

1. Will the group have access to experts in relevant disciplines?

2. Will there be a technical advisory group or will the technical decisions be made by the whole group?

3. How, and when, will technical advisory groups be formed, and who will be represented? How will their findings be presented to the group?

4. Will there be any independent evaluation or peer review of the group's recommendations?

5. Are there resources and plans for data gathering or monitoring the impact of the agreements on the ground?

A discussion answering the above questions will create cohesion in a collaborative process as it requires that decisions about data are made jointly by all participants.

One common approach to gathering additional scientific information is to create a forum for a scientific-intense debate, where contending groups, or interests, contract experts to support or confirm their position. This is called adversarial science for a good reason. This approach naturally sets up a scenario where scientists are pitted against each other and focused on proving their position, rather than presenting the best available science for a given situation. This often results in conflicting information, and after the process is finished, collaborative participants are no closer to a decision then they were before it began.

Another common approach to gathering additional information on highly complex issues where technical uncertainty compounds value and policy differences is called a *blue ribbon approach*. A technical advisory group is tasked with conducting studies, answering technical questions, and evaluating management proposals. This blue ribbon panel is usually made up of scientists with expertise in a field. They review relevant information and generate consensus on the science related to the issue. Members of the blue ribbon panel may participate actively in process meetings of the whole group but typically would not be considered decision-making members. The lack of personal contact between scientists and decision makers allows for misinterpretation of scientific information, which in turn can lead to poor decision making (Rofougaran & Karl, 2005). Further, while this approach is favored among many policy developers, it may lack legitimacy with stakeholders because they were not involved in the process. If stakeholders are not involved, valuable information may be missed or the wrong questions asked. Science-intensive policy processes, which often require specialized knowledge, must directly involve technical experts, scientists, and stakeholders in the scientific information gathering process (McCreary et al., 2001; Raitio, 2012; Raitio & Saarikoski, 2012; Saarikoski & Raitio, 2013; Saarikoski, Raitio, & Barry, 2013). We favor an approach that includes technical experts, scientists, decision makers, and stakeholders in a joint data gathering and analysis process.

Joint Fact Finding

In multiparty cases where the issue or scientific data may be controversial, a joint fact-finding approach offers an alternative to adversarial science or blue ribbon panels (Weible & Sbatier, 2009). Joint fact finding, although applied to other types of decision making (such as health and economics), was developed in the context of environmental mediation (Ehrmann & Stinson, 1999; Herman, Susskind, & Wallace, 2007; McCreary et al., 2001; Wondolleck & Yaffee, 2000). The core idea is that experts, stakeholders, and policy makers work together to produce a common knowledge base relevant for the decision-making situation under dispute. All participants pool relevant information and jointly determine the questions to be addressed; what information is needed; and the best process for gathering, analyzing, and applying or utilizing the information during negotiations. Integrating both expert knowledge and stakeholder knowledge and concern, it focuses the debate, creates shared concepts and definitions, promotes innovative solutions to policy problems, and can produce policy-relevant technical information accepted by a wide range of stakeholders and policy makers (Ehrmann & Stinson, 1999; Herman et al., 2007; McCreary et al., 2001; Saarikoski & Raitio, 2013; Wondolleck & Yaffee, 2000). "The goal is to marshal the most relevant, reliable information and analyses to create technically sound public policies, and to elevate the level of understanding of technical issues among responsible agencies and members of the public" (McCreary et al., 2001, p. 334). Inclusive inquiry, structured according to the principles of joint fact finding, could create more extensive and reliable policy. It also provides relevant and socially legitimate knowledge base for decision making as it gives rigor to scientific decisions and sets a legally defensible process (Tear et al., 2005).

Saarikoski and Raitio (2013) argue that fact finding can create more policy-relevant and scientifically robust decisions for forest management. Using two case studies of old-growth management, one in Finland and one in Canada, they argue that traditional science is insufficient in complex and highly political environmental decision-making situations. In Upper Lapland, Finland, traditional science failed to resolve the conflict between state forestry and traditional Sami reindeer herding over old-growth management. The reindeer herders argue that logging of old-growth forests destroys essential lichen pastures, whereas the forestry sector argues that the deterioration of pasture lands is caused by overgrazing, not forestry operations. Comparing the situation to a similar one in British

Columbia, Canada, the authors argue that if joint fact finding had been employed, the conflict could have been resolved. Joint fact finding played an important role in reaching the Canadian Great Bear Rainforest agreement, which increased the protection of old-growth from 9% to 33%. This decision met the needs and goals of all participants, strengthening relationships between participants in a once contentious process (Raitio, 2012; Raitio & Saarikoski, 2012; Saarikoski & Raitio, 2013; Saarikoski et al., 2013)

A well designed joint fact-finding process will improve the capacity of all participants and provide the opportunity to learn from all forms of knowledge to reach solutions (Rofougaran & Karl, 2005). It also offers those stakeholders with less experience the technical understanding necessary to make an informed decision, as it puts all members of the collaborative on equal footing, resolving areas of uncertainty, building trust in each other, and creating confidence in the process resulting in a strengthened relationship among participants (Andrews, 2002; Baldwin, Tan, White, Hoverman, & Burry, 2012; Brewer & Ley, 2012; Ehrmann & Stinson, 1999; McCreary et al., 2001; Wondolleck & Yaffee, 2000). Baldwin et al. (2012) discuss how a joint fact-finding process informed a community understanding of groundwater in Australia. They argue that it was the process of joint fact finding that brought diverse voices together to discuss in an open dialogue the scientific details of hydrology and ultimately produced a consensus-based decision. Through the process, all participants learned and, as a result, were able to craft a well-supported agreement. Others have argued for a fact-finding process in relation to water issues. Examining two communities in Southern California, Rofougaran and Karl (2005) conclude that the absence of an effective joint fact-finding process led the participants to distrust the science resulting in a stalemate. The authors believe if a joint fact-finding process was employed, the parties could have learned from each other and may have been able to reach a resolution.

Deciding when to use a joint fact-finding process will depend on the issue or situation. Scholars and practitioners recommend using the process in highly technical, scientifically intense decision-making forums that hinge on critical information. It can also be employed when there is deadlock or low trust between participants, as joint fact finding offers an opportunity to build trust, identify agreements, and narrow disagreements. When deciding, you will have to determine how much information can be gathered in light of political, financial, and related contexts. Joint fact finding can be expensive and time-consuming. You will have to consider cost, time, and the potential good of new information. If a fact-finding process will not likely yield beneficial data and cannot be effectively integrated into the dispute resolution process, it is better to consider another forum for gathering the necessary scientific information (Baldwin et al., 2012; Ehrmann & Stinson, 1999). However, if fact finding proves to be a feasible process, there are key design techniques that can increase the likelihood of success.

Each joint fact-finding process must be tailored or customized to the situation and have well-defined protocols (Innes & Booher, 2010; McCreary et al., 2001; Susskind et al., 2012). However, there are common techniques and steps that scholars and practitioners agree should be included. The first is designing the process so participants can have a face-to-face dialogue. This is crucial for the development of trust and provides an opportunity for participants to strengthen their relationships and build confidence in the process (Hubo & Krott, 2013; McCreary et al., 2001; Saarikoski & Raitio, 2013). The second technique is the use of a neutral third party. This is often the same mediator that is designing the entire collaboration process. They will be familiar with the issue and participants and can provide a seamless process design complimentary to the larger process. In addition to facilitating the face-to-face meetings, the mediator can coach technical experts in making their presentations understandable and accessible for all stakeholders (McCreary et al., 2001; Susskind et al., 2012). The third technique is the use of a single-text document to record deliberations and decisions. This method requires all participants to work on the same *single-text* such as a Google document, so changes and edits are not lost. The use of single text will help the process stay organized and will create cohesion among participants (McCreary et al., 2001; Susskind et al., 2012).

With the design techniques mentioned above in mind, the specific steps taken may include the following:

1. Define issue of concern, the specific problem to be resolved, and the timeline for decisions.

2. Define process for gathering information, including who manages the process (roles and responsibilities), how to select experts, how to determine confidentiality, and how the information will be used.

3. Define the questions to be asked and the method of analysis. Translate general questions into research questions; decide methodology, both qualitative and quantitative approaches; and outline possible limitations to each.

4. Develop a final report with the understanding that the process may not reveal definitive answers under continuing uncertainty but outline how findings will be integrated into possible options for agreement and contingency plans.

The scope of the process will be determined by the nature of the issue, the budget, and the time available. The important thing to remember is to outline a clear transparent process that has the buy-in of the entire group (Herman et al., 2007).

A strong educational phase will set up a solid platform to develop options for mutual gain, which is the next step in the policy development process.

Development of Options

Once the environmental problem has been jointly framed as a goal and the necessary information has been obtained and shared with all participants, the next step is to develop options for mutual gain. This step provides the opportunity to use creative problem-solving methods to generate mutual gain through brainstorming techniques.

Brainstorm

The first step in developing options is to use various brainstorming techniques to harness the creativity of the group (Carpenter, 1999; Fisher & Ury, 2011; Maser & Pollio, 2012; Susskind et al., 2012). To maximize the potential inventiveness of participants, it is important to create the correct atmosphere and conditions. Ground rules during this phase should include (a) no criticism or judgment of ideas, (b) focus on the future and potential situation, (c) no commitment of ideas at this stage, and (d) no option is off the table. There should also be a time limit to this step, influenced by the time frame in which a decision must be made. This will give the process a sense of urgency, which is necessary to move the process along (McKearnan & Fairman, 1999).

It is important to identify the purpose or goal of the brainstorming session. Because of the complexity of environmental conflict, it is often necessary to fraction the conflict, or break it up into smaller, more manageable portions (Susskind et al., 2012). Focusing on a specific issue will provide direction for the group and make developing options more manageable. Some issues, however, will not be as easily defined. For example, issues such as face or respect will need to be converted into something tangible and able to be negotiated (Daniels & Walker, 2001)

There are various brainstorming techniques that will assist the group members in developing creative options. These include (a) freethinking, which allows participants to freely call out ideas in random order; (b) turn taking, which requires each participant to generate an original idea or option; (c) small group, which breaks participants into smaller groups to generate more discussion; (d) bird's eye, which allows some members to view the brainstorming process of others in the group; and (e) worksheets, which uses worksheets designed to visually breakdown concerns, ideas, and possibilities.

Identify the Shared Interests of Group Members

After ideas or options have been generated, the areas of agreement, or what McCreary et al. (2001) call zones of agreement, should be identified. In this step, participants start with the zones of agreement or the most promising idea and consider ways to build on, expand, or narrow options.

After options have been invented and common interests have been identified, it is important to jointly establish objective criteria in order to assess which options are feasible.

Establishment of Criteria

Criteria are the governing principles of the negotiation and the standards by which you will judge each option. They will be influenced by the interests of all parties and should set up a measurable condition that the chosen option must meet in order to be a viable option for all parties involved. They are, in a sense, what success will look like (Susskind et al., 2012). While some practitioners place the establishment of criteria before the generation of options, to brainstorm options before establishing criteria is the classical approach in the field. This is to better encourage creativity and synergistic thinking that is not limited by already defined criteria. Although the criteria will vary for each process or negotiation, environmental scholars and practitioners have identified some common criteria (MacNaughton & Martin, 2002; Maser & Pollio, 2012; McKearnan & Fairman, 1999; Tear et al., 2005). These criteria include the following:

- Cost effectiveness: Is the option in question economically viable?
- Scientific reliability: Does the option adhere to professional standards of the scientific community and is it based on sound scientific evidence and reasoning?
- Social and professional legitimacy: Will the option have social legitimacy and acceptance with the professional organizations/constituents associated with the group as well as the general public?
- Timeliness: Is the option feasible within the timeframe necessary and will the option(s) provide a timely solution to the situation?
- Fairness: Is the proposed solution fair and equitable to all parties? Are the interests of all parties represented and addressed?
- Feasibility: Is the proposed solution feasible and does it directly address the problem, statement, or goals of the process?
- Legally defensible: What is the risk of legal action should the option be chosen? Is it legally defensible?
- Relationship enhancement: Does the proposed option strengthen the scientific and environmental community in which it impacts?

Criteria will be specific to a given policy or decision and should be jointly agreed upon by the entire group. While they do not dictate the decision, they provide a standard that any potential solution must meet in order to be accepted by the group.

Negotiation of Packaged Deals

Once options have been generated and criteria set, the next step is to evaluate the options in light of the established criteria. This will help participants narrow the range of options or create packages of proposals to consider (Fisher & Ury, 2011; Gunia, Swaab, Sivanathan, & Galinsky, 2013; Maser & Pollio, 2012; McCreary et al., 2001; McKearnan & Fairman, 1999; Susskind et al., 2012; Susskind & Cruikshank, 1987). It is important to remember that no decision has been made at this point. Decisions should be kept tentative and conditional. This allows for joint gains or trade-offs to be sought within packages linking decisions to each other in acceptable offers or trade-offs (Gunia et al., 2013; Maser & Pollio, 2012).

Participants at this stage should use good negotiation strategies to package ideas and proposals. Often, participants in negotiations have a zero-sum perspective or the belief that a gain to one side is a *loss* to the other. Having ideas packaged together can help avoid zero-sum thinking and create solutions that are mutually beneficial. To do this, there are a number of negotiation strategies outlined by scholars and practitioners in the field.

Bridging

This is perhaps the most commonly used negotiation strategy. Negotiators who use this strategy invent new options that meet each other's needs. Or in other words, look for an option that will bridge the interests of the parties in dispute. For example, the Jordan Valley Water Conservancy District brought together a group of 20 stakeholders, including federal, state, and county agencies; special interest groups; and private companies to discuss alternatives for cleaning up ground water contaminated by historical mining activities. Solutions for assessment and cleanup bridged many interests of private, governmental, and interest groups.

Expanding the Pie

Parties should avoid fixed-pie mentality and seek for ways to increase their resource base. **Expanding the pie** refers to finding ways to increase available resources so all parties can meet their objectives (Fisher & Ury, 2011; Walton & McKersie, 1965). In a dispute where a city wants to protect a fragile environmental resource and a citizens group wants access to the land for recreational purposes, they could expand the pie by a joint fundraising project to acquire additional land. This solution would provide the space to meet both interests instead of forcing the disputants to compete over the limited resource. Another example is the Juneau Airport Expansion project. This project was controversial because expanding the runway of the airport meant ruining critical wetlands. To expand the pie and gain additional resources, **mitigation** packages included acquiring additional land and creating wetlands.

Building Coalitions/Alliances

A second strategy to developing options for mutual gain is coalition building or forming alliances. Coalitions are defined as "subgroups whose purpose is to influence the decision of a larger group" (Polzer, Mannix, & Neale, 1995, p. 135). Stakeholders are likely to form alliances as a bargaining tool to gain power (Gray, 2003). Organizing groups or individuals with shared interests provides for a unified front built on common interest and purpose (Manring et al., 1990; Susskind & Cruikshank, 1987). Focusing on the development of policy concerning the California Marine Protection Act (MPA), Fox et al. (2013) outline how engaging additional support through previously formed coalitions allowed the group to address potential conflicts between military use areas and MPA planning in a way that was beneficial to both the collaborative group and the military.

Cost Cutting/Specific Compensation/Mitigation

This strategy refers to offering to compensate a party for costs incurred by accepting the other party's proposal. The negotiation of environmental standards may involve compensation such that the total environmental quality will remain on a similar or higher level. For example, farmers who agree to reduce the pumping of water from an aquifer may incur costs from resulting losses to their rice crops. To address this, a government agency might provide technical, or even financial, assistance for the farmers to convert to less water-intensive crops, which in turn may offer the farmers more economic security in the long term. In environmental policy negotiation, this is often called *mitigation*, or providing a compensation for impact on the environment.

Voogd (2000) provides an example of compensation in the Dutch planning practice regarding the treatment of polluted soils. Soils are classified according to different categories. Category A describes soils in which the amount of chemicals does not deviate from what would be expected in the soil under natural conditions. Category B is reserved for soils with a modest pollution and Category C is for soils designated as heavily polluted. Creating measures whereby soils can be designated Category A is very costly. Cleaning the last 10% or 20% is often as costly as cleaning the first 80% or 90%. Therefore, cleaning 80% is often accepted, provided compensation is given by cleaning up in whole, or part, another site that would otherwise not be cleaned up.

Nonspecific Compensation

In this strategy, one party is offered something in return for a concession (Daniels & Walker, 2001). The compensation is *nonspecific* because the compensation or trade-off does not directly relate specifically to the concession. Money exchange is the most common form of nonspecific compensation (Voogd, 2000).

Logrolling

In this strategy, the parties look for low-cost options to address the other party's high-priority issues. In a siting dispute, city officials may be willing to hold two additional public meetings (low cost) in exchange for the citizens agreeing to not go to the press during the negotiation period (high priority).

It is important to note that during this negotiation phase there will be a number of iterations of proposals or packages. It is important that participants understand that no agreement is final until the proposal addresses all concerns and meets the goals established early on in the process (McCreary et al., 2001). It may even be necessary to develop contingency agreements should a portion of the package be changed due to unexpected pressures or threats (McKearnan & Fairman, 1999).

Considering Culture

Forming Cultural Alliances and Building Coalitions

The conflict between Native Americans and their white rural neighbors over environmental issues is well documented. Yet there are cases focused on the alliances of some Native and white communities that have become a key element in the protection of natural resources. In eastern Montana and western South Dakota, some of the earliest alliances in the United States between Native Americans and white ranchers confronted mining corporations and later bombing ranges and toxic wastes (Grossman, 2005). Highlighting various case studies, Grossman (2005) argues that an alliance is more than a temporal agreement; it can represent a way to challenge racial or ethnic conflict by using the concept of place (environment) as a common building block. Building on Grossman's work, we identify several key elements or guidelines to consider when forming cultural alliances.

Most Successful Alliances are Formed at the Local Level

Efforts to improve interethnic relations at the governmental or large-scale level are often unsuccessful in improving relations at the social or local level. Negotiations in the Northwest United States over fishing and water rights represent intense treaty rights conflicts that have resulted in strong government-to-government relations between tribal and non-Native state and federal agencies. But this *top-down* cooperation has done little to improve relationships at a local level. Alliances based solely on institutional and government cooperation are not enough to adequately address environmental problems. In Washington and Oregon, the fishing conflict between the western Washington Tribes, the state government, and the white fishermen has led to widespread conflicts that in some cases have persisted until this day. In the 1960s and 1970s, non-Native fishing groups were at odds with many Native American tribes over treaty fishing rights. But in the early 1980s, some non-Native fishing groups began to rethink their opposition and many began working with the tribes to stop projects that threatened fish habitat, such as hydroelectric dams. Many of those alliances created locally between members of the community still persist today and continue to have success (Grossman, 2005). Alliances between culturally variant groups can harness their joint power, creating a strength each would not enjoy alone. Further, an environmental alliance built at the local level between groups can directly address racial differences because that is where the racism and divide between communities lives. While people-to-people alliances are important, they should not be seen as an alternative to government-to-government alliances. Local alliances between cultural groups should be developed in parallel to government-to-government alliances. Creating alliances at both levels can increase negotiation power and strengthen cultural community ties.

The Parameters of a Cultural Alliance Must Be Mutually Understood and Respected

A successful alliance will foster trust developed through mutual understanding of interests and a respect for the concerns of the others (Margerum,

2011). In Wisconsin, the Ho-Chunk Native Americans joined with white farmers to oppose Air National Guard low-level flights and a bombing range expansion. The expansion of the bombing range was important to the Ho-Chunk, while the expansion of the flight range was of most concern to the farmers. At the onset, these alliances enjoyed moderate success as the Ho-Chunk and local farmers aligned their resources to oppose the expansions. In the end, however, the Air National Guard met the demands of white farmers not to expand the flight ranges but continued to pursue the expansion of the bombing range. Many of the white farmers claimed victory and dropped their demand to oppose bombing range expansion, severing their alliance with the Ho-Chunk tribe and effectively worsening their relations (Grossman, 2005).

The Ho-Chunk example reflects a larger critique of alliances between whites and people of color. Alliances are often based on the assumption that the minority communities will set aside their particular concerns for a common universal good; many of the majority are not often willing to do the same. Alliances must be mutually understood and members of the alliance must have mutual respect for the concerns of their counterpart.

The Strongest Alliances Are Built on a Shared Sense of Place

The goal of a cultural alliance must be common mutual inclusion. This is different from merely crossing social boundaries or shifting political jurisdictions. It means configuring a community or home that includes all groups living in the same landscape. Native American resistance to multinational mining corporations in Wisconsin has been growing for over 3 decades. To protect tribal resources, the Mole Lake Chippewa joined with both their non-Native neighbors in the town of Nashville and local sport-fishing organizations to oppose the Crandon mine and the metallic mining district proposed by promine interests. Building on their shared sense of place, the alliance not only fought the mine proposal, but began to chart economic alternatives to mining development in their community. Cooperative relations between the town and the Mole Lake tribe were further strengthened when they received a $2.5 million grant from the federal government to promote long-term sustainable jobs in their community. Together with surrounding townships, the Menominee Nation, the Lac du Flambeau Tribe, and the Mole Lake Chippewa formed the Northwoods Niijii (the Chippewa word for "friends") Enterprise Community. Now Native American nations, sport-fishing groups, environmentalists, unionists, and local community residents are working together in a multiracial, rural-based grassroots alliance to address not only "endangered species, but endangered Native cultures and endangered rural economies as well" (Grossman & Gedicks, 2001). The above case study demonstrates the increased capacity a cultural alliance can have in addressing environmental conflicts.

Alliances between cultural groups are not exempt from facing differences or difficulties, but local people-to-people alliances that foster mutual understanding and respect and are built on enduring values, commonalities, and a shared sense of place can become a solid foundation for jointly addressing environmental issues and managing conflict.

Ratification of Agreement

The single-text document that has recorded decisions and negotiated iterations will become the written agreement of the group. After the group has reached agreements on all issues, the next step is for each member to endorse the agreement through the process of ratification. If the decision is unanimously supported, the report can declare as such. However, if there are aspects of the report that are not unanimous but the group has agreed to move forward with an agreement, dissention should be documented in a minority report (McCreary et al., 2001)

It is essential that an agreement is signed to prevent misunderstandings or misinterpretations and ensure accountability and commitment (Manring et al., 1990). Who signs the document depends on its anticipated use and political context, but typically all stakeholders who are part of the negotiation process would sign it.

Included in the agreement should be an account of the adaptability of the document and/or provisional strategies in light of new information or changing conditions. This will add to the longevity of the agreement and cultivate long-term capacity building (Susskind et al., 2012). Chapter 10 of this book will talk more of implementation, capacity building, and sustaining community relations.

Collaborative policy development is challenging and can seem overbearing to participants. As participants work through their differences and jointly develop options to address the environmental conflict or issue, having a well-thought-out process with specific steps will alleviate feelings of fatigue and provide signposts of progression for the group.

Case Study Application

Referring to your chosen case study from Appendix A, negotiate as a team and apply each policy development step outlined above as you create policy to address the conflict.

1. Prepare to negotiate: Identify the main issues, positions, interests, BATNA, and sources of power for each stakeholder.

2. Define the issue: Using the guidance above, develop a goal statement for your group.

3. Identify information gaps and opportunities for education between the parties: If additional information or data is needed, will you use a fact-finding process? If so, decide as a group how to proceed.

4. Using the brainstorm techniques suggested, develop options to address the issue and accomplish the goal of the collaborative process.

5. As a group, jointly establish criteria to apply to your options.

6. Using the negotiation strategies outlined above, develop package deals to address the issue.

7. Document and ratify your agreement.

Voices From the Field

Sustainability and Corporate Responsibility: Rio Tinto

James Cantrill, PhD

Professor and Department Head

Communication Studies

Northern Michigan University

Often, to put in place a durable system for managing natural resource conflicts, one must negotiate away the power to say "No!" and, in doing so, learn why the affirmation of mutual interests lays the foundation for a sustainable, trusting relationship.

In 2007, one of the world's largest mining conglomerates, Rio Tinto, secured preliminary federal and state permits to mine up to 300 million pounds of high-grade nickel—a strategic metal necessary for the production of everything from stainless steel to batteries that will power a large part of the emerging green economy, and for which the United States did not have a domestic source—in a remote region of Michigan's Upper Peninsula. Although the Eagle Project is small by global standards, with a production footprint of less than 130 acres, the underground ore body is in a matrix of sulfide-bearing minerals that, when extracted elsewhere in the past, has left a legacy of highly acidic mine drainage that has sometimes destroyed water quality in a region for generations. Precisely because of the environmental risks posed by the operation, along with the *boom and bust* social upheavals occasioned by most mining operations, Rio Tinto's efforts to permit the Eagle Project had been strongly opposed by wealthy land owners in the area of the mine, local and national environmental organizations, and the Keweenaw Bay Community of the Chippewa Nation that claimed religious and natural resource treaty rights to the site of the operation. The mining opponent's interests resulted in the filing of several, repeatedly unsuccessful, legal challenges and the State of Michigan creating the most stringent, nonferrous mining regulations ever adopted in the United States, as well as the company having to invest millions of dollars into using the best technology currently available to mitigate any potential environmental harm. Nonetheless, despite the issuing of final permits in 2010 and the adoption of safeguards, such as the construction of a reverse osmosis water treatment facility that would discharge water from the mine that is significantly purer than that found in local streams, the entrenched conflict would not go away.

Normally, one might expect a multinational corporation with vast financial resources and the backing of the local business community to simply marginalize those voices opposed to the Eagle Project and forge ahead despite the continuing outcry. But Rio Tinto is not your normal mining company. Since the mid-1990s, with an eye toward sustainability and corporate responsibility, the organization has required every operation and its subsidiaries to abide by not only a strict standard of environmental accountability, but also the engendering

(Continued)

(Continued)

of as much community support for its projects as possible. In the case of the Eagle Project, this commitment entailed recognizing its social license to operate depended on overcoming local distrust of corporate motivations and regulatory oversight, lack of scientific literacy, and a sense of powerlessness to protect health and hearth. So, in addition to other measures, Rio Tinto negotiated with its detractors a first-of-its-kind community environmental monitoring system, initially funded to the tune of $1.2 million. It is a relatively elegant initiative: A local watershed partnership organization opposed to the mine would be given free rein to use whatever means necessary to monitor all air and water quality aspects of the mining operation. To prevent even the appearance of corporate co-option, financing of the ongoing monitoring activities would flow from Rio Tinto to a neutral and local community foundation who would disburse funds accordingly. Rio Tinto would exempt itself from having the right to censor any findings from the monitoring process and gave the community foundation the final say in determining if the process was valid and reliable. In essence, the company empowered its opponents by providing a way and the means to initiate new civil action if it did not live up to its promises and the strictures under which the mine was permitted.

Once the monitoring agreement was in place, and just about the time that tunneling to the face of the nickel deposit 1000 feet underground was completed, the conflict dynamics radically changed. Staunch opponents of the Eagle Project began to soften their rhetoric, distrust began to recede, and antimine advocates began to publically express admiration for both the technological sophistication of the operation, as well as those who represented Rio Tinto's interests in the area. Indeed, those sentiments carried through to the summer of 2013 when Rio Tinto sold 100 percent of its interests in the Eagle Project to another company, Lundin Mining, who agreed to keep in place all of the conflict management processes that had been established thus far as a condition of sale.

Key Terms

BATNA	expanding the pie	Logrolling
Bridging	interests	mitigation
Coalitions/Alliances	interest-based negotiation	positions
criteria		principled bargaining
decision-making model	joint fact finding	ratification

CHAPTER 10

Communication Capacity Building

One of the most challenging aspects of any collaborative process is the communication between participants. A single phrase uttered in contempt can undo weeks of progress. Having good communication skills is imperative to the success of an environmental policy development process (d'Estree, 2003; Manring, Nelson, & Wondolleck, 1990; Rieman, Hessburg, Luce, & Dare, 2010; Singletary et al., 2008). Littlejohn and Domenici (2001) listed three requirements for developing healthy communication and dialogue among people united only by their diversity: (a) taking time to explore experiences, ideas, concerns, and doubts; (b) listening for both differences and commonalities in the experiences and stories, as well as values, expressed by all parties; and (c) asking open, nonjudgmental, and curious questions to learn more about the others. This chapter focuses on the communication skills necessary to work through differences and craft agreements that meet the needs of those involved in the decision-making process. The key to successful collaborative processes is training in listening, good communication skills, and problem solving (Davidson & Wood, 2004). Specific skills such as listening, communicating concerns, question asking, and **reframing** will be discussed, and the development of such proficiencies will be addressed through exercises, role plays, and scenario analysis.

Communication Competency

Our approach to communication views conversational exchanges as shared understanding or systems of meaning (d'Estree, 2003). Participants in conversation create and co-create their worldviews, including the problem to be addressed and potential solutions (Dewulf, Francois, Pahl-Wostl, & Taillieu, 2007; Gordon, 2011; Walker, 2007). Successful communicators recognize this dependency and seek to jointly establish possibilities in conversation by working off of each other. Daniels and Walker (2001) outline three dimensions of communication competence: (a) adaptability, the ability to assess situations and adapt their communicative behaviors accordingly; (b) appropriateness, knowing how and when to employ communication behaviors; and (c) effectiveness, the ability to achieve communicative goals. The key to competence is knowing and accepting that appropriate and effective communication is determined by others. Thus, it is necessary to seek to engage *with* others not merely speak at them.

Communication Capacity Building

Power-over communication, or what Floyd (2009) calls a "one-up," is a verbal message through which the speaker attempts to exert dominance or gain control over the listener. It is to verbally establish a hierarchy through tone, word choice, and cadence. Power-over communication is not well received by others as conversation and turns into a series of power messages, leaving behind the real intent of communicating, such as understanding perspectives or advocating your view.

The alternative to power-over is power-with, or what Floyd (2009) calls "one-across." This is a verbal message that seeks to neutralize relational control and power and establish commonality through tone, word choice, and cadence. This type of communication is inviting and engaging as communicators seek to understand and build upon the perspectives that each participant brings to the table. The following paragraphs focus on developing power-with communication skills to engage in conversation that will move participants toward understanding and agreement.

Listening and Acknowledgment

One of the most powerful, and indeed crucial, tools participants in a collaborative process must have is the ability to listen. Floyd (2009) calls *listening* the "cure for conflict" (p. 479). Active listening focuses on learning information and exploring problems (Davidson & Wood, 2004; Welton, 2002). It assumes a desire to learn from another person, thereby recognizing their perspective. Listening assumes acknowledgment and such acknowledgment is critical to the communicative process between participants (Collins, 2009; Davidson & Wood, 2004; Malouff, Calic, McGrory, Murrell, & Schutte, 2012; Welton, 2002). "Consensus building may be impossible unless the work of acknowledgement and recognition precedes the work of problem solving. . . . After recognition comes exploration, listening, learning, invention, proposals, and creative work" (Forester, 1999, p. 491). Once people feel heard, they are open to creatively addressing issues and working toward agreement.

In conflict, it is difficult to really listen to the other without hastily prejudging the other or focusing on what you will say next. To truly listen means to be present to the other, allowing the person to truly speak their mind or what Gordon (2011) calls "embracing the other" and being open to their experience (p. 48).

Active listening takes focus, commitment, and discipline and is dependent on motivation (Brownell, 2010; Daniels & Walker, 2001). If you are committed to listening and developing the necessary skills, you will be more effective in handling conflict.

Brownell (2010) presents a skill-based model of listening-centered communication. Creating an easy to remember acronym, HURIER, she identifies six critical components of good listening: **H**earing, **U**nderstanding, **R**emembering, **I**nterpreting, **E**valuating, and **R**esponding. Building on her work and incorporating the work of others, we present the **HURIER model** below.

Hearing

The first component identified by Brownell is hearing. To hear another is to make a decision about what to focus on within a context filled with many stimulus options. In order to do this, the listener must commit to understanding and prepare to listen by determining their listening goals, analyzing the listening context, and addressing the influence of listening filters such as culture, style, age, attitudes, and the like. (Thompson, Leintz, Nevers, & Witkowski, 2010). The hearer must optimize physical conditions for hearing and minimize psychological barriers. Body posture and eye contact must be directed towards the speaker so as to maximize attention and minimize distraction. Finally, the listener must receive and consciously attend to, collect, and distinguish between verbal and nonverbal messages (Bodie, Cyr, Pence, Rold, & Honeycutt, 2012).

Understanding

The second component of good listening is understanding. Brownell (2010) defines this as having decoded both the verbal and nonverbal components and having attended to and received the message. To understand, a listener must recognize assumptions and listen to understand, rather than evaluate, their message. They are to distinguish the main ideas from the supporting evidence by recognizing patterns and focusing on the essential message rather than the detail. This is done while continually checking perceptions for accurate comprehension (Thompson et al., 2010). While listening to their message, it is often tempting to make judgments, calculate the ways you disagree with them, or formulate your response while they are speaking, but if true listening is to happen, the listener must hear the entire message without interrupting and focus on the speaker rather than their own response (Wolvin, 2010).

Remembering

Remembering is the third component outlined by Brownell (2010). This step involves understanding how current information compares to previous understandings. This is often more difficult during conflict but is necessary for the hearer to make sense of what is being said.

Interpreting

The fourth component of listening is interpreting. This is the process of assigning meaning to the message and drawing inferences from the new information. The listener must be willing to suspend personal bias temporarily as they consider the context of the communication act and factor in the understood goals of the communicator (Bodie et al., 2012; Thompson et al., 2010). In this stage, there is an increased sensitivity to both verbal and nonverbal cues as the listener engages in mirroring. To mirror another speaker is to acknowledge and repeat key phrases from the conversation. This demonstrates that you are paying attention and understanding where they are coming from (Leach, Rogelberg, Warr, & Burnfield, 2009; Malouff et al., 2012; Yukl, 2010). To encourage the speaker, it is also necessary to ask clarifying questions to make sure you understand their message and intended meaning (Bodie et al., 2012).

Evaluating

The next step in Brownell's (2010) model is evaluating the new information and making an informed judgment about the relative merits of the message. It is in this step that we make verdicts about the accuracy and validity of the message by assessing the speaker's credibility, analyzing their logic and reasoning, and identifying emotional appeals. It is at this point that the listener accepts or rejects all or portions of the message. It is important for the listener to identify their preconceived notions, assumptions, and personal biases that may skew their evaluation.

Responding

The final component of the listening model is responding to the message of the speaker. The listener is to reflect on the message by first paraphrasing or summarizing their point before responding (Cohen, 2008). This allows the speaker to feel heard and also can clear up any misunderstandings on the part of the listener. The listener is to then react appropriately to the message and sender by choosing proper verbal and nonverbal responses while recognizing the impact of the response. Becoming familiar with response options and the impact is crucial to good listening. It is with this flexibility that a listener becomes competent. Listening does not end when responding, as the responder continually monitors the nonverbal and verbal cues of the initial speaker and shows empathy and respect for the speaker (Thompson et al., 2010).

Developing good listening skills is critical to conflict management. By understanding and following the model outlined above, participants in the collaboration can have what Wolvin (2010) calls true engagement. For without such engagement, participants will not be able to come to a common understanding of the issues or jointly develop potential solutions.

Activity

Listening and Summarizing

Instructions: Please break into groups of two and role-play the following scenarios, paying particular attention to how you listen, summarize, and respond. Make sure you summarize the other's words before you respond with your own thoughts or ideas.

Scenario A: In December, 2011, the city of Leviston, across St. Peter's River from Ottawa City, Canada, proposed development of a new traffic route to ease congestion on its main thoroughfares and create a potential new zone for industrial expansion. In accordance with provincial requirements, the city prepared an environmental impact assessment, which was open to public review and comment. A municipal counselor raised several serious concerns about the adequacy of the impact assessment and of the highway extension project.

    Party A: Municipal counselor—You are to communicate all of your concerns, in detail, regarding the proposed development to the project manager. They include public safety (the highway would entail a new railway crossing), increased traffic noise on several streets, and impacts on heritage and archeological resources. Be specific but develop your concerns.

    Party B: Project manager—You are to listen to the complaints of the municipal counselor and then summarize his concerns to the best of your ability. Do not respond with a rebuttal, merely summarize his comments and ask for clarification.

Scenario B: In February, 2013, the state of Utah placed a $5.00 canyon entrance fee to Bear Canyon, a widely popular canyon located in Glendale, Utah. The purpose of the fee was to generate funds for maintenance of the canyon and to increase awareness of and respect for the use of the canyon. At the base of the entrance live some of the wealthiest people in Glendale who use the canyon on a regular basis for recreational activities. On behalf of the homeowners, Barney Bennett has come to complain to your agency regarding the fee.

    Party A: Barney Bennett—You represent the homeowners in the area and are concerned at the high entrance fee. You understand the need for a fee for those who visit the canyon occasionally, but as a local member of the community who accesses the canyon on a regular basis (at least 3 times a week) you do not feel the fee is justified or fair. After all, you have to put up with the traffic of others coming into the canyon as the road is directly in front of your house and have not complained at all. You would like a break from the imposed fee.

    Party B: Agency representative—You are to listen to the complaints of Mr. Bennett and then summarize his concerns to the best of your ability. Do not respond with a rebuttal, merely summarize his comments and ask for clarification.

Listening for Narratives

    While listening to others in conflicts, especially conflict about environmental issues, it is essential to listen to the shared narratives (Lejano, Ingram, & Ingram,

2013). It is in narratives that deeply held values are shared. Values run deeper than interests and most often are not amenable to change, persuasion, rational argument, or even bargaining. They speak to our sense of self and are often associated to a specific environmental issue or place and are what scholars in the field call place-based identity values (Clarke, 2008; Forester, 1999; Gray, Peterson, Putnam, & Bryan, 2003). These identity values are not often articulated clearly but emerge through storytelling or personal narratives. Stories are accounts of a sequence of events, characters, and experiences that convey the meaning of this otherwise disparate assemblage. Hidden in narratives are taken-for-granted practices of power, culturally influenced beliefs, and experientially influenced sets of understanding (Goldberg, 2009). Stories help participants establish their identities vis-á-vis the other participants in the collaborative group, and when parties tell stories, they tell a lot about themselves, their histories, and their connections to the environment (Clarke, 2008). Listening to narratives and acknowledging their significance can help participants focus on, and potentially address, key issues of the conflict (Clarke, 2008; Lejano et al., 2013; Lewicki, Gray, & Elliot, 2003; Winslade & Monk, 2000).

Considering Culture

High- and Low-Context Cultures

In his 1976 book *Beyond Culture*, Anthropologist Edward T. Hall introduces the concept of high-context and low-context cultures. This refers to a culture's tendency to use high-context messages over low-context messages in communication as they relate to each other in interaction (Hall, 1976). In **high-context cultures**, nonverbal communication is emphasized and meanings are conveyed by context and behavior more than words. Thus, people rely on shared cultural understanding to give communication meaning. In **low-context cultures**, there is more verbal and direct communication with a minimal focus on contextual meaning. Words, rather than context, carry meaning and are assigned specific interpretations. This gives less leeway for implied meanings.

High Context	Low Context
Nonverbal communication emphasized	Verbal communication emphasized
Contextual, implied meaning	Specific, literal meaning
Indirect, covert	Direct, overt
Implicit message	Explicit message
Reactions reserved	Reactions on the surface

Although cultural context is relativistic rather than absolute, you can expect people living in some communities to demonstrate higher contexts than people living in other communities. Imagine that you are working with a conflict between sea turtle biologists and residents of a small coastal village in El Salvador. Suppose that most of the biologists grew up in Australia, Germany, New Zealand, or the United States, and those that did not grow up there received their education in these countries. Suppose that the villagers grew up in El Salvador or another Central American country. One of your most challenging tasks will be to facilitate communication strategies that help both groups adapt to the other cultural context. As members of low-context cultures, the biologists may feel that asking for assistance demonstrates a lack of expertise, while the relatively high-context villagers may interpret the failure to ask for their opinion as disrespect or even a personal insult.

Advocating Your View

Peter Senge (2006), author of *The Fifth Discipline: The Art and Practice of the Learning Organization,* outlines a method for using direct communication and advocating your view in an organizational setting. He suggests that when making your point or perspective known, the key is to make your own reasoning explicit, and then encourage others to explore your view and provide a different view. He argues that when inquiring into others' views it is necessary to ask questions about their reasoning and state any assumptions you are making about their view with evidence. It is important to not make it personal and to distinguish between the argument and the person. In a negotiation, it is oftentimes too easy to align a position with an individual. When the negotiation becomes personal, it is difficult to see beyond differences to the underlying issues and concerns. When this happens, suggestions are taken personally and disagreements are seen as attacks. Fisher and Ury (2011) suggest that in negotiation, one should separate the people from the problem. Or in other words, separate the substance from the relationship by focusing on specific issues rather than an organization or individual.

Activity

Advocating Your View

Team up with another member of the group and practice using direct communication with the following scenarios:

Scenario 1: You are a sergeant explaining to your colonel that he has to delay his military maneuvers to comply with the Endangered Species Act. A specific example would be the Desert Tortoise crossing the road in front of an Army caravan at White Sands Missile Range, New Mexico. The caravan was required to stop for 3 hours to wait for the tortoise to cross the road because the tortoise cannot be touched.

Scenario 2: You are a representative of the timber industry who, in response to a loss of income in the community, is proposing a timber harvest. You are speaking to an avid environmentalist who is opposed to any harvesting of timber in the area.

Communicating Your Concerns

Scholars of communication and conflict management advocate the use of *I* statements when addressing conflict or communicating concerns (Abigail & Cahn, 2011; Cohen, 2008; Daniels & Walker, 2001; Davidson & Wood, 2004). Using statements that begin with *I* communicates the impact of situations, actions, or another's communication on oneself without attacking or blaming the other. For example, instead of saying, "you are so inconsiderate when . . ." you would say, "I get frustrated when . . ." Using *I* statements allows you to own your own perspective and focus on actions that can be changed rather than making a definitive statement about a person or situation. "This is how I see the situation . . ." rather than "you are selfish and don't care about this community." The former focuses on impact of an action or situation, whereas the latter makes a character statement that will most likely spark a debate rather than an exploration of how to solve an issue. Using *I* statements also helps to avoid victim discourse, which is language that focuses solely on blame. While understanding a contribution to a situation is important in developing solutions, focusing on blame keeps the emphasis on the past instead of the future where potential solutions can be developed and implemented (Stone, Patton, & Heen, 2000). Instead, identify behavior or situational characteristics and name the consequences of those behaviors or situation on yourself.

In addition to using ***I* language**, it is also necessary to avoid vague or generalized statements and be specific in your concerns. Describe as accurately and objectively as possible the behavior you see that concerns you. This will help move the conversation from intangible themes, which are abstract and difficult to address, to a conversation about specific instances or issues that can more easily be attended.

In conflict, we often assume that the perspective of the other is the same as our own and then become frustrated when they do not act as we want them to act. Our judgments then become limited by our cognitive capacity (Gillespie & Richardson, 2011). We assign intent and meaning to actions, and then look for evidence to prove our assumptions correct instead of having an authentic conversation about perceived differences. To avoid this, check your assumptions about feelings, intentions, and meanings you perceive rather than assume them to be true. This is particularly important when interpreting nonverbal behavior. Checking assumptions can save time in any negotiation and move the conversation to the real issue more quickly.

A powerful tool or communication exercise to overcome divergences of viewpoints is perspective taking (Betancourt, 2004; Cohen, 2008; Gillespie & Richardson, 2011; Senge, 1994). This is the act of putting yourself in another person's shoes to recognize and legitimize their viewpoint, emotions, and interests. Asking them where they are coming from allows you to see the situation from a different and equally valid position and is a necessary step to move toward a common understanding of the issue and possibilities to solve concerns

In any discussion, the receiver should not be made to feel as though they are getting scolded. The goal is to articulate clearly the impact of behavior and request a change, not to rebuke and offend. Asking questions and involving them in a possible solution instead of talking at them can lead to a more authentic discussion, eventually solving the conflict. It is also a good idea to leave the discussion open or arrange to revisit the conversation in time.

How to Communicate a Concern

1. Name a specific behavior and name the consequence of the behavior

   When you do this_____, what happens (happened) for me/others is/was_____.

2. Check your assumptions

   What I assume is true is _____. Is this correct?

3. Articulate feelings, impacts, or responses

   I feel _____ (name the feeling or the response)

4. Give the other person an opportunity to speak and listen to understand their intent

   Will you tell me what is going on? (Ask questions, check assumptions, and clarify).

5. Be specific and detailed in your request for new/different behavior

   What I want from you is _____ (this must be a behavior)

6. Offer support to the change

   What do you need from me to support this change? What do you need me to do differently (behavioral)?

7. Leave the conversation open to an arranged revisit in the future

Activity

Communicating a Concern

Please team up with another person and use the following activity to practice giving constructive criticism.

Scenario A

Mediator: You are working with participants in a policy development process concerning the designation of critical habitat for the Florida Key Deer. One of the participants named Matt represents a local environmental organization and is very passionate and knowledgeable about the species. Matt can sometimes be

(Continued)

(Continued)

condescending to other participants in the group. Others have described him as elitist and patronizing. When he begins to speak, people begin rolling their eyes and instantly dismiss his comments, even when his comments may have merit.

Scenario B

Mediator: You are working with the Department of Environmental Quality (DEQ) and local farmers on a nonpoint source Total Daily Maximum Load (TMDL) process. One of the farmers is quite vocal and dominates group discussions, frequently talking over people or dismissing what they say. A few of the members have complained that they might stop coming to meetings because they feel their perspectives are not heard or valued.

Considering Culture

Developing Cultural Fluency

In their book *Conflict Resolution Across Culture: A Unique Experience of Bridging Differences*, Lebaron and Pillay (2006) define what it means to be culturally fluent in cross cultural communication and conflict resolution. **Cultural fluency** dynamically grows in a social context of interdependence between self and others, enhancing our ability to "anticipate, internalize, express and help shape our process of meaning-making" (p. 58). The authors further define each element of cultural fluency as they provide ways to develop **anticipatory capacity**, **embeddedness**, and **expressive capacity**.

Anticipatory Capacity

Anticipatory capacity is the ability to anticipate a range of possible scenarios about how relationships will evolve in unfamiliar cultural contexts. To build anticipatory capacity, LeBaron and Pillay (2006) suggest the following techniques:

- Observe patterns of being and doing demonstrated by others, taking into consideration how they characterize who they are and what they care about.
- Articulate what others' patterns of meaning making are, but keep your cultural interpretation tentative and subject to revision.
- Reflect on how your own meaning-making patterns have been shaped by reflecting on how you have come to perceive who you are and what you care about.
- Consider the interactions of both patterns (theirs and yours) and how they cocreate the present.
- Remain willing to reshape your imperative lenses by continually adding new insights gained from both observation and self-reflection.

To be able to abide in uncertainty and be open to surprises while at the same time anticipating differences places a communicator in a position to not only better understand, but work through, cultural differences.

Embeddedness

Lebaron and Pillay (2006) define *embeddedness* as one's ability to remain conscious of unfamiliar cultural influences that come to be embedded in our meaning making. Or in other words our ability to check our cultural assumptions and understand our unconscious patterns of thinking. To do this, they suggest the following:

- Acknowledge deep assumptions that affect your way of sense making.
- Ask yourself why you are unfamiliar with cultural outsiders when a difference is felt, keeping in mind how your own cultural assumptions have helped to shape the perceived difference.
- Explore a cultural assumption by naming it and articulating it.
- Reflect on your upbringing and how this has shaped you.
- Reflect on their upbringing and how their assumptions are shaped by their experience.

The idea of understanding the cultural assumptions of others is also called cultural perspective taking and can assist those involved in environmental conflicts in working through their differences. In Australia, a conflict between white and aboriginal Australians over forest management pitted two cultures against each other. When those involved in forestry, tourism, farming, and conservation were asked to compare their own feelings of spiritual or sentimental connection to the forest with the kinds of attachments they thought the other might have to their homelands, there was a shift in the conflict. It wasn't until both sides explored the cultural significance of the forest from the perspective of the other were they able to come to a settlement and sign the Western Australian Regional Forest Agreement (Trigger & Mulcock, 2005).

Expressive Capacity

To be able to communicate cultural differences during conflict, you need to be able to express your cultural assumptions in an authentic way that is understandable to others who are unfamiliar with your way of sense making. This skill is called expressive capacity and can be developed in the following ways:

- Articulate what you care about by unpacking and explaining the meaning.
- Encourage others to articulate their meaning making in the same way.
- Suspend value judgments as you probe and explore both meaning-making patterns.

Recognizing and communicating the interdependency of all participants in a collaborative process can help them productively navigate cross-cultural dynamics to co-create a constructive shared meaning and potential solutions.

Developing cultural fluency is critical to addressing environmental conflict in cross-cultural contexts. By learning how to anticipate difference, recognize cultural assumptions, and express those assumptions, participants in conflict will be more able to have genuine conversations that lead to the potential development of solutions.

Question Asking

Question asking is a vital communication skill in conflict management. Good questions can help gather important information, provide an opportunity to learn and explore options, support creative thinking, test assumptions, and provide a reality check (Senge, 2006). In Chapter 9, we discussed the importance of moving from positions to interests to move beyond bottom-line reasoning and support creative alternative development (Abigail & Cahn, 2011). Asking good questions can focus the conversation on interests and possibilities instead of blame and bottom lines (Senge, 2006). When using questions to explore options and generate alternatives, it is important to ask questions that do not demand justification, cross-examine, or hold judgment. The goal is not to interrogate but to understand, learn, and explore ideas (Bodie et al., 2012). Thus, questions should be open-ended and focused on possibility (Littlejohn & Domenici, 2001; Malouff et al., 2012). Daniels and Walker (2001) distinguish between different types of appropriate questions. *Clarification questions* are meant to better understand and focus on the who, what, or when. For example, "what is the city's main purpose for a landfill in this community?" *Probing questions* are meant to learn more, such as why and how. For example, "what concerns you about the development of a landfill in this community?" *Hypothesis questions* are meant to explore alternatives or introduce new perspectives such as, "are you open to other community economic development ideas?" Finally, *evaluative questions* are used to assess ideas and proposals. "What are the economic advantages of having a landfill in this community?" is an example of an evaluative question.

Question asking can also be a way to genuinely empower others and address interpersonal conflict. Asking a good question can allow another person to be heard, reduce aggressiveness and defensiveness, evoke willingness, and secure commitment (Welton, 2002). To ask a good question means to listen to the concerns of others and provide acknowledgment of their ideas and interests. Questions should be focused on future possibilities and not previous events. They should be thoughtful and constructive and lead others to explore new areas of thought in a safe manner. This will allow creative ideas to emerge and potential solutions to develop.

┌─ Activity

Conflict Management and Choice Making

The object of this exercise is to practice the art of question asking through assisting another person to think through a choice. The goal is to assist them in coming up with choices or solutions that are clear, realistic, and acceptable to them.

Instructions: Ask the other person to describe a conflict or a choice (decision) they have to make. Ask them to be as specific as they can and to describe the circumstance and people involved. Do not give any advice. Ask clarification, probing, hypothesis, and evaluative questions to empower them to make their own decision.

Sample questions to empower others include the following:

Describe/Define an Outcome

- What do you want?
- What is most important to you in this conflict?
- What experience are you looking for?
- What is at stake for you in this situation?
- What are the givens in this situation?
- How would you like this experience to end? For you? For the other person?
- How will you know when the conflict is over? What does resolution look like?
- What can you do now to end the conflict?

Determine Long-Term Interest

- Where do you want to be with this conflict 2 months from now? Six months? A year from now?
- How do you want to feel about this down the road?
- What can you do now to get what you want?

Explore Options/Alternatives

- What have you done so far to get what you want?
- What are you willing to do to solve this conflict?
- What are you *not* willing to do to solve this conflict?
- What are your alternatives? Worst? Best?
- What are the consequences of each alternative?
- What is the best option you have now to deal with this issue?

Reframing

Frame theory contends that collaborative group members bring experiences that shape their respective frames for conflict (Campbell & Docherty, 2004; Goffman, 1974; Gray, 2004). Originally developed by Goffman (1974) and built on by others, frame theory suggests that social events are governed by frames, which provide an "organization of experience" and help individuals make meaning out of everyday activity (p. 11). This includes previous attitudes toward the issue, previous interactions with the other participants, or previous experience in similar negotiations. They are, in effect, how participants frame the issues, prioritize elements of the conflict, and make sense of the situation. Thus, a frame can be considered a sense-making device (Dewulf et al., 2007; Gray, 2004; Weick, 1995; Wondolleck & Yaffee, 2000). "When we frame a conflict, we develop interpretations about what the conflict is about, why it is occurring, the motivations of the parties involved, and how the conflict should be settled" (Gray, 2003, p. 12). The cognitive frames people develop of a situation lead to various behaviors and approaches and affect their decision-making process in terms of both the nature of the situation as well as the choices available to them. "An important challenge in these cross-disciplinary endeavors is dealing with the diversity of frames or perspectives that people use to make sense of the issues" (Dewulf et al., 2007, p. 14). Framing then plays an important role in the creation, evolution, and perpetuation of environmental conflicts.

Scholars have used frame analysis to better understand environmental conflicts and their potential for collaborative resolution. Riemer (2004) demonstrated how frame analysis can help make sense of environmental and cultural conflict of Chippewa spearfishing in northern Wisconsin. Fischer and Marshall's (2010) analysis of landscape frames in the Scottish moorlands and Fletcher's (2009) analysis of language used to frame climate change in the U.S. identify similar opportunities (Dewulf et al., 2007; Fischer & Marshall, 2010; Fletcher, 2009). Robinson (2013) used frame analysis to understand how communities in Vancouver, Canada, and Stockton, California, strategically positioned themselves politically in relation to the privatization of water. Similarly, Dewulf et al. (2007) analyze dialogue during an interdisciplinary research collaborative centered on conflict over water management and contend that in order to achieve improved water management, participants must understand and acknowledge each other's social frames. They developed a template of steps participants from different backgrounds can use to develop common sense-making or mutual framing. Steps include (a) understanding each other's frames, (b) acknowledging differences, (c) translating other's frames into one's own terms, (d) exploring each other's frames, and finally (e) integrating frames by constructing a new and jointly created system of meaning.

Lewicki et al. (2003) and Brummans et al. (2008) offered framing as an especially promising approach to intractable environmental conflict. Frame analysis enables a more complete understanding of a conflict's interaction dynamics (Brummans et al., 2008; Lewicki et al., 2003). Similarly, Peterson (2003) argues that practitioners need to develop a deep understanding of conflict participants' frames before they suggest possibilities for improving the situation. By analyzing communication interactions of dispute participants, environmental practitioners (process mediators) can discover the operative frames parties bring to a negotiation and can then use that knowledge to encourage more productive relations among stakeholders (Gray, 2003; Webb & Raffaelli, 2008).

Mediators can also provide disputants with opportunities to engage in *frame shifts* or reframe conflicts in more productive ways (Brummans et al., 2008; Lewicki et al., 2003). Reframing is the art of shifting the meaning people make of their experience of issues, events, relationships, and circumstances. Reframing occurs when participants develop a new way of interpreting or understanding the issue and engage in perspective taking (d'Estree, 2003; Gray, 2003, 2004). Practitioners can encourage reframing by helping disputants develop more realistic expectations and identify potential shifts within the conflict. This can be done with process techniques such as imaging, narrative forums, group modeling, or perspective taking exercises to lead participants to strategic framing of the problem to be solved (Dewulf et al., 2007; Gray, 2004). As they learn to interpret their situations differently, disputants become more open to new alternatives and possibilities for resolution (Lewicki, Saunders, & Minton, 1999; Moore, 1996; Putnam, Burgess, & Royer, 2003).

In addition to reframing exercises, mediators can help parties shift their frames by use of communicative reframing through the isolation of negative words and reframing those words into something neutral or positive (Asah, Bengston, Wendt, & Nelson, 2012). A reframe is built on positive intent and should always be an expansion of an idea to create the possibility of more interpretations, options, and alternatives (Asah, Bengston, Wendt, & Nelson, 2012; Folger, Poole, & Stutman, 2012; Lewicki et al., 1999; Moore, 1996). Communication techniques include the following:

- *Using different words to interpret the meaning of something differently or cast an event, action, or person in a different light.* For example, if someone is described as having "constantly irritating behavior," a reframe might sound like, "They approach things differently" or "have a different style of communicating."
- *Turning a negative into a neutral or positive.* For example, a criticism of some- one might sound like, "he's nitpicky and can't get beyond the fine print and footnotes." A reframe might be, "he pays careful attention to details."
- *Turning a demand into an interest.* A demand such as, "It's not fair that we should have to pay for a permit into the canyons when it's our back yard. It makes sense that people who don't live here should have to pay for entrance, but it's insulting that we have to pay when we've been taking care of this place for years. It's our land—we pay taxes—what are they for if not access to our land?" This could potentially be reframed by responding to the interest of the speaker. "You want a fair permitting process and would like your connection to this area to be taken into account."
- *Turning a complaint into a request.* A complaint against a development com- pany might sound like, "Our community has put up with that company's lies for long enough. Sure they provide jobs, but at what cost? The lives of our children? The health of our community? It has been their way long enough. They never listen to what we want. They have to pay and things will be our way for a change." A reframe focused on what the participant is requesting might sound like, "You want your desires to be heard and acknowledged. You want immediate change and action to be taken as well as compensation for your loss."

It is important to note, however, that when introducing new language, it has to make sense within the existing frame (Lakoff, 2010). Therefore, it is a good idea to test the reframe with the participant. Simply asking "is that a fair interpretation of your concern?" will allow the participant to correct any misunderstandings while empowering them by giving them another opportunity to clarify their concerns. It is also appropriate to ask the participant questions that will lead to their own reframing. "Is there a different explanation for this situation? Could the person's actions be interpreted differently?" These are examples of questions to ask to lead the participant to their own reframing.

When reframing, use empowering words that elicit a more positive response, such as explore, consider, generate, gather, put together, discuss, describe, collect, look for, sound out, think out loud about, propose, suggest, and come up with.

Avoid using negative blocking verbs such as judge, assess, label, evaluate, rate, compare, categorize, grade, rank, order, analyze, criticize, classify, diagnose, monitor, assume, and claim.

It is very important to not change anything factual about what the person has said, deny or minimize anything they have said, or patronize or condescend when reframing. Your intent must not be manipulative. Disingenuous reframes will make a stakeholder feel like they are being handled and will only act to escalate conflict. If done with a genuine intent to better understand someone's perspective and move the collaborative forward, reframing negative or combative comments from participants during a collaborative or the general public during public involvement activities helps to reduce hostility, enhance the desirability of the options and alternatives presented, validate perspectives, enhance communication between stakeholders, and help to establish a common ground as a basis of agreement (Folger et al., 2012; Lewicki et al., 1999).

Activity

Reframing

Keeping in mind the direction above, reframe the following statements as if you were responding.

"I've worked with this agency/organization in the past and they're not interested in a fair agreement. They don't care about our children or their future. They are only concerned with looking good on paper and are only asking our input because it's required for the NEPA process. I'm sick of putting in my time when in the long run it won't do a damn bit of good."

_____

_____

_____

"If we had all the money that environmentalists do, we could hire professional lobbyists to stand up for our beliefs. They buy billboards spreading propaganda against logging and mining, usually using grant money from the very people they attack."

_____

_____

_____

"No one has even asked us what we want. This is our home. They think that just because we are poor, they can come in here and force us out so they can build their fancy new federal courthouse. We're not going to just sit by and let that happen. We have our rights."

_____

_____

_____

"When I agreed to come to this meeting, I didn't agree to sit and listen to this crap. The greens have been dictating to everyone how they should live their lives for decades. I will decide where I will and won't drive my ATV and I don't feel I should have to answer to some out of town environmentalists who don't even know what it's like to live here."

_____

_____

_____

Conclusion

The focus of this chapter has been the art of developing good communication skills to help participants in a collaborative process be more successful. Learning how to better communicate concerns can reduce hostility, improve relationships, and help resolve disputes (d'Estree, 2003).

Case Study Application

As you move through the policy development process steps outlined in Chapter 7, use and practice the communication techniques suggested above. Pay careful attention to how you listen, acknowledge, ask questions, and reframe your words as you negotiate your interests in the collaborative process. Practice advocating your view and communicating concerns through power-with communication. Listen and acknowledge the perspectives of others, ask good questions, and use reframing as a technique to meet each other on common ground.

Voices From the Field

Understanding Cultural Impact: Uses of the Yellowstone River Cultural Inventory Reports

Damon M. Hall

Center for Sustainability

Saint Louis University

The Yellowstone River (Montana, USA) is the nation's longest undammed river. In addition to the recreational amenities this natural feature offers, the river also

(Continued)

(Continued)

exhibits natural flood cycles when upstream mountain snow melts each June. In 1996 and 1997, the valley experienced severe floods, prompting riverfront landowners to build hardscape structures to reduce stream bank erosion. Conflict arose over the unknown negative effects of these new structures on the river's ecology.

Funded by the U.S. Army Corps of Engineers (USACE) and the Yellowstone River Conservation District Council (Council), the Yellowstone River Cultural Inventory (YRCI) was one study within a comprehensive research project examining the cumulative impacts of bank stabilization projects on the river's social and ecological systems. Researchers conducted and documented in-depth conversations with 313 riverfront landowners, recreationalists, civic leaders, Native Americans, and agriculturalists along 515 river miles to assess the diversity and magnitude of concerns about riverbank erosion, general river management, user conflicts, understandings of the river's natural features and processes, and long-term desires for the river. A 787-page report was generated to share these findings with government agencies and interested members of the public. The report design enabled resource agencies to systematically listen to citizens organized by topic. The report conglomerated the spectrum of river users' comments, concerns, and ideas for management in verbatim quotes organized by both topic and geographic area.

The USACE used the report to provide content for the public comment and social and cultural resources sections of the Yellowstone River Cumulative Effects Study (2011) and Upper Yellowstone River Special Area Management Plan (2009). The Council used the reports to assess public information needs in specific geographic reaches. The reports enabled them to produce targeted educational and outreach materials for their programming. The Council also used the reports to identify pressing conservation practices desired most by residents. This led to an emphasis on exotic invasive vegetation management as a top priority.

Other local, state, and federal agencies indirectly involved in the cumulative effects study also used the YRCI. The U.S. Environmental Protection Agency wrote about the YRCI as a means of engaging the public in a regional newsletter. When the Montana Fish, Wildlife, and Parks Agency acquired approximately 3900 acres of riverfront land, they used the relevant geographic segment of the YRCI to inform planning the new Yellowstone River State Park's recreational amenities and infrastructural needs.

Individual resource managers have used the reports in unique ways. A water quality specialist with the Montana Department of Environmental Quality working in eastern Montana has given colleagues in Helena (the capitol) copies of the Eastern geographic segments to illustrate how Eastern Montanans' concerns differ from Western Montanans. When a new agent joins his region, he requires them to read the report to improve their understanding of how Eastern Montanans think about resource management and agencies. A Montana Fish, Wildlife, and Parks fisheries biologist has used the fisheries relevant sections in his publications and interactions with citizens.

Citizens involved in water planning also use the reports. In 2013, the Montana Department of Natural Resources and Conservation established the

Yellowstone River Basin Advisory Council (BAC) to solicit public input on basin-wide water planning issues for Montana's 2015 State Water Plan. Several BAC delegates reported reading the YRCI reports to prepare for their responsibilities in water planning. A regional grassroots environmental organization used portions of the YRCI reports to evidence their position and advocate recommendations concerning the Upper Yellowstone River Special Area Management Plan.

The Western Heritage Center in Billings, Montana, has used the reports to develop a museum exhibit documenting the voices of the Yellowstone River. Although this use falls outside of natural resource management, it does speak to the spectrum of uses and broad appeal of this type of cultural assessment document.

Further Reading

Gilbertz, S., Horton, C. C., Hall, C., & Hall D. M. (2007). *Yellowstone river cultural inventory*. United States Corps of Engineers and the Greater Yellowstone River Conservation District Council. Available at http://www.yellowstonerivercouncil.org/dev/resources.php

Hall, D. M., Gilbertz, S., Horton, C., & Peterson, T. R. (2012). Culture as a means to contextualize policy. *Journal of Environmental Studies and Sciences*, 2(3), 222–233.

DOI: 10.1007/s13412-012-0077-9

Key Terms

anticipatory capacity	embeddedness	*I* language
Communication Competency	expressive capacity	low-context cultures
	high-context cultures	reframing
cultural fluency	HURIER model	

CHAPTER 11

Implementation and Evaluation

This chapter focuses on practical application of your preparatory work, from the initial assessment through design. We discuss contingency factors that could assist or impede **implementation** of your project and how to address potential challenges. Factors to consider include timelines, funding sources, political climates, the discovery of additional and new science, and unforeseen outside forces. We also will address how to create **contingency plans**. Once you have implemented a process, you also will need to evaluate it. In this chapter, we will outline some approaches to evaluation that are appropriate for collaborative environmental conflict management (ECM) processes. In the implementation stage of ECM, it is important to understand and discuss not only how a decision will be carried out but also what challenges and opportunities may come as a result of the decision. We will then discuss the importance of evaluating not only the process, but also the solution. After reading this chapter, you should have a better understanding of implementation and evaluation phases of ECM, including how to appropriately evaluate both process and solution. You will have the opportunity to apply the implementation and evaluation steps to the case studies that were introduced in Chapter 5.

Implementation

The results of your conflict assessment (see Chapter 5) will have provided you with the basic factors to consider when implementing the program you have designed (see Chapters 6 and 7). Your assessment should have suggested specific techniques that are most likely to succeed when working with stakeholders in that specific conflict (see Chapter 8). The collaborative process you design and implement needs to guide participants through complex decision-making tasks that contribute to policy development within the existing legal system (see Chapters 3 and 9). Because the success of your process will be dependent on the participants' abilities to communicate effectively, you will need to devote considerable effort to building that capacity (see Chapter 10). You will use many of the strategies and techniques discussed earlier in this book to implement your design plan.

Factors to Consider

Contingent factors that could assist or possibly impede the proposal must always be considered. These include the following:

1. *Affected parties*—What people, groups, or organizations will benefit from your proposal? What people, groups, or organizations believe they will be hurt by or lose from your proposal?

2. *Externalities*—What factors should be considered as *givens* in the situation that pertains to your proposal but seem outside or external to your decision? This might include disagreements that may arise in the future, partially as a result of this process.

3. *Funding sources*—How will your proposal be funded? Who will be responsible for the cost of implementation?

4. *Implementation responsibility*—Who will implement (operate or manage) your improvements, options, and proposals? Who will be the administrators (people, groups, organizations, or agencies)? Is it flexible? Is it achievable?

5. *Key players*—Who are potential blockers? What parties may have the desire and/or power to block your proposal? Who are the potential supporters? What parties can provide key support for your improvements?

6. *Obstacles*—Can you foresee any obstacles to the implementation of your proposal?

7. *Timelines*—What is the proposed schedule for implementation?

8. *Values and beliefs*—What mind sets, values, and beliefs are important to consider when implementing the proposal?

Dietz and Stern (2008) suggest a set of factors that will be important to consider when implementing any sort of management or resolution of environmental conflict:

1. Diagnosis (conclusions from your assessment)

2. Iterations (how you will adapt tools and techniques as the process moves forward)

3. Monitoring of the process (who will do this, and how will they share their observations)

4. Opportunities for collaborative choice of techniques to meet potential difficulties

Your diagnosis provides an important starting point, because it should suggest specific techniques that you consider most likely to succeed in a specific conflict. You will use these techniques to implement your design plan. Imagining multiple iterations will encourage you to think about options for adapting to changing needs of the participants. Monitoring the process will enable you to determine when these changes are needed. It is vital that you know in advance whether you will have assistance with this task or whether you must conduct all monitoring activities yourself. Finally, by involving participants in the choice of techniques, you encourage them to take ownership of the process. At the same time, you need to balance this with the resource constraints. Just because a participant is eager to try a specific technique is not adequate justification for doing so. You remain responsible for ensuring that the process makes careful use of available resources, including both time and money.

Developing Contingency Plans

One widely used approach to contingency planning is known as **SWOT analysis** (Bonacorsi, 2007; Bradford, Duncan, & Tarcy, 2000). We will explain what a SWOT analysis is, how to conduct one, and finally we will provide an example. SWOT stands for Strengths, Weaknesses, Opportunities, and Threats. Internal factors are labeled as strengths and weaknesses, while external factors are labeled as opportunities and threats. Developing a SWOT matrix involves identifying the internal and external factors that are favorable and unfavorable to achieving project objectives. Your conflict assessment (Chapter 5) should give you a basis for beginning a SWOT analysis. To further develop the analysis, you should work with those who have agreed to participate in the conflict management process. The results of a SWOT analysis can guide your decisions regarding how to implement your design (Chapters 6 and 7).

You might begin the SWOT by characterizing the strengths and weaknesses of the group and your proposed process. Strengths are characteristics of the group or the process that give it an advantage. They are resources that can be used as the basis for resolving the conflict, or at least improving the situation. Examples of potential strengths could include the positive reputation of the group or individual members, the know-how of group members, and direct access to decision makers. Weaknesses are characteristics that place the group or process at a disadvantage. Examples of potential weaknesses would include a poor reputation with others, ignorance of legal and procedural aspects, and minimal access to decision makers.

Next, you must relate your internal analysis to an analysis of the group's external environment. Opportunities are elements from the external environment that the group could exploit to its advantage. They refer to possibilities for growth and development. Examples could include widespread awareness of unfulfilled community needs, availability of new technologies for managing the natural resource in conflict, or changes in the legal/regulatory regime that may open new decision space. Finally, threats are elements from the external environment that could cause trouble for the group. They refer to potential risks. Examples could include shifts in community preferences away from the goals of the group, emergence of politically powerful actors who oppose the group's goals, or changes in the legal/regulatory regime that shrink decision space.

You can summarize your SWOT analysis in a matrix based on Table 11.1. It should help you understand the fit between the internal environment (relationships within the group) and the external environment and suggest how to exploit that fit.

TABLE 11.1 Basic Template for a SWOT Analysis

	Strengths	Weaknesses
Opportunities	S-O strategies	W-O strategies
Threats	S-T strategies	W-T strategies

Once you have created a matrix, you should think about what it suggests for implementation. Items in the S-O block and the W-T block are likely to be of immediate importance. You need to implement the process in a way that enables the group to pursue opportunities that are a good fit to the group's strengths. At the same time, items in the W-T block suggest the need for a defensive plan to minimize weaknesses that make the group susceptible to external threats. Information in the W-O block and the S-T block may be less urgent, but still require attention. Items in the W-O block suggest strategies to overcome weaknesses, which would enable the group to pursue its opportunities. Items in the S-T block suggest strategies for using the group's existing strengths to reduce its vulnerability to threats.

Be rigorous in the way you develop your SWOT matrix and in the ways you apply it. Try to limit claims to precise, verifiable statements. Carefully prioritize the items in your matrix, so you spend most of your time working with the most significant issues. Make sure that the strategies generated are carried through into specific implementation steps. Finally, use it in conjunction with other steps in the process, from the conflict assessment through the design process.

Applying SWOT

The Fairbanks, Alaska, interior field office of the U.S. Bureau of Land Management (BLM) manages a unique subarctic boreal forest that is rich in resources, history, and opportunity. It encompasses over 8.7 million acres, including the White Mountain National Recreation Area; the Steese National Conservation Area; and the Birch, Beaver, and 40-mile Wild and Scenic Rivers. Together, this represents the majority of the BLM managed lands in the state of Alaska. The organization conducted a SWOT analysis to clarify the strengths, weaknesses, opportunities, and potential threats posed by proposed management plans (see Table 11.2). They used the information to devise strategies that would help them decide how to deploy their limited resources.

They identified as **strengths** their (a) use of both traditional and culturally validated science in monitoring efforts and their (b) cooperative relationships with other agencies, local governments, tribes, and residents.

They identified as **weaknesses** the (a) upcoming loss of institutional knowledge because several of the senior staff who had been instrumental in developing the land management plans were about to retire and the (b) difficulty of balancing the use and conservation of public land and other resources in eastern interior Alaska based upon conflicting demands of various laws, regulations, and policy.

They identified as **opportunities** the possibility of (a) educating the public about legal requirements, administrative process, and general land management responsibilities and (b) improving their communication by making information about the BLM more readily available.

TABLE 11.2 Partial Table for the SWOT Analysis		
	Strengths	**Weaknesses**
	1. Multiple approaches to science 2. History of cooperating with other groups	1. Coming loss of institutional knowledge 2. Balancing use and conservation of resources
Opportunities 1. Educating new residents 2. Improving communication with the public	**S-O strategies** Develop a volunteer program for interested residents.	**W-O strategies** Ensure that incoming personnel engage with participants in the new volunteer program.
Threats 1. Changing demographics 2. Changing legal interpretations	**S-T strategies** Collaborate with existing groups to develop programs to educate the public, especially those representing new demographics.	**W-T strategies** Preemptively identify potential conflicts between use and conservation that are especially likely with new demographics.

Source: U.S. Department of the Interior, Bureau of Land Management.

(Continued)

(Continued)

They identified as **threats** the (a) changing demographics of the region and (b) shifting interpretations of relevant laws and policies from Washington, DC.

Applying the SWOT analysis to the implementation stage of their process helped them focus their efforts where they could be most successful and allowed them to make plans to address the challenges they faced. For example, they built on existing strengths by designing a new volunteer program, especially for groups with whom they already had a strong cooperative relationship, and then they attempted to improve their relationship with the general public by engaging those volunteers in outreach activities to reach new members of the community who represented different demographics.

Evaluation

The very complexity of environmental conflicts means that they provide exceptional opportunities for continual learning and improved approaches. As such, the final step in a collaborative decision-making process is evaluation of the process, including both design and implementation. Those engaged in ECM must be able to demonstrate that collaborative approaches can be an effective tool for building a sense of common purpose among participants, and that they can contribute to more environmentally sound decisions. This means that ECM professionals need to "conduct more rigorous assessments of its utility under different conditions" (O'Leary, Nabatchi, & Bingham, 2004, p. 325). O'Leary et al. (2004) also point to

the need for scholars and practitioners to understand interventions as procedures targeted at aggregate rather than dyadic relationships, as complex systems embedded in even larger complex systems, as time-extended phenomena, and as elements ripe for evaluation of their impact on substantive environmental outcomes. (p. 325)

Collaborative processes should be evaluated by a variety of parties, including (but not limited to) those who have participated in, convened, designed, and facilitated them. Ideally, a collaborative decision-making process should receive formal evaluation from someone who has not been a part of the process, but is familiar with collaborative techniques and procedures used. An evaluator or evaluation team should be involved from the onset of the project or included as early as possible. This ensures that the evaluator is able to observe as much as possible of the collaborative process. Participants, including designers and facilitators, should also assess the process and indicate which content material and activities they found more and less useful. They should also be encouraged to indicate ways in which they feel the process could be improved. The process of decision making and the facilitator and their techniques should also be evaluated by the outside observer and the participants. The content of the proposal should also be evaluated and compared with the stated goals and objectives of the group. Although improved relationships between participants should emerge from collaborative decision-making processes, the goal is progression and improvement.

It is always best to evaluate the process at multiple points during the overall application (Dukes, Firehock, Leahy, & Anderson, 2001). If evaluation is only done after the final decision has been made, an accurate and timely description of the process cannot be provided. There are numerous benefits to conducting regular evaluations throughout the process. This enables facilitators to change the management plan based on the responses to the evaluation. It also can be used to measure incremental improvements or deterioration of the situation and can safeguard against future criticisms and litigation.

Evaluators should consider a multiple-method approach to the evaluation that incorporates a variety of research techniques such as observation, interviews, and surveys. For this reason, although we focus on a specific approach to evaluation, we do not limit the discussion to this approach. Because there are always limitations on the time and money available for evaluation, it will be up to you to decide which approaches to use. The results of your assessment (see Chapter 5) should guide your decisions regarding how best to evaluate the process.

Evaluating the Process

Process evaluations should convey to participants the characteristics of effective collaboration. Questions to consider might include the following: Was the opportunity for engagement improved? Were there opportunities to share data and learn new information? Was creative thinking encouraged? Were you given opportunity to improve your communication and/or collaboration skills? The type or nature of questions you ask will depend on the issue and design of the collaboration (Wade, 2004). Although you will want to adapt any form to fit your process, we offer the following as a starting point for your process evaluation (Figure 11.1).

It is important to evaluate the process dynamics multiple times during a process to guide iterative changes (Wade, 2004). Participants who have been involved in the process design or modification will have a stronger commitment to the process (Peterson & Feldpausch-Parker, 2013). Participants should also have the opportunity to learn how the group has responded to the questions asked in such an evaluation. This will provide transparency to the process and can lead to increased trust between participants.

Unifying Negotiation Framework

We will focus on the **Unifying Negotiation Framework** (UNF), which was designed "to support public administrators' ability to evaluate the results of collaborative management effort" (Daniels, Walker, & Emborg, 2012, p. 5). We like its approach to evaluation, largely because it presents a highly nuanced notion of discourse as the organizing concept for understanding and managing environmental

FIGURE 11.1   Sample Process Evaluation Form

(p. 1)

Name (may or may not be appropriate to include):

Date:

1. How much have you learned from group activities? A. a lot B. a little C. nothing	2. Have you participated in group activities? A. a lot B. a little C. not at all
3. Have you enjoyed the group activities? A. a lot B. a little C. not at all	4. How effective has your group been in allocating time and accomplishing its tasks? A. very B. somewhat C. barely D. not at all
5. I would evaluate our movement toward resolving the conflict as: A. poor B. fair C. average D. good E. excellent Give reasons for your rating. Please include specific examples.	6. What, if any, aspects of your own behavior do you need to change to be a more effective group member? Please give specific examples.
7. What, if any, aspects of other group members' behavior need to change to enhance the group's ability to resolve the conflict or improve the situation? Please give specific examples.	8. What, if anything, did the facilitator do that encouraged the group to move toward resolving the conflict or improving the situation? Please give specific examples.
9. What, if anything, did the facilitator do that inhibited the group from resolving the conflict or improving the situation? Please give specific examples.	

Example Process Evaluation Form

(p. 2)

10. Incidence of productive and counterproductive communication behaviors. **Check** any you engaged in and **circle** any you observed in others.

Productive Communication	Counterproductive Communication
__ asked, gave information	__ monopolized discussion
__ asked, gave reactions	__ called attention to self
__ asked, answered questions	__ chronic interruptions
__ restated ideas/points in articles	__ criticized others (put downs)
__ restated ideas/points of discussants	__ changed subject often
__ asked for/gave examples	__ frequent irrelevant comments
__ asked for/gave summary	__ withdrawn, did not participate
__ asked for/gave evidence or support for ideas	__ apologized when asked to support ideas
__ redirected group to return to task	__ OTHER–please specify:
__ monitored time	
__ encouraged, supported, and elaborated ideas from other participants	
__ OTHER–please specify	

conflicts, and it provides a comprehensive, yet flexible framework for evaluating the processes designed to manage these conflicts. Their notion of discourse is very similar to our use of the word *communication* throughout this book, leading them to emphasize that "public issues and policy responses to them are . . . socially constructed through the intersections of history, culture, society, and materiality" (Daniels et al., p. 9). Other researchers, such as Eden and Bear (2012), have also demonstrated the importance of integrating multiple dimensions of any situation into efforts to manage environmental conflicts. This is why it is so important to understand the laws and policies (Chapter 3) that are relevant to an environmental conflict, and why assessment (Chapter 5) must include both archival research into the situation as well as personal interviews with potential participants.

Further, the developers of the UNF recognize that cultural context is always important. Along with numerous other researchers, they have found that stakeholder participation must be conducted in a way that is consistent with the local culture (Bawole, 2013; Perz, 2002; Vedeld, Jumane, Wapalila, & Songorwa, 2012). This involves deep awareness of culture that influences basic design, rather than simply applying different techniques. They have experimented with the UNF on multiple continents, and have found it "equally applicable in Australia, Angola, or Alaska" (Daniels et al., 2012, p. 6).

To illustrate the importance of their focus on communication, you might recall that we cautioned about overuse of consensus building (see Chapter 2) earlier in this book. Daniels et al. (2012) recognize that a successful ECM process "can build consensus, but it may also identify deeply seated dissensus [or disagreement] just as usefully" (p. 9). Their point is that consensus is better thought of as a tool that may or may not be appropriate for resolving/managing a specific conflict. The bigger question is how to encourage communicative interaction that empowers all participants and contributes to improved environmental quality. The relative success or failure of an ECM process should be evaluated by how well it accomplishes these two objectives.

The UNF provides a "cognitive structure" (Daniels et al., 2012, p. 9) for your evaluation and suggests important concepts you might query. It does not provide cookie cutter clarity, but guidance for designing an individualized evaluation, based on the specifics of your situation. This means, of course, that the approach is not likely to be especially useful to an evaluator who lacks a basic understanding of the communication dynamics of conflict. On the other hand, it provides a powerful tool for an evaluator who has such an understanding.

Daniels et al. (2012) suggest visualizing the UNF as a simple matrix. The rows of the matrix illustrate different levels of social aggregation, from the individual to the large system. The six columns of the UNF provide categories for evaluating the success of a process. They identify culture, institutions, and agency as "**highly contextual factors**" (p. 10). They identify actor orientation and experience, cognition, and incentives as "**individualistic factors**" (p. 10). They argue that the ideal design space for a collaborative process is at the midpoint of the matrix. Effective stakeholder processes need to include more than an individual but not so many people that they become lost in the crowd. Further, although your design must account for both your participants' culture and their individual experiences, it is unlikely to change either.

We suggest an adapted version of the UNF as an evaluation guide (Table 11.3).

When evaluating a collaborative ECM process, an observer needs to learn whether and how the process contributed to meaningful choice for its participants. By this, we mean that the individuals or groups making a choice actually have sufficient power and ability to enforce their choices. This will always happen within a political context, which is set by institutions that were probably in existence before your process began and will probably continue to exist after your process finishes. So, a careful assessment of a process should identify what meaningful choices the relevant institutions allow your participants and focus on how the process worked with the relationship between the institutions and stakeholders to open up greater choice for participants. For example, if you are attempting to help residents of a rapidly developing municipality resolve a conflict over zoning, you will need to account for the requirements put in place by a diverse set of institutions ranging from local homeowner associations to state agencies charged with maintaining water quality. Although those requirements need to be recognized, your process should enable residents to discover options for more effectively negotiating the space between themselves and the preexisting institutions. The categories of incentives and cognition work together similarly. The participants in any process will already have well-developed cognitive patterns for processing information and learning. An effective design will need to build on those patterns and encourage further learning in order to identify incentives that motivate people to behave in ways that help them build positive relationships within the group and support improved environmental management. People have reasons for what they do. As an ECM professional, your job is not to criticize your participants' reasons for action but to understand them, and then encourage joint development of incentives that build from existing cognitive patterns.

If you find it difficult to start filling in the template shown in Table 11.2, we recommend that you turn to the SWOT matrix you have already constructed. You will find that the opportunities and strengths, as well as the threats and weaknesses map nicely onto your evaluation. An evaluation based on the UNF is something you can implement at various points during the process. It will provide you with guidance as you make needed changes over time.

TABLE 11.3 Evaluation Template Based on the Unifying Negotiation Framework

	Institutions	Meaningful Choice	Incentives	Cognition
System				
Group				
Individual				

Evaluating the Results

You may recall from Chapter 1 that one of the characteristics of environmental conflict is its complexity. That complexity includes, but is not limited to, interconnections between biophysical, economic, political, and social systems (Dukes, 2004). Depending on the configuration of these elements, the expected (or necessary) results of the collaborative process will vary.

You probably will need to coordinate with at least one natural resource management agency to develop an appropriate instrument for evaluating the results of the collaborative effort. For example, if you are facilitating a group of stakeholders concerned about the status of endangered species anywhere in the U.S., you will not be able to properly evaluate success without close cooperation from the Ecological Services division within the U.S. Fish and Wildlife Service to learn what constitutes an improvement to the current situation for that species. If the conflict also includes transportation issues, such as a proposal to widen a highway, you probably will need to coordinate with the Department of Transportation in the state where you are working. Imagine further that the endangered species in question is a bird that has been known to fly into electric power lines, which are stretched along the edges of the highway, and may need to be moved as part of the highway expansion. This will require you to coordinate with both the utility that provides the power (perhaps a private-sector entity) and the state or regional authority responsible for managing electric power in the region.

If the previous paragraph leaves you a bit dizzy thinking of all the challenges associated with evaluating the results of your ECM process, you are not alone. Luckily, all of the agencies we have mentioned in this example have considerable experience with such complexity. This does not necessarily mean they will be easy to work with. Like your stakeholders, you will be dependent on historical relationships between the various organizations. You can contribute to a positive working relationship with these various institutions by remembering that, although the public process is your priority, it is only one of many parts of the situation from their perspective. The natural resource management agencies are tasked with properly managing some aspect of the environment. The energy authority is tasked with providing reliable and low-cost electricity to residents. The utility is tasked with providing the electricity in a way that satisfies the authority, while also making sufficient profit to justify continuing as a business. All of these entities will be held legally responsible if they fail in their assigned tasks.

As a process facilitator, you need to help them understand that you are managing a public process that is intended to provide a solution to whatever environmental problem has given rise to the conflict. The solution is unlikely to be absolute, but it should constitute an improvement over the current situation. Ideally, your evaluation of the solution should directly measure the biophysical system that led to the conflict. For example, if the conflict swirls around water quality of a river, you should work together with the appropriate technical personnel to support efforts to monitor changes in that river's water quality. If the conflict emerged from the city's failure to meet federal clean air standards, you should collaborate with appropriate technical personnel to monitor changes in air quality. If you are unable to evaluate the results in such a direct way (perhaps you cannot get access to the baseline data needed to determine improvement), you can try indirect measures, such as modeling.

As collaborative approaches to ECM have multiplied, questions about their effectiveness have emerged. One of the most strongly supported suggestions for improving effectiveness is to integrate evaluation into the process, and use the evaluation as a basis for adapting the process (Susskind, Camacho, & Schenk, 2012). Whatever approach you take to evaluating the results of the collaborative, it is vital that you include the stakeholders in this process. They need to know that the process they have invested so many hours in has contributed to a material improvement in their environment. Despite the complexity of environmental conflicts, a well-designed, carefully implemented, and thoroughly evaluated public process has a good chance of improving both human relationships and environmental quality.

Case Study Application

Referring to your chosen case study from Appendix A, conduct a SWOT for the project and your chosen option. This will help you decide which policy decisions are most central to the project, and how you can facilitate positive relations between the diverse stakeholders in the case.

Voices From the Field

Adapting a Process Based on Evaluation

Dialogue on *Allemansrätten*

Lotten Westberg, PhD

Postdoctoral Research Fellow in Environmental Communication

Swedish University of Agricultural Sciences

Allemansrätten is a part of the Swedish cultural heritage that can be traced to the earliest historical texts. Sometimes translated into English as *All Man's Right*, *allemansrätten* refers to every person's right to access, walk, cycle, and ski on any land that is not in the immediate vicinity of a dwelling house or under cultivation. Visitors may pick flowers, mushrooms, and berries. Campers may even have small campfires. Along with the right comes the responsibility to avoid causing damage to the land. Since 1994, *allemansrätten* has been formally

(Continued)

(Continued)

designated in the Swedish Constitution as a limited right of access to nature that also requires users to protect the private property they access. Although a similar practice may once have been common in many European settings, it has survived most strongly in the Nordic countries of Finland, Iceland, Norway, and Sweden.

During the 21st century, many traditional access practices that had previously been individual or small group recreation activities have been commercialized. For example, companies have organized to sell the berries picked on private land and tourism entrepreneurs are selling their services as guides for hiking across private land. This has contributed to antagonism between those who defend the traditional right of public access and those who want to minimize or do away with it as a way of strengthening private ownership.

To deal with the controversy, *Naturvårdsverket*, the Swedish agency responsible for environmental management, decided to convene a dialogue process consisting of 20 invited representatives of landowner associations, government agencies, nonprofit organizations, and organizations that use the right of public access for commercial purposes. The purpose of the process was to increase mutual understanding among group members, to encourage them to acknowledge their concerns, to jointly identify the problems with current practice of *allemansrätten*, and to agree upon recommendations on how to handle these problems.

Limitations and preconditions of the process included the following:

1 Any proposed solutions should be applicable within the current legal interpretation of *allemansrätten*. *Naturvårdsverket* correctly believed that to do otherwise risked deluding group members to expect the process to directly influence legislation and engage in other political activities beyond the agency's mandate.

2 The dialogue process would consist of a series of six full days of meetings spread over one year. It would be guided by an experienced facilitator.

Within these preconditions, the facilitator worked with the group members to design the process.

Meeting 1 was devoted to laying a foundation for understanding the preconditions and the process framework, especially the communication form (dialogue).

Meeting 2 was an Open Space meeting designed to allow hundreds of participants to engage with the issue. Because the dialogue group was limited to only 20 actors, the facilitator encouraged the group to formally include these additional people.

Meeting 3 was intended to provide time for the dialogue group to develop their objectives and to construct agendas for the remaining meetings (4-6). This included deciding what questions were most important to investigate. They used notes from the Open Space session to supplement their own concerns. During this meeting, it became evident that participants were unable to follow a dialogic form of conversation. Instead, they repeatedly reverted to attempts to persuade others of the validity of their own viewpoints. Eventually, they began voicing concerns that the dialogue process would not legitimize their individual perspectives. Group members were not able to agree on an agenda for the remaining meetings.

Meeting 4 moved in a different direction, because the facilitator had realized group members were unable to engage in dialogue and had serious reservations about participating in a dialogue-based process. Based on her evaluation, the facilitator devoted this meeting to clarifying not only *what* the dialogue process framework was, but *why* it could be useful for the participants to gain a better understanding of each other's perspectives, and *how* a dialogue process could facilitate this goal.

Meeting 5 was the first time group members were able to begin jointly identifying the central issues of concern. They began to listen to each other with a goal of understanding different logics, rather than simply waiting until the other person finished talking. By the end of this meeting, group members began to propose useful informational content for future meetings.

Meeting 6 was dominated by constructive dialogue among group members. Contradictory perspectives were examined constructively, and participants began to think about the nuances of their own, as well as others', perspectives.

In retrospect, the convening agency realized that a formal assessment would have provided them a more realistic approach to the conflict. They had not realized how hostile group members felt before the process began, nor had they realized how much time participants would need to explore the dialogue process.

Key Terms

contingent factors

contingency plans

highly contextualized factors

implementation

individualistic factors

SWOT analysis

Unifying Negotiation Framework

CHAPTER 12

Sustaining Community Relations

n this chapter, we will first discuss how (and why) to sustain positive relationships after the conclusion of the formal Environmental Conflict Management (ECM) process. We will conclude with a brief summary of the book and a final case from the field. Although reading one book will not make you an expert on conflict management and resolution, it should have provided you with a framework for approaching environmental conflict with confidence. Throughout the book, we have explained important concepts about conflict, suggested approaches that are especially applicable to environmental conflict, identified and defined terms you should be familiar with, and provided exercises so that you can practice some of the techniques suggested.

Sustaining Positive Community Relationships

In the first half of this chapter, we'll explain what we mean by positive community relationships, and then we will briefly discuss some of the important dimensions of those relationships. We use the word *dimensions* rather than *components* to indicate the fluid relationship between community relations and the individual dimensions. For example, the first dimension we will discuss is **social capital**. Social capital is a dimension, rather than a component, of community relations. At the same time social capital contributes to positive community relations, those positive relationships also increase social capital. On the other hand, weak social capital may contribute to negative community relations that, in turn, further weaken a community's social capital.

Before going further, we need to explain what we mean by *community relations*. Basically, the term refers to the ways residents feel about their community and their involvement in it. Positive community relations develop out of positive experiences associated with democratic self-governance. They emerge when residents believe and act on the belief that everyone has a stake in the community's future (Weber, 2012). This means that residents are comfortable with their own rights and responsibilities in the community, are willing to extend those rights and responsibilities to others, and see their community as an institution that is working to meet the needs of its members (Fagotto & Fung, 2009).

We do not mean to suggest that the mediator or facilitator becomes responsible for the entire community. Rather, our point is that conflict and its management occurs within a larger social context. Because whatever agreements are reached will need to be implemented in that larger context, it matters. After the formal process is completed, it is unlikely that the collaborative group will continue to work with the same intensity. Depending on the situation, it may continue in another form or may even disband. You can help members of the collaborative think about what happens after the process is completed and can encourage them to think about how to sustain positive relationships that will contribute to the implementation of their agreement.

Social Capital

Social capital has been defined quite differently by numerous social scientific disciplines (for example, Adler & Kwon, 2002; Ostrom & Ahn, 2003; Paxton, 2002). Most definitions include some sort of statement about the relationship between perceived benefits of group membership and observance of group norms. Social capital is important to sustaining community relations because "the ability to secure benefits through membership in the community motivates observance of group norms" (Peterson, Peterson, Peterson, Allison, & Gore, 2006, p. 118). This framework underscores the critical role existing ties play in building and sustaining new partnerships and other collaborative relationships (Margerum, 2011; Putnam, 2000). Because it is very common to work with the same people in different contexts or collaborative opportunities, these strong, networked relationships can facilitate the initiation and implementation of new projects.

Both new collaborative efforts and ongoing collaborative efforts are more likely to be successful in communities with high levels of existing social capital (Sabatier, Leach, Lubell, & Pelkey, 2005). These communities already have social networks in place that make it easier to find stakeholders who can connect to other members of the community and provide insight into local needs (Lejano, Ingram, & Ingram, 2013). For example, McConney and Phillips (2012) found that the presence of existing networks based on previous collaborative efforts was the key to sustained planning in fisherfolk organizations in the Caribbean. Margerum (2011) highlights the California agency CALFED as an excellent example of sustaining collaborative relationships. He points out that CALFED was able to implement and maintain improved water management and restoration practices for the Sacramento and San Joaquin River basin through sustained and ongoing community relations. The social relations of the many local, state, and federal agencies and other stakeholders who joined together on various projects laid a pathway of success for continued and future collaborations such as ecosystem restoration, water quality assessment, and levee system integrity analysis. At the same time, social capital is not the panacea for environmental conflicts (Peterson et al., 2006). It can exclude new residents and the new information they offer that is critical to effectively managing environmental issues.

Free Flow of Information

Continued positive relations among collaborative participants, as well as between group members and the larger community, are crucial to maintain, even after the formal process has concluded. As with social capital, free flow of information can contribute to more positive community relations. At the same time, those positive community relations make it more likely that information flow will continue. Without that information flow, knowledge transfers do not occur and the larger community fails to become part of the solution. Many times members of the social networks described above have an in-depth understanding of the critical environmental issues faced by the community. In healthy communities, where conflict agreements are effectively implemented, information is openly shared across diverse interest groups (Lejano et al., 2013; Margerum, 2011).

Developing and maintaining channels for the free flow of information is especially important in cases where there are ongoing implementation efforts. Even if only a few of the original participants are directly involved in implementation, success requires the support of long-term relationships (Lejano et al., 2013; Margerum, 2011). Implementation and mitigation efforts may also change over time, and input from both the original members of the collaborative process and other community residents will be necessary to adapt to new science and changing demands.

When to Consider Ongoing Engagement

As stated earlier, extensive efforts to sustain community relations are not necessary. If the collaborative project was narrow or short in scope, there would be no reason to continue. Further, even if consensus is reached and collaborative members agree on how to move forward, there may exist poor interpersonal dynamics among members. In order for community relations to be authentically sustained, the interpersonal dynamics and relations made during the consensus-building phase must be healthy and built upon trust and good communication. If trust has not been properly fostered and patterns of good communication have not been adequately developed, efforts to continue relationships may be a waste of time and energy. The following two measures can help gauge how important it is to devote energy towards sustaining community relations.

Leadership

Leading the efforts to sustain community relations does not typically fall on the facilitator but is usually the responsibility of the convener or another designated person, such as a key organizational staff person or a willing member of the collaborative process. The designated leader works to maintain and enhance the networks that support their project implementation. Included in this are management tasks of organizing, planning, and communicating as well as the ongoing responsibility of gathering, combining, collecting, analyzing, and sharing data with the other stakeholders and the general public. Whoever is tasked with the role of leadership at the conclusion of the collaborative process must have the personality and skills to follow through and lead the community efforts by inspiring trust, encouraging continued commitment, and planning opportunities for true engagement.

Funding

Continued efforts to build and sustain relationships take staff, time, and resources. Even the planning of a biannual follow-up meeting requires time to strategize and organize. Organizations that fund collaborative efforts must be aware of the relationship between funding stability and effectiveness. Although the CALFED collaborative has seen much success, it continues to struggle with a lack of sustained long-term funding commitments from the state of California and the federal government. This has limited what they can do and how effective their efforts have been (Margerum, 2011).

Features of Successful Efforts

Certain characteristics can be seen as required (but not necessarily sufficient) to sustain positive community relationships. They increase the likelihood that members will remain engaged and authentic relations will be sustained.

Tailored Approach With a Well-Articulated Purpose and Focus

Efforts to sustain community relations can take many forms and should be tailored to the project needs and collaborative goals. Common activities include quarterly meetings, implementation workshops, cosponsoring of community events, or educational outreach programs. Whichever event or activity is implemented, it must align with the purpose and mission of the collaborative process. Further, sustained community relations and all activities must have a well-articulated purpose and a clear focus. Meetings or events must be well planned and executed. Community members and stakeholders who take time out of their schedule and spend money to go to a meeting or an event must feel their efforts are appreciated and worthwhile. Likewise, organizations that maintain their involvement and/or provide resources demonstrate that they are willing to sustain the group and efforts of the collaborative must receive benefits for their participation. Their time must be respected and well spent and the benefits of participating must exceed the cost. If efforts to sustain community relations have a focused purpose, it will be that much easier to foster commitment and secure the personal dedication of individuals as well as organizations. Support and backing from members of the collaborative is imperative.

Trust

We have identified trust as a key factor in building relationships throughout the collaborative process and it is equally important during postprocess efforts to successful community relation efforts. The public and associated agencies and organizations are more likely to trust public institutions with which they have an ongoing relationship (Margerum, 2011). Further, trust is central to ongoing policy effectiveness, as it becomes an existing, credible, and regulatory infrastructure that accepts and reinforces the desired policy direction and can set a strong precedent for future collaborations (Lejano et al., 2013; O'Leary, Nabatchi, & Bingham, 2004; Wondolleck & Yaffee, 2000).

Communication

In Chapter 10, we discussed the importance of good communication between participants and stakeholders during a collaborative process. Good communication must continue after the consensus-building process to sustain community relations. This includes face-to-face interaction. Contact between members of the collaborative must be part of any effort to sustain community relations. Face-to-face interaction provides opportunities for real conversations in real time allowing participants to sustain their developed relations, reorient and recommit to the agreement, and discuss any necessary adaptive measures or future projects.

Case Examples

The Blackfoot challenge (BC) is a comprehensive collaborative governance that includes the U.S. Fish and Wildlife Service (USFWS), ranchers, environmentalists, timber interests, recreation groups, state and local agency administrators, other federal agency officials, watershed landowners, and citizens. Watershed governance in the Blackfoot River area of Montana began in the early 1990s and continues today as a successful example of a strong collaborative governance institution and enhanced collective decision capacity within the community. What began as a conversation has turned into a network with monthly meetings to address specific concerns, annual barbecues, and extensive education and outreach programs focused on teaching citizens the value of cooperative conservation approaches to environmental management. When asked what made their efforts a success, members of the collaborative stated relationships built on trust, communication, and a common purpose (Weber, 2012).

Another good example of sustaining community relations post a consensus-building process is provided by the Bureau of Land Management (BLM) in the northwestern United States. The Owyhee desert crosses Southwestern Idaho, Northern Nevada, and Eastern Oregon and consists of six million acres of volcanic rock, sagebrush, and rocky canyons managed by the BLM. With the rising population in the west, more people are rediscovering the value of these arid lands, and the renewed interest has challenged the BLM to redefine the way it meets its multiple-use mandate. Ranching, mining, and military training have to be balanced with recreation, wildlife, and conservation. Equally important are Native American sites and artifacts. As part of a program called *Wings and Roots*, the BLM regularly meets with local tribes and other stakeholders to discuss management policies and engage them in implementation efforts. This relationship has continued to be strengthened over the years as meetings provide a forum to discuss and address issues and concerns (Erchia, 2009, p. 69; West, 2014).

Sustaining community relations is a critical part of the environmental conflict management process. If the context supports continued engagement efforts and activities are implemented with purpose and are designed to build trust and enhance communication, social capital can be built and community relationships will be strengthened.

Considering Culture

Sustaining Community Relations

Environmental issues can often serve as entry points for addressing cultural conflict, creating opportunities to come together and solve other forms of conflict between groups promoting and sustaining strong community relations. "Resolving environmental issues together can serve as a bridge for building cooperation and trust in post-conflict situations" (Jarraud & Lordos, 2012, p. 261). Instead of being the source of conflict, environmental issues can be leveraged and potentially alleviate existing tensions in a community. They can help reduce or replace distrust, uncertainty, and suspicion with shared knowledge and a tradition of cooperation.

EcoPeace and Friends of the Earth Middle East (FoEME) is a unique organization at the forefront of the environmental peacemaking movement. As a trilateral organization that brings together Jordanian, Palestinian, and Israeli environmentalists, their primary objective is the promotion of cooperative efforts to protect shared environmental resources, sustain regional development, and create the necessary conditions for peace and cultural cooperation in the region. In 2001, FoEME launched the *Good Water Neighbors* (GWN) program to raise awareness of the water problems shared by Palestinians, Jordanians, and Israelis. The program identifies cross-border communities whose mutual dependence on shared water resources is used as a basis for cooperation on sustainable water management. In 2013, a total of 28 communities grouped by a shared water resource were involved in the GWN. Not only has the program initiated projects and created real improvements in the water sectors of participating communities, it has promoted peace between communities, laying the groundwork for other cultural conflict and power asymmetries to be addressed and good community relations to be sustained (Sagive et al., 2013, p. 41). Working together on solving environmental problems is often the simplest way to longer term, systematic, and fundamental cooperation on a number of fronts.

Conclusion and Collaborative Process Overview

The increased importance of addressing complex and difficult environmental problems through the use of collaborative processes will continue to be central to environmental conflict management. In Chapter 2 we explained that this book would help you learn how to implement collaborative approaches to environmental problems that include the following aspects:

1. Welcome diversity and advocate acceptance of multiple perspectives

2. Value public involvement

3. Enhance collaboration and communication skills

4. Provide opportunities for deliberation and dialogue

5. Promote creative thought and constructive debate

6. Involve effective implementation of proposals

7. Encourage joint problem solving and inclusive decision making

8. Forge relationships between different stakeholders involved in conflict

9. Create a forum for shared voices

10. Urge continual progress

11. Advance social responsibility on the part of participants

Although the book has taken an interdisciplinary approach to the process of managing environmental conflict, it remains grounded in the idea that conflict is a communicative phenomenon. As we've illustrated throughout this book, there are common dimensions of ECM or collaborative processes that cut across different scales and types of conflicts. We have presented a generic framework that can be adapted to a broad variety of environmental conflicts.

This framework consists of the following four elements:

1. **Assessment**—identifying knowledge about the key players, the key issues, and the potential for collaboration

2. **Design**—the creation of a process structure to address the issues

3. **Development**—utilizing communicative and procedural skills to foster trust, cultivate creativity, enhance the decision-making process, and craft solutions that produce mutual gain for all parties involved

4. **Implementation**—decide how a decision will be carried out but also what challenges and opportunities may come as a result of the decision

By following this process, you should be able to gain a basic understanding of most environmental conflicts and develop a positive way to manage them. The exercises, worksheets, and role plays included in the text should have provided you opportunities to apply these steps, using some of the strategies and techniques suggested. The overall strategy is to help disputants achieve a collaborative perspective toward their conflict. To do this, we have suggested ways to help them negotiate options, communicate concerns, and generally work through their differences. We hope these tools will improve your understanding of the complexities of environmental conflict and give you the skills to take the necessary steps to develop sound, adaptable, socially legitimate, and implementable solutions that use the most appropriate science and technology.

Voices From the Field

We Are One Team!

Expanding a Turtle Conservation Team to Include the Entire Community

Michael J. Liles

Executive Director, Eastern Pacific Hawksbill Initiative–El Salvador

Hawksbill Conservation Program, *Bahía de Jiquilisco*, El Salvador

Conflict over sea turtles is one of today's greatest conservation challenges. The values that diverse stakeholders place on sea turtles vary dramatically, according to social contexts. For example, sea turtles draw interest from the international conservation community because of their complex life cycles and precarious conservation status. At the same time, sea turtles often are viewed as a subsistence resource in low-income communities where they nest. The divergence of these perspectives has fueled conflict among stakeholders for many decades.

The conflict in El Salvador heated up in 2009 when the central government passed a moratorium that prohibited local residents from collecting sea turtle eggs for human consumption. The decision to approve the moratorium stemmed from international pressure, with a key factor being an assessment conducted by the United States Agency for International Development (USAID). Given the importance of sea turtle egg sales to coastal communities, *tortugueros* (i.e., local sea turtle egg collectors) were outraged that without forewarning, the Salvadoran government had declared this income source they had depended on for decades illegal. The shock of the 2009 mandate instantly damaged relationships of trust among *tortugueros*, local nonprofit organizations (NGOs), and the central government that had been gradually building over many years. Suspicions and rumors about who participated in the establishment of the moratorium permeated coastal communities, making it critical for local NGOs—most of which had no knowledge of the mandate prior to its approval—to begin rebuilding relationships.

Recognizing the socioeconomic realities of coastal communities and the role of sea turtles in those realities, the Eastern Pacific Hawksbill Initiative (ICAPO, acronym is in Spanish) established a collaborative conservation program for hawksbill turtles in El Salvador that connected international conservation priorities with human well-being at the local level. The approach of this program centers on *tortugueros* as key contributors to hawksbill research and conservation, which is fundamentally different than previous approaches, which had limited the role of coastal residents to superficial levels. An essential component of ICAPO's conservation program is the purchase of hawksbill eggs from *tortugueros*, who now sell them to hatcheries for conservation. This has gained acceptance among coastal communities as a socially just conservation strategy.

To engage other coastal residents in turtle conservation, ICAPO worked with *tortugueros* and Fauna and Flora International, to develop an innovative competition that draws from a deep-rooted passion—the soccer World Cup—which is an unrivaled cultural phenomenon that has the ability to fuel excitement, destroy division, and strengthen relationships throughout Central America. The result was the Hawksbill Cup, which emulates the soccer World Cup. For the Hawksbill Cup, the hawksbill nesting season represents the championship match between the two most important nesting sites for hawksbills in the eastern Pacific Ocean—*Bahía de Jiquilisco* in El Salvador and *Estero Padre Ramos* in Nicaragua. The winner is determined by which team—Team *Bahía* or Team *Estero Padre Ramos*—scores more hawksbill conservation goals (e.g., number of nests protected, number of hatchlings produced, hatching success of nests, etc.) during the season. The scoring system was cooperatively designed by *tortugueros* and environmental NGOs to fit conservation objectives, while simultaneously ensuring that each team has an equal chance of winning.

In 2012 and 2013, the Hawksbill Cup contributed to the achievement of record-breaking results at both locations, including 166 individual hawksbills tagged, 775 nests protected (a 96% protection rate), 77,686 hatchlings produced, and more than 200 local egg collectors participating directly in research and nest protection. These results are even more impressive given that before 2008 so few adult hawksbills were sighted in the eastern Pacific Ocean that they were believed to be extirpated and that few, if any, hawksbill eggs escaped human consumption.

In addition to the conservation achievements, the Hawksbill Cup has transformed the relationships that *tortugueros* have with each other, with coastal communities, with environmental NGOs, and with hawksbills. At both sites, *tortugueros* speak enthusiastically about the human connection generated by the Hawksbill Cup—the camaraderie within and between competing teams, the trust that has developed between local residents and turtle biologists, and the excitement of uniting around a common goal infused with passion. The shared passion exhibited by both teams is exemplified in videos they have created to build the spirit of competition (see the videos at www.hawksbill.org). The Hawksbill Cup slogan of "We are one team!" rings throughout the videos of both teams. No matter which team wins the competition in a given year, all participants form one team in the fight to protect hawksbills in the eastern Pacific Ocean.

(Continued)

(Continued)

Further Reading

Liles, M. J., Gadea, V., Henriquez, A., Altamirano, E., Melero, D., Urteaga, J. . . . Gaos, A. (2014). The Hawksbill Cup: A social innovation helps save sea turtles through sport. *State of the World's Sea Turtles Report 9,* 30–31. Ross, CA: Oceanic Society.

Liles, M. J., Peterson, M. J., Lincoln, Y. S., Seminoff, J. A., Gaos, A. R., & Peterson, T. R. (2014). Connecting international conservation priorities with human well-being in low-income nations: Lessons from Hawksbill turtle conservation in El Salvador. *Local Environment,* pp. 1–22.

Case Study Application

Discussion and activities: Referring to your chosen case study in Appendix A consider the following:

1. Discuss as a group the benefits of sustaining community relations. Make sure to direct your conversation to the specifics of your project.

2. After you have discussed the benefits, spend some time discussing who will take the lead on sustaining efforts and where funding will come from.

3. Last, discuss the level of engagement your collaborative group will take and identify a number of activities and events focused on sustaining community relations. Make sure you plan with purpose to ensure commitment and continued trust building and ongoing communication.

Key Terms

assessment	development	social capital
design	implementation	

Appendix A:
Application Case Studies

Case Study 1: Sandspit Watershed Committee

This case study addresses the management of salmon fishing in British Columbia touching on issues such as endangered species, environmental justice, tourism, economic development, water quality, policy regulation, and international relations.

Background Information

One of the most enduring icons of the Pacific Northwest, Pacific salmon have been the lifeblood of generations of fishermen and are an integral part of communities up and down the West Coast. Salmon are anadromous, which means they are born in fresh water but migrate to the oceans to mature. The Sandspit Watershed is the second largest producer of Pacific salmon in British Columbia, Canada. The life cycle of salmon, their dependence on freshwater for spawning, and their long migration and stay at sea makes them the target of a wide range of users. The challenges of managing this fishery, involving a diversity of stocks with both healthy and vulnerable populations, and a complex chemistry of competing interests has given rise to turmoil, anger, and recrimination. Several species of hatchery fish were introduced into the Columbia River to mitigate the economic loss caused by dams to commercial salmon harvest. Extensive efforts to preserve the wild fish have not worked well and some populations of wild fish have declined to where they are now protected by the Endangered Species Act (ESA). Recovery of these ESA fish is an important factor in any proposal for fish management. A problem arises with the harvest of hatchery fish that are comingled with ESA protected fish. Even with abundant hatchery fish, fishing opportunity is controlled by the impact on ESA fish which necessarily has to be very low. After years of angry confrontation, the parties in the dispute are unable to resolve the issue. The legislature is unable to spend the time to resolve such a complex technical issue and the result has been to maintain the status quo. There is little trust between the various groups; however, various parties have been called together to foster communication and cooperation among the parties in order to conserve, protect, and rebuild the salmonoid resources of the Sandspit Watershed through a process of consensus decision making. Among the issues to be discussed are health, access and fishing rights, and use of the salmon.

Stakeholders

A preliminary list of stakeholders includes the following:

The Department of Fisheries and Oceans (DFO): As the agency in charge of salmon regulation, your main concern is the life and health of the salmon.

The Province of British Columbia: As a political entity, you are concerned for the rights of your constituents as well as the economic welfare of your province.

The First Nations of the Sandspit Watershed: These native tribes not only rely on salmon as their main sustenance, but place high cultural and symbolic value on them as well. Treaty rights guarantee them full access and do not limit their take. As an indigenous culture, they feel that they have first rights to the salmon.

Aqua Corp: Aqua Corp Power Company owns a majority of damns on the Columbia River and provides about two-thirds of the regional power requirements of the Pacific Northwest.

The Sandspit River commercial salmon industry: This industry relies on salmon fishing as their main source of income. The commercial fishermen do not feel their access can be compromised.

The Sandspit River sport fishermen: These fishermen rely on the salmon for recreational fishing and are members of the various organizations of sports fishermen. They feel that it is unfair that tribal members are allowed, what seems to them, unlimited access.

Salmonwatch: A nongovernmental organization concerned with the health and treatment of salmon. They understand tribal fishing rights but represent community citizens who feel those fishing rights have been abused.

Facts and Data

For the past 20 years, the department of fisheries has operated an experiment called Select Area Fisheries Enhancement (SAFE) to imprint juvenile fish in the bays and estuaries of the lower Columbia. These fish are harvested by nets that capture 95% of all the returning hatchery fish with almost no impact to ESA fish. A new bill has been proposed (HB 2734) that would move more hatchery fish to the SAFE areas and restrict netting to these areas. Those who support the bill argue the approximately 80 Oregon commercial fishermen in the Columbia would get as many or more fish as permitted today but with little or no impact to wild fish. The continued use of nets is needed to minimize the numbers of straying fish.

The economic impact of the change proposed by HB 2734 to the commercial industry and our ability to buy salmon in a restaurant or a supermarket is neutral or positive.

Salmon issues can be confusing because there are seven species and several key river systems, each with their own management issues. In addition, some of the species have genetic variants that return to the rivers at different times of the year. This adds additional complexity for fish management in rivers like the Columbia, as some stakeholders and the general public group all salmon together.

The First Nations tribe just put out a statement to the press. It reads,

> It is the policy of the confederated First Nation tribes that the health of the Columbia Basin and the Pacific Ocean be restored, and that all salmon and other native fish species be restored to the same population levels and to all rivers in which they lived prior to the treaty of 1855. We hereby declare that a state of emergency exists in the Columbia Basin and Pacific Ocean which requires immediate action.

Case Study 2: Woodpecker County Water Supply

This case study addresses water quality in Woodpecker County, Texas, touching on issues such as quantity, quality, use, water rights, economic development, land use planning, environmental justice, and policy regulation.

Background Information

Woodpecker County, Texas, had been a rural area with a population of about 15,000 since the mid-1950s. The county's surface water was fully allocated by 1954. Since then, additional water has been provided by the Pecan aquifer, which underlies most of the county.

During the 1980s and 1990s, the county's population grew. People can buy property in Woodpecker County for less than half the cost of neighboring Osprey County. Therefore, many people who work in Osprey County but cannot afford to live there reside in Woodpecker County. These residents tend to have lower-than-average incomes, and most are young families with school-aged children. This means that Woodpecker County has an increased need for infrastructure without a matching increase in the tax base.

Approximately 30,000 people live in the county now. Just over 25,000 of those live in Jasperville (the county seat), Grandview, and Idenheim, three communities that grew up along the old railroad line. Fewer than 4,000 people live on small rural acreages that produce premium quality tomatoes, cucumbers, and other truck crops for regional markets. The remaining residents raise livestock on large ranches. Despite steady industrial growth in neighboring Osprey County, unemployment in all three Woodpecker County communities has risen steadily during the last decade. The three grade schools are seriously overcrowded, the county high school is at risk of losing its state accreditation, and street repairs have been put on hold.

Residents have responded to the economic squeeze in different ways. Members of the Jasperville Chamber of Commerce formed the Jasperville Economic Development Council (EDC). With the support of the city and the commission, Jasperville's EDC has approached ACME Corporation, a nationwide company that builds and manages retirement communities, regarding a purchase by ACME of 150 acres of the Old Dirkson Farm from the county and has drawn up plans for a retirement center. The Dirkson family, a prominent family in the area, donated their farm to Woodpecker County and Jasperville in 1949 (while retaining 49% of ownership rights). Although the property had been turned into a community park, over the years it has become run-down and more of a liability than an asset.

The retirement center consists of a 60-unit condominium complex called Sunnydale. The plan calls for a 36-unit, 6-story tower and three 8-unit single story structures; a restaurant; and recreational facilities, including two tennis courts, indoor and outdoor pools, and a golf course. The condominiums are designed primarily for middle-to upper-income retirees.

Although both the county commission and the city council approved the proposal unanimously, members of the community are concerned about the impact of the new development on the area's water supply. A group of concerned farmers in the area protested the proposal, arguing that the new development would put Woodpecker County's family farmers out of business. At a recent community meeting, a dozen produce farmers testified that the deep wells called for in ACME's plan would cause their more shallow wells to go dry. Although Woodpecker County has rich soil, the farmers cannot continue to produce crops without a certain amount of irrigation. Another shallow well in danger of becoming nonfunctional is the one on the Dirkson property (originally dug by the Dirksons), which is used to irrigate the park and supply water for public restrooms and a drinking fountain.

Stakeholders

A preliminary list of stakeholders includes the following:

ACME: Your interests lie in the development of Sunnydale retirement center. Woodpecker County is ideal for the development of an older community, as its warm weather and temperate climate are attractive to snowbirds from northern states. There also already exist community organizations and clubs geared toward involving older community citizens.

Jasperville's Economic Development Council (EDC): Your interests lie in the economic development of your community. You are sympathetic to the local farmers' argument but must also consider the livelihoods of those in the area who do not farm.

Local Farmers' Representative: Your interests lie in maintaining a lifestyle that not only has flourished in this community for generations but is your sole means of survival. The deep wells called for in ACME's plan would cause your more shallow wells to go dry. Although Woodpecker County has rich soil, you could not produce crops without sufficient irrigation.

U.S. Fish and Wildlife: As a federal agency, your main concern is the sustaining of habitats to support the several unusual plant and animal species, one of which has been listed as threatened.

Dirkson Family Landowner: Your family has been prominent in the community for as long as most people in the area can remember. In 1949, after you donated a portion of your land to the county, the county agreed to keep the land (now a park) in good condition. However, over the years, the county has not made maintenance of that land a priority, arguing that they do not have the funds. Selling the land to ACME would provide financial relief for your family and would alleviate maintenance burdens the park has caused.

Jasperville City Council: As representatives of Jasperville community members, your concern is your constituents. You would like to see the historical culture of your community continue, but you know that Jasperville would also benefit from the new economic development.

Grandview City Council: As a representative of Grandview, you would like to see the Sunnydale development take place, as it will provide jobs for members of your community. However, you are nervous that the farmers in your area will also have water supply problems if Sunnydale is developed.

Idenheim City Council: As a representative of Idenheim, you would like to see the Sunnydale development take place, as it will provide jobs for members of your community. However, you are nervous that the farmers in your area will also have water supply problems if Sunnydale is developed.

Facts and Data

Data and additional facts important to this case study are as follows: Jasperville's Economic Development Council (EDC) has discovered low-cost power and water supplies and has recently acquired 180 acres of relatively undeveloped, county-owned land on the edge of town.

A hydrological engineer who has recently retired from Texas A&M has prepared a fact sheet handout showing the geological relationship between the Old Dirkson Farm and the Pecan aquifer. She has shown that at least half of Woodpecker County's wells would run dry due to the lowering of the aquifer by wells proposed in ACME's plan. In addition, the water in excess of the Pecan aquifer's storage capacity leaks out into Woodpecker Spring, also located on the Old Dirkson Farm. The spring flow supports several plant and animal species, one of which has been listed as threatened by the U.S. Fish and Wildlife Service. If ACME's water supply plans for Sunnydale are implemented, excess water will no longer be available to leak out of the aquifer into the springs.

Case Study 3: North Umpqua Hydroelectric Relicensing

This case study addresses dam relicensing in Douglas County, Oregon, touching on issues such as energy development, endangered species, tourism, environmental justice, water flow, and policy regulation.

Background Information

The North Umpqua Hydroelectric project is located in Douglas County, Oregon, near the headwaters of the North Umpqua River. PacifiCorp owns the project, and its facilities include eight hydroelectric developments constructed between 1947 and 1956. The project generates 185 megawatts of power. Each development typically consists of a dam, a waterway, a penstock, roads, and a powerhouse. The project also includes 117 miles of electric transmission line, three reservoirs, and four forebays, which provide limited water storage. The last reservoir (downstream), called Soda Springs Reservoir, is operated to reregulate downstream flows and reduce the effect of flow fluctuations resulting from peak power generation at the upstream developments. The project operates under a PERC license, which expired in 1995. While relicensing proceeds, the project operates on a year-to-year license.

The project is located completely on lands administered by the Forest Service. The river is home to five native anadromous fish species, three of which are experiencing population decline (sea-run coastal cutthroat trout, Coho salmon, and Pacific lamprey). An abundance of fish (native and nonnative) in both the river and the reservoirs has led to the development of a strong sport fishing industry. Unfortunately, some of the introduced fish compete for food and habitat resources with and/or are predators to anadromous and native fish.

Other recreational opportunities offered by the river, its tributaries, and the reservoirs are whitewater boating, hiking, camping, bicycling, swimming, sightseeing, boat angling, nonmotorized boating, nature study/observation, and automobile touring.

PacifiCorp is interested in initiating a collaborative watershed analysis process to address and resolve specific resource concerns that have been voiced by the many and varied stakeholders.

Stakeholders

A preliminary list of stakeholders includes the following:

PacifiCorp: PacifiCorp's main interest is to generate power inexpensively. They are also concerned about relationships.

Forest Service (FS): The North Umpqua project is completely on Forest Service land (Umpqua National Forest). The Forest Service feels a certain obligation to seek on-site, in-kind mitigation for both fish passage and terrestrial impacts caused from piping and project development. The Forest Service is also concerned with meeting the directives of the Northwest Forest Plan of December, 2006.

U.S. Fish and Wildlife Service (USFWS): Although the mandate for fish passage belongs to the National Marine Fisheries Service (NMFS), for this particular project the USFWS is involved because of terrestrial species affected by the project. Specifically, the USFWS argues that the lack of migration and increased animal casualties limits the genetic pool and threatens the continued survival of certain species in that area.

National Marine Fisheries Service (NMFS): The NMFS has the mandate to ensure fish passage and survival or explain why fish passage is not prescribed.

Oregon Department of Environmental Quality (ODEQ): The ODEQ has the mandate to issue water quality permits (Section 401 permits). They have identified water quality measures that PacifiCorp has to take to meet ODEQ standards. Negotiation between PacifiCorp and the ODEQ is technically independent of the relicensing process; however, ODEQ is invited to the table because water quality is linked so closely to other issues and concerns of stakeholders.

Oregon Department of Fish and Wildlife (ODFW): The ODFW has the mandate to prescribe fish passage or explain why fish passage is not prescribed. It also has the mandate to manage resident and sport fishing in the state of Oregon, which sometimes conflicts with the restoration of native fish. This area of the country is also known for its world-class sports fishing.

Oregon Water Resources Department (OWRD): The OWRD is responsible for issuing water rights, including the right to divert water out of a water body for purposes other than natural uses.

Klamath Native American Tribe: The Klamath Tribe once lived in the southern Cascade Range, some 100 miles long and 25 miles wide, which was originally dotted with marshes, lakes, rivers, and streams. In 1864, the Klamath signed a treaty and moved to their reservation around Upper Klamath Lake. In 1954, a Termination Act was passed, which resulted in the U.S. Government terminating the Klamath Reservation. The land was subsequently turned into the Winema National Park. Although the project area is not on reservation land, the Klamath tribe has had fishing rights in the area and has interest in the free run of anadromous fish.

Audubon Society: The Audubon Society chapter in the area represents a coalition of nongovernmental environmental organizations and interests (including Oregon trout). They would like to see a more natural flowing system and would like the hydrograph to more accurately reflect natural flow patterns. They would also like to see the lower dam breached.

Douglas County, Oregon: The current PacifiCorp project generates a lot of revenue for Douglas County and they are in full support of relicensing the dam.

Facts and Data

Data and additional facts important to this case study are as follows:

PacifiCorp is currently capturing seeps (water run-off) from groundwater run-off without water rights. Because PacifiCorp has historical use of water in the area (meaning the current dam project was initiated before water rights laws were established), they feel they are justified in acquiring seepage water. This has caused conflict between PacifiCorp and the OWRD, which issues and manages water rights in Oregon.

Recently in the local paper, there was a series of editorials citing PacifiCorp's North Umpqua dam as an eyesore. Citizens complained that it takes away from the beauty of the area and advocated breaching the dam and using mitigation measures to clean it up.

The project splits the mountain, causing migration problems. There are miles of open canals, and the number of animals that fall in and drown is high.

In an attempt to resolve the logging standoff in the Northwest, then President Clinton met with the Forest Service leaders in the Northwest to create the Northwest Forest Plan, published in December, 1996. Forest Service officials in the area are now faced with the task of interpreting and implementing directives of the plan. The plan contains only a small paragraph regarding small-scale hydroelectric power proposals, which is difficult to interpret.

The effects of a hydroelectric power project are long term because licenses issued are good for 30 to 50 years. Decisions about allowing hydropower development to proceed, the total effects of a project on the watershed, and mitigation measures generally need to assume a 30 to 50 year time period. In the past several years, the Forest Service has negotiated millions of dollars' worth of mitigation on hydropower projects, including recreation facilities, watershed restoration work, and road obliteration and maintenance. If the mitigation projects are compatible with the Forest Service's standards and guidelines, benefits can be accrued for the mitigated resource (i.e., mitigation) as well as for the public (i.e., production of power).

Case Study 4: Cyprinus Lake Phosphorus Total Maximum Daily Load (TMDL)

This case study addresses water quality assessment in rural Saline County, Georgia, and touches on issues such as development, water quality (point and nonpoint source pollution), agriculture, and policy regulation.

Background Information

Cyprinus Lake is a large, shallow lake located in rural Saline County, Georgia. Major tributaries to the lake, all of which discharge into the northern end of the lake, include the Mykiss River, Mud Creek, and Willow Creek. The communities of Youngstown (population 60,000) and Prattville (population 2,600) are located along the Mykiss River and Willow Creek, respectively. The Mud Creek drainage is predominantly used for agriculture, but it is increasingly being used for retirement homes that are being built along the river corridor and recreation. An existing rural-residential subdivision (Lakeside) is located on the south end of the lake. Most homes in the subdivision were constructed in the early 1950s and operate on septic systems grandfathered in under state code.

The Cyprinus Lake Watershed encompasses approximately 300,000 acres in a valley between West Mountain and the Blue Mountains, at a moderately high elevation. A portion of the watershed is steeply sloped forested land, while the area immediately adjacent to the lake and major tributaries is generally gently sloping agricultural and residential land. Only minor changes in local relief occur on the valley floor, and elevation increases sharply in the forested lands. Anthropogenic features such as ponds, irrigation ditches, and diversions dominate the flow of water within the watershed. Beneficial uses of Cyprinus Lake include domestic and agricultural water supply, cold-water aquatic life, salmonoid spawning, and primary and secondary contact recreation.

Historically, the lake has hosted a healthy population of rainbow, brown, and lake trout; whitefish; and crappie. The current fishery consists of carp, stocked rainbow trout, and white crappie. Until recently, timber harvest and agriculture (livestock grazing) dominated the local economies. These industries are being rapidly replaced by the recreation industry (lake and woodland) and specialty crop agriculture within the watershed.

In the mid-1990s, it was observed that phosphorus was entering the lake from point (permitted) sources and nonpoint sources (primarily spring runoff and irrigation returns). In 2001, high phosphorus inputs and drought conditions combined to produce dense mats of blue-green alga in the lake. In September, several domestic dogs and some livestock died as a result of ingesting toxins produced by the blue-green alga. The high pollutant loads and reduced water volume resulted in decreased dissolved oxygen levels due to algal growth and decay, warmer water temperatures, and increased sediment-phosphorus release. These changes resulted in a substantial fish kill in the south end of the lake that included nearly all species of fish.

Under section 303(d) of the Clean Water Act (CWA), Cyprinus Lake has been identified as water-quality limited due to excessive phosphorus loading from the surrounding watershed. The nuisance of algae growth has impaired beneficial uses of the lake, specifically agriculture water supply (toxic algal blooms), cold water aquatic life (low dissolved oxygen and warm temperatures), and primary and secondary contact recreation (toxic algal blooms). The lake has been listed by the state as a high priority for TMDL development.

Water-quality studies of Cyprinus Lake revealed that a 40% reduction (1,200 lb/year) in phosphorus loading is required to restore good water quality and fully support designated beneficial uses. As the phosphorous is coming from all sources all over the watershed, reductions can be targeted throughout the watershed. Phosphorus reductions do not have to be evenly applied as long as the total reduction goal for the lake is reached.

Stakeholders

A preliminary list of stakeholders is listed below.

Youngstown Municipal Wastewater Treatment Plant (WWTP): This WWTP is the largest total phosphorus discharger to the watershed (70% of the point source load, 630 lb/year). Already operating an activated sludge process, upgrading to reduce total phosphorus loading would require additional treatment capability costing approximately $68 per pound of phosphorus removed. Rate increases and state revolving fund loans are available to help offset these costs to some degree.

Prattville Wastewater Treatment Plant: This WWTP is a very small total phosphorus discharger to the watershed (5% of the point source load, 45 lb/year). Currently operating a lagoon system, upgrading to reduce total phosphorus loadings would require additional treatment capability costing approximately $200 per pound of phosphorus removed. Rate increases and state resolving fund loans are available to help offset these costs to some degree.

Methuselah Paints: This industrial discharger represents a very small total phosphorus load to the watershed (5% of the point source load, 45 lb/year). Upgrading to reduce total phosphorus loading would require additional treatment capability costing approximately $500 per pound of phosphorus removed. Cost increases passed directly to the consumers are the only available measure to help offset these costs.

Jonah Fish Farms: This permitted discharger represents 20% (180 lb/year) of the total phosphorus point source load to the watershed. Upgrading to reduce total phosphorus would require additional treatment capability costing approximately $25 per pound of phosphorus removed. Cost increases passed directly to the consumers of federal and state agricultural program funds (cost share) are available to help offset these costs.

Gideon's Orchards: Nonpoint source loading from this land use represents 15% (225 lb/year) of the total phosphorus nonpoint source load to the watershed.

Upgrading to reduce total phosphorus loading would require establishing and implementing best management practices, costing approximately $30 per pound of phosphorus removed. Cost increases passed directly to the consumers and federal and state agricultural program funds are available to help offset these costs.

Field of Promise Stables: Nonpoint source loading from this land use represents 10% (150 lb/year) of the total phosphorus nonpoint source load to the watershed. Upgrading to reduce total phosphorus loading would require establishing and implementing best management practices, costing approximately $60 per pound of phosphorus removed. Cost increases passed directly to the customers and federal and state agricultural program funds (cost share) are available to help offset these costs.

Local Agricultural Growers: This land use represents the largest nonpoint total phosphorus loading to the watershed (60% of the nonpoint source load, 900 lb/year). Upgrading to reduce total phosphorus loadings would require establishing and implementing best management practices, costing approximately $40 per pound of phosphorus removed. Federal and state agricultural program funds (cost share) are the only available measure to help offset these costs.

Lakeside Home Owners Association: Nonpoint source loading from this land use represents 15% (225 lb/year) of the total phosphorus nonpoint source load to the watershed. It also represents a bacterial concern for contact recreation in the waters in the south end of the lake. Upgrading to reduce total phosphorus loading will require the construction of a new WWTP area, as existing lots are too small to accommodate new septic tanks and drain fields that conform to current state standards. Construction and operating costs for a new WWTP are projected to be approximately $243 per pound of phosphorus removed. State revolving fund loans can be applied to offset these costs to some degree, but the majority of the cost must be borne as hookup fees and monthly charges.

U.S. Environmental Protection Agency (EPA): The Clean Water Act charges the EPA and state agencies with ensuring that waters of the U.S. meet water quality standards and fully support the designated beneficial uses. The EPA is further charged with oversight and enforcement of discharge permits in the state.

Georgia Department of Environmental Quality, Division of Water Quality (GDEQ): Under section 303(d) of the Clean Water Act (CWA), the GDEQ identified Cyprinus Lake as water-quality limited due to excessive phosphorus loading from the surrounding watershed and has listed it as a high priority for TMDL development. In their report, recommendations were made for implementing a plan to clean up Cyprinus Lake. Although they do not have any regulatory teeth for nonpoint source cleanup, their expertise with the history of the lake and regulatory connections places them in a position to provide oversight and guidance.

Facts and Data

Data and additional facts important to this case study are listed below.

The initial assessment process for establishing TMDL has determined that 30% (900 lb/year) of the total phosphorus loading is from point sources (e.g., wastewater treatment plants, industrial discharges, and aquaculture). Nonpoint sources (e.g., agriculture, livestock grazing, and failing septic systems) account for 50% (1,500 lb/year) of the total phosphorus loading, and natural sources account for 20% (600 lb/year).

Reductions in nonpoint source loading are essentially voluntary and cannot be enforced through fines and other legal action. In most cases, contributors to the local economy, being primarily agricultural and rural residential, do not have the financial means to implement the necessary changes on their own and must rely on outside funding to allow management changes to be implemented. Change would be relatively straightforward, however, at a lower cost per pound of phosphorus than cost per pound for industrial or municipal dischargers. Additionally, such improvements can be carried out in an incremental fashion until cumulative efforts result in the desired level of water quality in the runoff water. For example, an agricultural land owner that used flood irrigation could switch a portion of his fields to sprinkler irrigation until the desired water quality criteria were met in the irrigation drain water.

Reductions in point source loading are regulated by discharge permits under the jurisdiction of the Environmental Protection Agency. These reductions are nonvoluntary, can be enforced through fines and other legal action, normally come at a higher economic cost, and generally cannot be implemented incrementally. For example, if a WWTP is currently operating a traditional lagoon system and must reduce their total phosphorus output substantially, they generally must construct an additional treatment system (biological-nutrient removal, chemical precipitation, etc.), rather than add components onto existing systems.

Case Study 5: Bowcrest Mountain Ski Resort

This case study addresses ski resort development in Big Pine, North Dakota, and touches on issues such as permitting, endangered species, wildlife management, economic development, tourism, and policy regulation.

Background Information

Bowcrest Mountain is a ski resort operating in a 4,500 acre, special use permit area on U.S. Forest Service land. The ski resort's base area (which includes lodges, rental shops, a hotel, and a parking lot) is located on private land owned by the resort. The ski resort currently has approximately 450 acres of skiable terrain, most of which caters to intermediate and advanced skiers. The number of skiers that can safely and comfortably use this amount of terrain is approximately 3,000 at any given time. The parking lots, lodges, and other base areas of the facilities can comfortably accommodate approximately 2,000 skiers at any given time.

The ski resort seldom has visitation exceeding 3,000 at any given time except during Christmas vacation (December 20 through January 1) and President's weekend. During these periods, visitation sometimes exceeds 6,000 skiers at a time. Approximately 70% of the resort's annual income is earned during these peak visitation periods.

The ski resort is adjacent to the town of Big Pine, North Dakota. Forty miles southwest is the town of Canmore, North Dakota. Each town has a population of less than 25,000.

The majority of the economic revenue in Big Pine is associated with the operation of the ski resort, with the service industry being the biggest employer in town. Living expenses are very high in Big Pine; most workers in Big Pine commute from Canmore where the housing is more affordable. However, recent growth in the skier visitation to Bowcrest Mountain has resulted in a scarcity of affordable housing in Canmore as well. Consequently, workers have begun to obtain housing in the surrounding communities of High River and Okotoks, which are approximately 75 miles northeast of Big Pine. Both of these communities are essentially supported by farming and ranching.

The ski resort has approached the forest service with a proposal to expand its special use permit by 2,000 acres on an adjacent, undeveloped mountain. The ski resort proposes to clear 700 acres of skiable terrain on this mountain bringing the total amount of skiable terrain at the resort to 1,150 acres. An additional four ski lifts (high-speed quads) would be constructed to access the terrain. To provide facilities for skiers using the new terrain, the ski resort proposes to construct additional base area facilities (e.g. lodges, hotels, and parking) at the bottom of the undeveloped mountain. These facilities would be constructed on private land owned by the ski resort.

The additional proposed terrain (700 acres) and base areas facilities would allow the resort to safely and comfortably accommodate 7,000 skiers, which is the maximum number the ski resort typically experiences during peak visitation weekends.

The additional terrain would also allow the development of a snowboard terrain park to cater to the expanding snowboarder market.

The additional terrain would require increased snowmaking capacity, including increased water withdrawal and transport capabilities. The infrastructure for the snowmaking would be built on both private and public land. Additional water for snowmaking would be taken from Bow River, which flows by the current ski resort base facilities. The ski resort currently has a withdrawal tight of 10 cubic feet per second (cfs) of water from Bow River. In order to provide adequate snowmaking on the additional proposed terrain, the ski resort would have to construct another diversion structure on Bow River at the base of the mountain in the proposed expansion area. An additional 15 cfs of water would have to be withdrawn at this diversion structure.

Stakeholders

A preliminary list of stakeholders includes the following:

U.S. Army Corps of Engineers: You have identified several wetland and riparian areas on the resort's private land and are also concerned that Bow River consistently goes below its state-mandated minimum instream flow.

U.S. Fish and Wildlife Services: You are concerned that critical habitat for the Canada lynx may be impacted along with the habitat for other big game species. You are also worried about the potential impact to the North Dakota River system.

U.S. Forest Service: You oversee the majority of the land potentially impacted. Responsibilities include managing unbroken stands of Douglas fir and spruce and protecting cultural resources found on Forest Service land.

North Dakota Division of Wildlife: This agency is concerned that critical habitat for the Canada lynx may be impacted along with the habitat for other big game species. They are also worried about the potential impact to the North Dakota River system.

North Dakota State Historical Preservation Office: This agency has identified historic and prehistoric sites that are eligible for the National Registry of Historic Places and requires mitigation measures to preserve these locations.

City of Big Pine: Big Pine community members rely on the ski resort for business and economic viability. The community stands to benefit by the expansion of the resort.

City of Canmore: This community has also benefited from the popularity of the ski resort. However, affordable housing has become scarce due to the growing popularity of the area.

Cities of High River and Okotoks: These communities are both primarily ranching communities and would like to preserve that rural identity. However, due to the cost of housing in the surrounding areas, growth has become an issue for both communities and housing costs are beginning to skyrocket.

Bowcrest Mountain Ski Resort: The resort considers itself the financial stability of Big Pine and needs this expansion to remain financially viable.

Blood Indian Tribe: This Tribe used to live and hunt along these ridgelines in the proposed project area. The boundaries of their reservation do not include the ridgelines, but the land still holds special spiritual significance to their people.

Facts and Data

Data and additional facts important to this case study are listed below.

The town next to the ski resort depends almost entirely on ski resort tourism for its economic survival. When the ski resort is withdrawing its maximum water right (10 cfs) during late January and early February, Bow River consistently goes below the state mandated minimum instream flow of 73 cfs.

Bow River is a tributary of the North Dakota River. Any water depletions of the North Dakota River will have the potential to impact endangered fish in the North Dakota River system.

The ridgelines in the proposed project area have been identified as having special tribal significance to several Native American Tribes, specifically the Blood Indian Tribe.

The immediate area was once heavily logged and mined. Several logging and mining structures are still located on both the existing ski resort and the mountain proposed for expansion.

Most of the terrain at the existing ski resort is vegetated with stands of Douglas fir and spruce, interspersed with cleared ski trails that have been revegetated with a mixture of native species and introduced wheatgrass, ryegrass, and bluegrass. The undeveloped mountain is covered almost entirely of unbroken stands of Douglas fir and spruce

This area represents a potential habitat for Canadian lynx, a federally listed threatened species. The valley between the two mountains contains a tributary of Bow River, as well as North Dakota Division of Wildlife designated critical wintering habitat for mule deer. A wildlife habitat mitigation area for preserving and enhancing potential habitat for Canada lynx is located near the project area.

Several wetlands and other waters of the U.S. associated with Bow River's riparian zone are found on the ski area's private land.

The immediate area of the ski resort and its proposed expansion was once heavily logged. There are historical dams and logging and mining camps associated with historical operations throughout the area. Many of these structures would likely be eligible for listing in the National Register.

Case Study 6: Wolf Reintroduction in the State of Minnesota

This study addresses wolf reintroduction in the state of Minnesota and touches on issues such as wildlife management, endangered species, economic development, agriculture, and environmental justice.

Background Information

In 2010 a federal judge ruled in favor of reintroducing the gray wolf in the state of Minnesota, and against the American Farm Bureau in a lawsuit that sought to block the project. The Minnesota government turned down a proposal made by the Minnesota Department of Fish and Wildlife Services to contract with the Cree Indian tribe to manage the wolf reintroduction. Since the beginning of the proposal, there has been controversy in the community as some members feel the wolf reintroduction will jeopardize the safety of their children and will only lead to the reintroduction of the grizzly bear, which used to also live in this area. This will hinder camping and recreational activities and make the outdoors unsafe. Others are also concerned for their agricultural businesses, as the wolves are believed likely to prey on cattle. Most of the tension has been under the surface until a recently reported incident where a wolf killed and fed on a farmer's calf. The farmer, in retribution, grabbed his shotgun and killed the wolf. This has led to a division within the community as fear and unease has increased.

Stakeholders

A list of preliminary stakeholders includes the following:

Cree Indian Tribe: As this is the first time a Native American tribe has led the reintroduction of an endangered species, the Cree are particularly proud of their status. The wolf represents more than an opportunity to be involved in a reintroduction of an endangered species, to the Cree the wolf is sacred and a major part of their ancestral culture. As such the reintroduction represents a resurgence of their culture as well as environmental wholeness.

Minnesota Cattle Association/Minnesota Farm Bureau: Members of these organizations are concerned that the wolves will prey on their cattle. After the cited incident of the wolf killing, a meeting was called in which their main objective was to seek ways to halt the project before the wolf problem became out of hand.

Minnesota ATV and Outdoor Recreation Association: Members of this organization are concerned that the wolf reintroduction will hamper their outdoor activities and become a barrier to their rights to a safe outdoors. They have also heard talk of a possible reintroduction of the grizzly bear that would even further endanger their activities. They want the reintroduction stopped.

Minnesota Independent Miners Association: Members of this organization are concerned that the wolf reintroduction will limit their mining or industrial activities. They see no need for a reintroduction of an animal that has been absent from these areas for some time and feel the proposal is not only a waste of time but of taxpayers' money.

Local Environmental Groups: Local environmental groups are in complete support of the wolf reintroduction as they view it as a step towards environmental wholeness in the area.

Local Citizens Groups: Many local citizens are concerned about the reintroduction and fear for their children. Rumors of wolves carrying away small children plague some citizens. They also feel the wolf reintroduction may lead to the reintroduction of the grizzly bear.

Local Political Leaders: Although they can see the benefits of the reintroduction, local political leaders want to support their constituents and make sure their concerns or fears are addressed.

Minnesota Department of Fish and Wildlife Services: While the federal government turned down their proposal, they are in support of the reintroduction and have even offered to work closely with the Cree tribe throughout the reintroduction. Their main concern is that the reintroduction is handled properly and in a timely manner.

Facts and Data

Wolves live and hunt in packs of around six to ten animals. They are known to roam large distances, perhaps 12 miles (20 kilometers) in a single day. These social animals cooperate on their preferred prey—large animals such as deer, elk, and moose. When they are successful, wolves do not eat in moderation. A single animal can consume 20 pounds (9 kilograms) of meat at a sitting. Wolves also eat smaller mammals, such as birds, fish, lizards, snakes, and fruit.

A pair of lawsuits filed in early 2011 has put the recovery plan in jeopardy. Interestingly, while one of the lawsuits was filed by the Minnesota Farm Bureau, the other was filed by a coalition of concerned environmental groups including the Minnesota Conservation League and Audubon Society. The latter group pointed to unofficial wolf sightings as proof that wolves had already migrated down to Minnesota from the north, which they argued made the plan to reintroduce an experimental population in the same area unlawful.

References

Abigail, R. A., & Cahn, D. D. (2011). *Managing conflict through communication*. Boston, MA: Allyn & Bacon.

Adler, P. S., & Kwon, S. W. (2002). Social capital: Prospects for a new concept. *Academy of Management Review, 27*(1), 17–40.

Allison, S. A. (2002). *Community-based conservation planning: The case of the endangered Houston Toad in Bastrop County, Texas*. College Station: Texas A&M University.

Anderson, C. M. (2004). How institutions affect outcomes in laboratory tradable fishing allowance systems. *Agriculture and Resource Economics Review, 33*(2), 193–208.

Anderson, R., Baxter, L. A., & Cissna, K. N. (2004). *Dialogue: Theorizing difference in communication studies*. Thousand Oaks, CA: Sage.

Andrews, C. J. (2002). *Humble analysis: The practice of joint fact finding*. Westport, CT: Praeger.

Armstrong, A., & Stedman, R. C. (2013). Culture clash and second home ownership in the U.S. northern forest. *Rural Sociology, 78*(3), 318–345.

Arnstein, S. (1969). A ladder of citizen participation. *Journal of the American Insitute of Planners, 25*, 216–224.

Asah, S. T., Bengston, D. N., Wendt, K., & Nelson, K. C. (2012). Diagnostic reframing of intractable environmental problems: Case of a contested multiparty public land-use conflict. *Journal of Environmental Management, 108*, 108–119.

Axelrod, R. S., VanDeveer, S. D., & Downie, D. L. (Eds.). (2011). *The global environment: Institutions, law, and policy* (3rd ed.). Washington, DC: CQ Press.

Baldwin, C., Tan, P.-L., White, I., Hoverman, S., & Burry, K. (2012). How scientific knowledge informs community understanding of groundwater. *Journal of Hydrology, 474*, 74–83.

Bascharach, S. B., & Lawler, E. J. (1981). *Bargaining: Power, tactics, and outcomes*. San Francisco, CA: Jossey-Bass.

Bawole, J. N. (2013). Public hearing or "hearing public?" An evaluation of the participation of local stakeholders in environmental impact assessment of Ghana's Jubilee oil fields. *Environmental Management, 52*(2), 385–397.

Beckenstein, A. R., Long, F. J., Arnold, M. B், & Gladwin, T. N. (1996). *Stakeholder negotiations: Exercises in sustainable development*. Boston, MA: Richard Irwin.

Beierle, T. C., & Cayford, J. (2002). *Democracy in practice: Public participation in environmental decisions*. Washington, DC: Resources for the Future.

Berardo, R., & Gerlak, A. K. (2012). Conflict and cooperation along international rivers: Crafting a model of insitutional effectiveness. *Global Environmental Politics, 12*(1), 101–120.

Berks, F. (2004). Rethinking community-based conservation. *Conservation Biology, 18*(3), 621–630.

Betancourt, H. (2004). Attribution-emotion processes in White's realistic empathy approach to conflict and negotiation. *Peace and Conflict: Journal of Peace Psychology, 10*(4), 369–380.

Biggs, S. (1989). Resource-poor farmer participation in research: A synthesis of experiences from nine national agricultural research systems. *OFCOR Comparative Study Paper* (Vol. 3). The Hague, The Netherlands: International Service for National Agricultural Research.

Bingham, G. (1986). *Resolving environmental disputes: A decade of experience.* Washington, DC: The Conservation Foundation.

Bingham, L. B. (2006). The new urban governance: Processes for engaging citizens and stakeholders. *Review of Policy Research, 23*(4), 815–826.

Birkhoff, J., & Lowry, K. (2003). Whose reality counts? In R. O'Leary & L. B. Bingham (Eds.), *The promise and performance of environmental conflict resolution* (pp. 27–50). Washington, DC: Resources for the Future.

Bjornberg, K. E. (2009). What relations can hold among goals, and why does it matter? *Critica, 41*(121), 47–66.

Blackstock, K. L., Kelly, G. J., & Horsey, B. L. (2007). Developing and applying a framework to evaluate participatory research for sustainability. *Ecological Economics, 60,* 726–742.

Blackstock, K. L., Waylen, K. A., Dunglinson, J., & Marshall, K. M. (2012). Linking process to outcomes: Internal and external criteria for a stakeholder involvement in River Basin management planning. *Ecological Economics, 77,* 113–122.

Bodie, G. D., Cyr, K. S., Pence, M., Rold, M., & Honeycutt, J. (2012). Listening competence in initial interactions: Distinquishing between what listening is and what listeners do. *International Journal of Listening, 26,* 1–28.

Bonacorsi, S. (2007, October). SWOT Analysis. *Ezine.* Retrieved from http://ezinearticles.com/?SWOT-Analysis&id=785617

Booher, D. E. (2004, Winter). Collbaorative governance practices. *National Civic Review, 93*(4), 32–46.

Bots, P., & van Daalen, E. (2007). Functional design of games to support natural resource management. *Simulation & Gaming, 38*(4), 512–532.

Boulding, K. E. (1989). *Three faces of power.* Thousand Oaks, CA: Sage.

Bradford R. W., Duncan, P. J., & Tarcy, B. (2000). *Simplified strategies for strategic planning: A no-nonsense guide for busy people who want results fast!* Worchester, MA: Chandler House Press.

Brewer, P. R., & Ley, B. L. (2012). Whose science do you believe? Explaining trust in sources of scientific information about the environment. *Science Communication, 35*(1), 115–137.

Brownell, J. (2010). The skill of listening-centered communication. In A. D. Wolvin (Ed.), *Listening and human communication in the 21st century* (pp. 141–157). Oxford, UK: Wiley-Blackwell.

Bruce, A., Lyall, C., Tait, J., & Williams, R. (2004). Interdisciplinary integration in Europe: The case of the fifth framework programme. *Futures, 36,* 457–470.

Bruce, C. (2006). Modeling the environmental collaboration process: A deductive approach. *Ecological Economics, 59,* 275–286.

Brummans, B., Putnam, L., Gray, B., Hanke, R., Lewicki, R., & Wiethoff, C. (2008). Making sense of intractable multiparty conflict: A study of framing in four environmental disputes. *Communication Monographs, 75,* 25–51.

Bryer, T. A. (2013). Designing social media strategies for effective citizen engagement: A case example and model. *National Civic Review, 102*(1), 43–50.

Bryer, T. A., & Zavattaro, S. M. (2011). Social media and public administration: Theoretical dimensions and introduction to the symposium. *Administrative Theory & Practice, 33*(3), 341–361.

Burger, J., Harris, S., Harper, B., & Gochfeld, M. (2010). Ecological information needs for environmental justice. *Risk Analysis, 30*(6), 893–905.

Campbell, M. C., & Docherty, J. S. (2004). What's in a frame? (That which we call a rose by any other name would smell as sweet). *Marquette Law Review, 87*, 769–781.

Carlozzi, C. (1999). Make your meeting count. *Journal of Accountancy, 187*, 53–55.

Carlson, C. (1999). Convening. In L. Susskind, S. McKearnan, & J. Thomas-Larmer (Eds.), *The consensus building handbook* (pp. 169–197). Thousand Oaks, CA: Sage.

Carpenter, S. (1999). Choosing appropriate consensus building techniques and strategies. In L. Susskind, S. McKearnan, & J. Thomas-Larmer (Eds.), *The consensus building handbook* (pp. 61–97). Thounsand Oaks, CA: Sage.

Carson, R. (1962). *Silent Spring*. Boston, MA: Houghton Mifflin.

Carvalho, A., & Peterson, T. R. (2012). *Climate change politics: Communication and public engagement*. Amherst, NY: Cambria.

Chase, L. C., Decker, D. J., & Lauber, T. B. (2004). Public participation in wildlife management: What do stakeholders want? *Society and Natural Resources, 17*, 629–639.

Choi, A. S. (2011). Current status and issues of local participation in the major DMZ projects of Gangwon Province. *Korean Journal of Local Government Studies, 15*(1), 163–186.

Clarke, T. (1999). Constructing conflict: The function of synecdoche in the endangered wolf controversy. *Wicazo Sa Review: Journal of Native American Studies, 14*(1), 113–127.

Clarke, T. (2002). An ideographic analysis of Native American sovereignty in the state of Utah: Enabling denotative dissonance and constructing irreconcilable conflict. *Wicazo Sa Review: Journal of Native American Studies, 17*(2), 43–63.

Clarke, T. (2008). *Native Americans and nuclear waste: Narratives of conflict*. Verlag, Germany: VDM.

Clarke, T. (2010). Goshute Native American Tribe and nuclear waste: Complexities and contradictions of a bounded constitutive relationship. *Enviornmental Communication: A Journal of Nature and Culture, 4*(4), 387–405.

Cohen, M. H. (2008). Professional communication and teamwork. *Creative Nursing, 14*(1), 17–23.

Collins, S. D. (2009). *Listening and responding*. Mason, OH: Thomas Higher Education.

Conley, A., & Moote, A. (2001). *Collaborative conservation in theory and practice: A literature review*. Tucson: Udall Center for Studies in Public Policy, University of Arizona.

Conley, A., & Moote, M. A. (2003). Evaluating collaborative natural resource management. *Society and Natural Resources, 16*, 371–386.

Cox, R. (2006). *Environmental communication and the public sphere*. Thousand Oaks, CA: Sage.

Crowfoot, J. E., & Wondolleck, J. M. (1990). Environmental dispute settlement. In J. E. Crowfoot & J. M. Wondolleck (Eds.), *Environmental disputes: Community involvement in conflict resolution* (pp. 17–31). Washington, DC: Island Press.

Cullen, D., McGee, G. J. A., Gunton, T. I., & Day, J. C. (2010). Collaborative planning in complex stakeholder environments: An evaluation of a two-tiered collaborative planning model. *Society and Natural Resources, 23*, 332–350.

Cullen-Unsworth, L. C., Hill, R., Butler, J. R. A., & Wallace, M. (2012). A research process for integrating indigenous and scientific knowledge in cultural landscapes: Principles and determinants of success in the Wet Tropics World Heritage Area, Australia. *The Geographical Journal, 178*(4), 351–365.

Daniels, S. E., & Walker, G. B. (2001). *Working through environmental conflict: The collaborative learning approach.* Westport, CT: Praeger.

Daniels, S., Walker, G. B., & Emborg, J. (2012). The unifying negotiation framework: A model of policy discourse. *Conflict Resolution Quarterly, 30*(1), 3–31.

Davidson, J., & Wood, C. (2004). A conflict resolution model. *Theory into Practice, 43*(1), 6–13.

Davidson, S. (1998). Spinning the wheel of empowerment. *Planning, 3*, 14–15.

DeLopez, T. T. (2001). Stakeholder management for conservation projects: A case study of Ream national park, Cambodia. *Environmental Management, 28*(1), 47–60.

Dempsey, S., Dutta, M., Frey, L., Goodall, H. L., Madison, D. S., Mercieca, J., . . . Miller, K. (2011). What is the role of the communication disicpline in social justice, community engagement, and public scholarship? A visit to the CM Café. *Communication Monographs, 78*(2), 256–271.

Depoe, S., & Delicath, J. (2004). Introduction. In S. Depoe & J. Delicath (Eds.), *Communication and public participation in environmental decision making* (pp. 1–10). Albany: State University of New York.

Depoe, S. P., John, W. D., & Elsenbeer, M.-F. A. (2004). *Communication and public participation in environmental decision making.* Albany: State University of New York Press.

d'Estree, T. P. (2003). Achievement of relationship change. In R. O'Leary & L. B. Bingham (Eds.), *The promise and performance of environmental conflict resolution* (pp. 111–128). Washington, DC: Resources For The Future.

Dewulf, A., Francois, G., Paul-Wostl, C., & Taillieu, T. (2007). A framing approach to cross-disciplinary research collaboration: Experiences from a large-scale research project on adaptive water management. *Ecology and Society, 12*(2), 1–24.

de Zuniga, H. G. (2012). Social media use for news and individual's social capital, civic engagement, and political participation. *Journal of Computer-Mediated Communication, 17*, 319–336.

Dietz, T., & Stern, P. C. (2008). *Public participation in environmental assessment and decision making.* Washington, DC: National Academies Press.

Doremus, H., Andreen, W. L, Camacho, A., Faber, D. A., Glicksman, R. L., Goble, D., . . . Huang, Y. (2011). *Making good use of adaptive management.* Washington, DC: Center for Progressive Reform.

Dukes, E. F. (2004). What we know about environmental conflict resolution: An analysis based on research. *Conflict Resolution Quarterly, 22*(1-2), 191–211.

Dukes, E. F., Firehock, K. E., & Birkhoff, J. E. (2011). *Community-based collaboration: Bridging socio-ecological research and practice.* Charlottesville: University of Virginia Press.

Dukes, E. F., Firehock, K., Leahy, M., & Anderson, M. (2001). *Collaboration: A guide for environmental advocates.* Charlottesville: University of Virginia.

Durant, R. F., O'Leary, R., & Fiorino, D. (2004). Introduction. In R. F. Durant, D. Fiorino, & R. O'Leary (Eds.), *Environmental governance reconsidered: Challenges, choice and opportunities* (pp. 1–27). Cambridge, MA: MIT Press.

Eden, S., & Bear, C. (2012). The good, the bad, and the hands-on: Constructs of public participation, anglers, and lay management of water environments. *Environment and Planning A, 44*(5), 1200–1218.

Edwards Aquifer Recovery Implementation Program Steering Committee. (2014). *About EAHCP.* Retrieved from http://www.eahcp.org/index.php/about_eahcp/history/earip_steering_committee

Ehrmann, J. R., & Stinson, B. L. (1999). Joint fact finding and the use of technical experts. In L. Susskind, S. McKearnan, & J. Thomas-Larmer (Eds.), *The consensus building handbook* (pp. 375–399). Thousand Oaks, CA: Sage.

Elias, A. A. (2008). Towards a shared system model of stakeholders in environmental conflict. *International Transactions of Operational Research, 20*, 65–91.

Elias, A. A. (2012). A system dynamics model for stakeholder analysis in environmental conflicts. *Journal of Environmental Planning and Management, 55*(3), 387–406.

Elias, A. A., Jackson, L. S., & Cavana, R. Y. (2004). Changing positions and interests of stakeholders in environmental conflict: A New Zealand transport infrastructure case. *Asia Pacific Viewpoint, 45*(1), 87–104.

Endres, D., Sprain, L., & Peterson, T. R. (2009). *Social movement to address climate change: Local steps for global action.* Amherst, NY: Cambria.

Erchia, T. (2009). *Owyhee County natural resources plan.* Denver, CO: Bureau of Land Management.

Eurobarometer. (2007). *Scientific research in the media.* E. P. O. A. Sector (Ed.). Brussels, Belgium: European Commission.

Fagotto, E., & Fung, A. (2009). Sustaining public engagement: Embedded deliberation in local communities. *Occasional Research Papers.* Retrieved from http://kettering.org/wp-content/uploads/Sustaining_Public_Engagement.pdf

Falkner, R. (2008). *Business power and conflict in international environmental politics.* New York, NY: Palgrave Macmillan.

Fischer, A., & Marshall, K. (2010). Framing the landscape: Discourse of woodland restoration and moorland management in Scotland. *Journal of Rural Studies, 26*, 185–193.

Fischer, A., & Young, J. C. (2007). Understanding mental constructs of biodiversity: Implications for biodiversity management and conservation. *Biology Conservation, 136*, 271–282.

Fisher, R., & Ury, W. (2011). *Getting to yes: Negotiating agreement without giving in* (2nd ed.). New York, NY: Penguin Books.

Fletcher, A. L. (2009). Cleaning the air: The contribution of frame analysis to understand climate policy in the United States. *Environmental Politics, 18*, 800–816.

Floyd, K. (2009). *Interpersonal communication: The whole story.* Boston, MA: Mcgraw Hill.

Folger, J. P., Poole, M. S., & Stutman, R. K. (1997). *Working through conflict* (3rd ed.). New York, NY: Longman.

Forester, J. (1999). Dealing with deep value differences. In L. Susskind, S. McKearnan, & J. Thomas-Larmer (Eds.), *The consensus building handbook* (pp. 463–493). Thousand Oaks, CA: Sage.

Fox, E., Hastings, S., Miller-Henson, M., Monie, D., Urgoretz, J., Frimodig, A., . . . Serpa, P. (2013). Addressing policy issues in a stakeholder-based and science-driven marine protected area network planning process. *Ocean & Coastal Management, 74*, 34–44.

Freeman, R. E. (1984). *Strategic management: A stakeholder approach.* New York, NY: Basic Books.

Gillespie, A., & Richardson, B. (2011). Exchanging social positions: Enhancing perspective taking within a cooperative problem-solving task. *European Journal of Social Psychology, 41*, 608–616.

Goffman, E. (1974). *Frame analysis: An essay on the organization of experience.* New York, NY: Harper & Row.

Goldberg, R. M. (2009). How our worldviews shape our practice. *Conflict Resolution Quarterly, 26*(4), 405–431.

Gordon, M. (2011). Listening as embracing the other: Martin Buber's philosophy of dialogue. *Educational Theory, 61*(2), 207–219.

Gray, B. (2003). Framing of environmental disputes. In R. Lewicki, B. Gray, & M. Elliot (Eds.), *Making sense of intractable environmental conflicts: Concepts and cases* (pp. 11–34). Washington, DC: Island Press.

Gray, B. (2004). Strong opposition: Frame-based resistance to collaboration. *Journal of Community & Applied Social Psychology, 14*, 166–176.

Gray, B., Peterson, T., Putnam, L. L., & Bryan, T. A. (2003). Comparing natural resource cases. In R. J. Lewicki, B. Gray, & M. Elliott (Eds.), *Making sense of intractable environmental conflicts* (pp. 159–189). Washington, DC: Island Press.

Grimble, R., Chan, M. K., Aglionby, J., & Quan, J. (1995). *Trees and trade-offs: A stakeholder approach to natural resource management.* London, England: International Insitute for Environment and Development.

Grossman, Z. (2005). Unlikely alliances: Treaty conflicts and environmental cooperation between Native American and rural white communities. *American Indian Culture and Research Journal, 29*(4), 21–43.

Grossman, Z., & Gedicks, A. (2001). Native resistance to multinational mining corporations in Wisconsin. *Cultural Survival Quarterly, 25*(1), 1.

Gunia, B. C., Swaab, R. I., Sivanathan, N., & Galinsky, A. D. (2013). The remarkable robustness of the first-offer effect: Across culture, power, and issues. *Personality and Social Psychology Bulletin, 39*(12), 1457–1558

Gunton, T. I., Day, J. C., & Williams, P. (2003). Collaborative planning and sustainable resource management: The North American experience. *Environments: A Journal of Interdisciplinary Studies, 31*(2), 4–19.

Hall, E. T. (1976). *Beyond culture.* Garden City, NY: Anchor Press.

Hand, L. C., & Ching, B. D. (2011). You have one friend request: An exploration of power and citizen engagement in local governments' use of social media. *Administrative Theory & Practice, 33*(3), 362–382.

Harris, F., & Lyon, F. (2013). Transdisciplinary environmental research: Building trust across professional cultures. *Environmental Science & Policy, 31*, 109–119.

Haynes, M. E. (2006). *Meeting skills for leaders: A practical guide for more productive meetings* (3rd ed.). Boston, MA: Course Technology.

Hays, S. P. (1987). *Beauty, health, and permanence: Environmental politics in the United States, 1955-1985.* New York, NY: Cambridge University Press.

Henkel, S. (2007). *Successful meetings: How to plan, prepare, and execute top-notch business meetings.* Ocala, FL: Atlantic.

Henry, J. (2004). Decide, announce, defend: Turning the NEPA process into an advocacy tool rather than a decision-making tool. In S. P. Depoe, J. W. Delicath, & M.-F. A. Elsenbeer (Eds.), *Communication and public participation in environmental decision making* (pp. 99–112). New York: State University of New York.

Herman, K., Susskind, L., & Wallace, K. (2007). A dialogue, not a diatribe. *Environment, 49*(1), 20–34.

Hjortso, C. N., Christensen, S. M., & Tarp, P. (2005). Rapid stakeholder and conflict assessment for natural resource management using cognitive mapping: The case of Damdoi Forest Enterprise, Vietnam. *Agriculture and Human Values, 22*, 149–167.

Hofstede, G. (1984). *Culture's consequences: International differences in work related values.* Thousand Oaks, CA: SAGE.

Hofstede, G. (2001). *Culture's consequences: Comparing values, behaviors, institutions, and organizations across nations* (2nd ed.). Thousand Oaks, CA: SAGE.

Hopke, J. E. (2012). Water gives life: Framing an environmental justice movement in the mainstream and alternative Salvadoran press. *Environmental Communication, 6*(3), 365–382. doi: 10.1080/17524032.2012.695742

Huang, Y.-H., & Bedford, P. (2009). The role of cross-cultural factors in integrative conflict resolution and crisis communication: The Hainan incident. *American Behavioral Scientist, 53*(4), 565–578.

Hubo, C., & Krott, M. (2013, August). Conflict camouflaging in public administraton: A case study in nature policy in Lower Saxony. *Forest Policy and Economics, 33*, 63–70.

Hunter, D., Salzman, J., & Zaelke, D. (2010). *International environmental law and policy.* New York, NY: Foundation Press.

Innes, J. E. (1999). Evaluating consensus building. In L. Susskind, S. McKearnan, & J. Thomas-Larmer (Eds.), *The consensus building handbook: A comprehensive guide to reaching agreement* (pp. 631-675). Thousand Oaks, CA: Sage.

Innes, J. E., & Booher, D. E. (2010). *Planning with complexity: An introduction to collaborative rationality for public policy.* New York, NY: Routledge.

Islam, G., & Zyphur, M. (2009). Rituals in organizations: A review and expansion of current theory. *Group and Organizational Management, 34*, 114–139.

Jarraud, N. S., & Lordos, A. (2012). Particpatory approaches to environmental conflict resolution in Cyprus. *Conflict Resolution Quarterly, 29*(3), 261–281.

Jeffrey, P. (2003). Smoothing the waters: Observations on the process of cross-disciplinary research collaboration. *Social Studies of Science, 33*(4), 539–562.

John, D. (2004). Civic environmentalism. In R. F. Durant, D. J. Fiorino, & R. O'Leary (Eds.), *Environmental governance reconsidered: Challenges, choices, and opportunities* (pp. 219–254). Cambridge, MA: MIT Press.

John, K. H., Youn, Y. C., & Shin, J. H. (2003). Resolving conflicting ecological and economic interests in the Korean DMZ: A valuation based approach. *Ecological Economics, 46*(1), 173–179.

Johnson, D. E., & Dagg, S. (2003). Achieving public participation in coastal zone environmental impact assessment. *Journal of Coastal Conservation, 9*, 13–18.

Kaplan, A. M., & Haenlein, M. (2010). Users of the world, unite! The challenges and opportunities of social media. *Business Horizons, 53*(1), 59–68. doi:10.1016/j.bushor .2009.09.003

Keough, H. L., & Blahna, D. J. (2005). Achieving integrative, collaborative ecosystem management. *Conservation Biology, 20*(5), 1373–1382.

Kietzmann, H. H., Hermkens, K., Mccarthy, I. P., & Silvestre, B. (2011). Social media? Get serious! Understanding the functional building blocks of social media. *Business Horizons, 54*, 241–251.

Krolikowska, K., Kronenberg, J., Maliszewska, K., Sendzimir, J., Magnuszewski, P., Dunajski, A., & Slodka, A. (2007). Role-playing simulation as a comunication tool in community dialogue: Krakonosze Mountains case study. *Simulation Gaming, 38*, 195–210.

Kunde, J. E. (1999). Dealing with the press. In L. Susskind, S. McKearnan, & J. Thomas-Larmer (Eds.), *The consensus building handbook* (pp. 435–462). Thousand Oaks, CA: Sage.

Lakoff, G. (2010). Why it matters how we frame the environment. *Environmental Communication: A Journal of Nature and Culture, 4*(1), 70–81.

Lawrence, A. (2006). No personal motive? Volunteers, biodiversity, and the false dichotomies of participation. *Ethics, Place and Environment, 9*, 279–298.

Layzer, J. A. (2002). Citizen participation and government choices in local environmental controversies. *Policy Studies Journal, 30*(2), 193–207.

Layzer, J. A. (2012). *The environmental case: Translating values into policy*. Washington, DC: CQ Press.

Leach, D. L., Rogelberg, S. G., Warr, P. B., & Burnfield, J. L. (2009). Perceived meeting effectiveness: The role of design characteristics. *Journal of Business and Psychology, 24,* 65–76.

LeBaron, M., & Pillay, V. (2006). *Conflict across cultures: A unique experience of bridging differences*. Boston, MA: Intercultural Press.

Lee, S. F. (2008). How should team meetings flow? R.a.!R.a.! Approach as a meeting process. *Journal for Quality & Participation, 31(1), 25–28.*

Lejano, R., Ingram, M., & Ingram, H. (2013). *The power of narrative in environmental networks*. Cambridge, MA: MIT Press.

Leopold, A. (1949). *A Sand County almanac and sketches here and there*. Oxford, UK: Oxford University Press.

Lester, L., & Hutchins, B. (2012). The power of the unseen: Environmental conflict, the media, and invisibility. *Media Culture Society, 34(7),* 847–863.

Leventhal, L. (2006). Interest-based negotiation: Conditioned for success with evidence from Kaiser Permanente. *Dispute Resolution Journal, 61(3),* 50–58.

Lewicki, R., Gray, B., & Elliot, M. (2003). *Making sense of intractable environmental conflicts: Concepts and cases*. Washington, DC: Island Press.

Lewicki, R. J., Saunders, D., & Minton, J. (1999). *Negotiation*. Burr Ridge, IL: McGraw-Hill Higher Education.

Littlejohn, S. W., & Domenici, K. (2001). *Engaging communication in conflict: Systemic practice*. Thousand Oaks, CA: Sage.

Lloyd, J. (2009). The listening cure. *Continuum: Journal of Media & Cultural Studies, 23(4),* 477–487.

Locke, E. A., & Latham, G. P. (2006). New directions in goal-setting theory. *Association for Psychological Science, 15(5),* 265–268.

Lockwood, M. (2010). Good governance for terrestrial protected areas: A framework, principles and performance outcomes. *Journal of Environmental Management, 91(3),* 754–766.

Loew, B. (2000). Multiple species habitat conservation planning: Goals and strategies of local governments. *Environmental Management, 26,* S15–S21.

Luyet, V., Schlaepfer, R., Parlange, M., & Buttler, A. (2012). A framework to implement stakeholder participation in environmental projects. *Journal of Environmental Management, 111,* 213–219.

Lynam, T., De Jong, W., Sheil, D., Kusumanto, T., & Evans, K. (2007). A review of tools for incorporating community knowledge, preferences, and values into decision making in natural resource management. *Ecology & Society, 12(1),* 5.

MacNaughton, A., & Martin, J. G. (2002). *Environmental dispute resolution: An anthology of practical solutions*. Chicago, IL: American Bar Association.

Malouff, J. M., Calic, A., McGrory, C. M., Murrell, R. L., & Schutte, N. S. (2012). Evidence for a need-based model of organizational-meeting leadership. *Current Psychology, 31,* 35–48.

Mann, C., & Adsher, J. (2014). Adjusting policy to insitutional, cultural and biophysical contect conditions: The case of conservation banking in California. *Land Use Policy, 36,* 73–82.

Manring, N. J., Nelson, K. C., & Wondolleck, J. M. (1990). Structuring an effective environmental dispute settlement process. In J. E. Crowfoot & J. M. Wondolleck (Eds.), *Environmental disputes: Community involvement in conflict resolution* (pp. 75–97). Washington, DC: Island Press.

Margerum, R. D. (2011). *Beyond consensus: Improving collaborative planning and management.* Cambridge, MA: MIT Press.

Mascarenhas, M., & Scarce, R. (2004). "The intention was good": Legitimacy, consensus-based decision making, and the case of forest planning in British Columbia, Canada. *Society & Natural Resources, 17,* 17–38.

Maser, C., & Pollio, C. (2012). *Resolving environmental conflicts.* New York, NY: CRC Press Taylor & Francis Group.

Maxwell, J. P., & Brown, S. R. (2000). Identifying problems and generating solutions under conditions of conflict. *Operant Sujectivity, 23*(1), 31–51.

McConney, P., & Phillips, T. (2012). Collaborative planning to create a network of fisherfolk organizations in the Caribbean. In B. E. Goldstein (Ed.), *Collaborative resilience: Moving through crisis to opportunity* (pp. 207–230). Cambridge, MA: MIT Press.

McCreary, S., Gamman, J., & Brooks, B. (2001). Refining and testing joint fact-finding for environmental dispute resolution: Ten years of success. *Mediation Quarterly, 18*(4), 329–348.

McKearnan, S., & Fairman, D. (1999). Producing consensus. In L. Susskind, S. McKearnan, & J. Thomas-Larmer (Eds.), *The consensus building handbook* (pp. 325–373). Thousand Oaks, CA: Sage.

Meadowcroft, J. (2004). Deliberative democracy. In R. F. Durant, D. J. Fiorino, & R. O'Leary (Eds.), *Environmental governance reconsidered: Challenges, choices, and opportunities* (pp. 183–217). Cambridge, MA: MIT Press.

Meijer, A. (2012). Co-production in an information age: Individual and community engagement supported by new media. *International Society of Voluntary and Nonprofit Organizations, 23*(4), 1156-1172.

Men, L. R., & Tsai, W.-H. S. (2013). Beyond liking or following: Understanding public engagement on social networking sites in China. *Public Relations Review, 39,* 13–22.

Mitchell, R. K., Agle, B. R., & Wood, D. J. (1997). Toward a theory of stakeholder identification and salience: Defining the principle of who and what really counts. *Academy of Management Review, 22,* 853–886.

Moore, C. W. (1996). *The mediation process: Practical strategies for resolving conflict* (2nd ed.). San Francisco, CA: Jossey-Bass.

Nash, R. (2001). *Wilderness and the American mind.* New Haven, CT: Yale University Press.

National Science Board. (2008). Science and technology: Public attitudes and understanding. In *Science and Engineering Indicators 2008.* Washington, DC: U.S. Government Printing Office.

Negotiated Rulemaking Act of 1990, Pub. L. No. 101–648, 104 Stat. 4969 C.F.R. (1990).

Nelson, K. C., Manring, N. J., Crowfoot, J. E., & Wondolleck, J. M. (1990). Maximizing organizational effectiveness. In J. E. Crowfoot & J. M. Wondolleck (Eds.), *Environmental disputes: Community involvement in conflict resolution* (pp. 152–182). Washington, DC: Island Press.

Oetzel, J. G., & Ting-Toomey, S. (2013). *The SAGE handbook of conflict communication: Integrating theory, research, and practice.* Thousand Oaks, CA: Sage.

O'Leary, R. (1995). Environmental mediation: What do we know and how do we know it? In J. W. Blackburn & W. M. Bruce (Eds.), *Mediating environmental conflicts: Theory and practice* (pp. 17–36). Westport, CT: Quorum Books.

O'Leary, R., & Bingham, L. B. (2003). *The promise and performance of environmental conflict resolution.* Washington, DC: Resources for the Future.

O'Leary, R., Durant, R. F., Fiorino, D. J., & Weiland, P. S. (1999). *Managing for the environment: Understanding the legal, organizational, and policy challenges.* San Francisco, CA: Jossey-Bass.

O'Leary, R., Nabatchi, T., & Bingham, L. B. (2004). Environmental conflict resolution. In R. F. Durant, D. J. Fiorino, & R. O'Leary (Eds.), *Environmental governance reconsidered: Challenges, choices, and opportunities* (pp. 323–354). Cambridge, MA: MIT Press.

Oravec, C. (1981). John Muir, Yosemite, and the sublime response: A study in the rhetoric of preservationism. *Quarterly Journal of Speech, 67*, 245–258.

Oravec, C. (1984). Conservationism vs. preservationism: The "public interest" in the Hetch Hetchy controversy. *Quarterly Journal of Speech 70*, 444–458.

Osterrieder, A. (2013). The value and use of social media as communication tool in the plant sciences. *Osterrieder Plant Methods, 9*(26), 1–6.

Ostrom, E. (1990). *Governing the commons: The evolution of insitutions for collective action.* New York, NY: Cambridge University Press.

Ostrom, E., & Ahn, T. K. (2003). *Foundations of social capital.* Cheltenham, UK: Edward Elgar.

Ostrom, E., Burger, J., Field, C. B., Norgaard, R. B., & Policansky, D. (1999). Sustainability-Revisiting the commons: Local lessons, global challenges. *Science, 284*, 278–282.

Overseas Development Administration. (1995). *Guidance note on how to do stakeholder analysis of aid projects and programmes.* London, England: Author.

Ozerol, G., & Newig. (2008). Evaluating the success of public participation in water resources management: Five key constituents. *Water Policy, 10*, 639–655.

PacifiCorp (2001, June). North Umpqua hydroelectric project settlement agreement, FERC No. 1927-008: Settlement agreement: Protection, mitigation, and enhancement measures. Accessed at http://www.pacificorp.com/content/dam/pacificorp/doc/Energy _Sources/Hydro/Hydro_Licensing/North_Umpqua_River/2001_2002_Annual_ Report.pdf

Parkins, J. R., & Mitchell, R. E. (2005). Public participation as public debate: A deliberative turn in natural resource management. *Society & Natural Resources: An International Journal, 18*(6), 529–540.

Paxton, P. (2002). Social capital and democracy: An interdependent relationship. *American Sociological Review, 67*(2), 254–277.

Perz, S. G. (2002). The changing social contexts of deforestation in the Brazilian Amazon. *Social Science Quarterly (Blackwell Publishing Limited), 83*(1), 35–52.

Peterson, M. N., Peterson, M. J., & Peterson, T. R. (2005). Conservation and the myth of consensus. *Conservation Biology, 19*, 762–767.

Peterson, M. N., Peterson, M. J., & Peterson, T. R. (2006). Why conservation needs dissent. *Conservation Biology, 20*, 576–578.

Peterson, M. N., Peterson, T. R., Peterson, M. J., Lopez, R. R., & Silvy, N. J. (2002). Cultural conflict and the endangered Florida Key deer. *Journal of Wildlife Management, 66*(4), 947–968.

Peterson, T. R. (1997). *Sharing the Earth: The rhetoric of sustainable development.* Columbia: University of South Carolina Press.

Peterson, T. R., & Feldpausch-Parker, A. M. (2013). Environmental conflict communication. In J. G. Oetzel, & S. Ting-Toomey (Eds.), *The SAGE handbook of conflict communication: Integrating theory, research, and practice* (2nd ed., pp. 513–537). Thousand Oaks, CA: Sage.

Peterson, T. R., & Horton, C. C. (1995). Rooted in the soil: How understanding the perspectives of landowners can enhance the managment of environmental disputes. *Quarterly Journal of Speech, 81*, 139–166.

Peterson, T. R., Peterson, M. N., Peterson, M. J., Allison, S. A., & Gore, D. C. (2006). To play the fool: Can environmental conservation and democracy survive social capital? *Communication and Critical Cultural Studies, 3*, 116–140.

PEW Research Center. (2014). The state of the news media 2014: An annual report in American Journalism. In Pew Research Journalism Project (Ed.), *Pew research center's project for excellence in journalism* (11th ed.). Washington, DC: Author. http://www.journalism.org/packages/state-of-the-news-media-2014/

Phillips, B. A. (2001). *The mediation field guide: Transcending litigation and resolving conflicts in your business organization.* San Francisco, CA: Jossey-Bass.

Pocewicz, A., & Nielsen-Pincus, M. (2013). Preferences of Wyoming residents for siting of energy and residential development. *Applied Geography, 43,* 45–55.

Polzer, J., Mannix, E., & Neale, M. (1995). Multiparty negotiation in its social context. In R. Kramer & D. Messick (Eds.), *Negotiation as a social process* (pp. 123–142). London, England: Sage.

Postmes, T., Spears, R., & Cihangir, S. (2001). Quality of decisions and group norms. *Journal of Personality and Social Psychology, 80,* 918–930.

Putnam, L. L. (2013). Definitions and approaches to conflict and communication. In J. G. Oetzel & S. Ting-Toomey (Eds.), *The SAGE handbook of conflict communication: Integrating theory, research, and practice* (pp. 1–32). Thousand Oaks, CA: Sage.

Putnam, L. L., Burgess, G., & Royer, R. (2003). We can't go on like this: Frame changes in intractable conflicts. *Environmental Practice, 5*(3), 247–255.

Putnam, R. (2000). *Bowling alone: The collapse and revival of American community.* New York, NY: Simon and Schuster.

Raitio, K. (2012). Discursive institutionalist approach to conflict management analysis: The case of old-growth forest conflicts on state-owned land in Finland. *Forest Policy and Economics,* 97–103.

Raitio, K., & Saarikoski, H. (2012). Governing old-growth forests: The interdependence of actors in Great Bear Rainforest in British Columbia. *Society & Natural Resources, 25*(9), 900–914.

Ramirez, R. (1999). Stakeholder analysis and conflict management. In D. Buckles (Ed.), *Cultivating peace: Conflict and collaboration in natural resource management* (pp. 101–126). Washington, DC: World Bank Insitute.

Rauschmayer, F., Berghofer, A., Omann, I., & Zikos, D. (2009). Examining processes or/and outcomes? Evaluation concepts in European governance of natural resources. *Environmental Policy and Governance, 19*(3), 159–173.

Rauschmayer, F., & Wittmer, H. (2006). Evaluating deliberative and analytical methods for the resolution of environmental conflicts. *Land Use Policy, 23*(1), 108–122.

Ravnborg, H. M., & Westermann, O. (2000). Understanding interdependencies: Stakeholder identification and negotiation for collective natural resource management. *Agricultural Systems, 73*(1), 41–56.

Reed, M. S. (2008). Stakeholder participation for enviornmental management: A literature review. *Biological Conservation, 141,* 2417–2431.

Reed, M. S., Graves, A., Dandy, N., Posthumus, H., Hubacek, K., Morris, J., . . . Stringer, L. C. (2009). Who's in and why? A typology of stakeholder analysis methods for natural resource management. *Journal of Environmental Management, 90,* 1933–1949.

Renn, O. (2004). The challenge of integrating deliberation and expertise: Participation and discourse in risk management. In T. MacDaniels & M. Small (Eds.), *Risk analysis and society: An interdisciplinary characterization of the field* (pp. 289–366). Cambridge, UK: Cambridge University Press.

Rieke, R. D., Sillars, M. O., & Peterson, T. R. (2012). *Argumentation and critical decision making* (8th ed.). Boston, MA: Pearson/Allyn and Bacon.

Rieman, B. E., Hessburg, P. F., Luce, C., & Dare, M. R. (2010). Wildfire and management of forests and native fishes: Conflict or opportunity for convergent solutions? *BioScience, 60*(6), 460–468.

Riemer, J. W. (2004). Chippewa spearfishing, lake property owners/anglers, and tourism: A case study of environmental social conflict. *Sociology Spectrum, 24*, 43–70.

Robinson, J. L. (2013). *Contested water: The struggle against water privatization in the United States and Canada.* Cambridge, MA: MIT Press.

Rofougaran, N. L., & Karl, H. A. (2005). San Francisquito Creek—The problem of science in environmental disputes: Joint fact finding as a transdiciplinary approach toward environmental policy making (pp. 1–24). Denver, CO: United States Geological Survey.

Rothman, J. (1997). *Resolving identity-based conflict: In nations, organizations, and communities.* San Francisco, CA: Jossey-Bass.

Rowley, T. (1997). Moving beyond dyadic ties: A network theory of stakeholder influences. *Academy of Management Review, 22*(4), 887–910.

Saarikoski, H., & Raitio, K. (2013). Science and politics in old-growth conflict in Upper Lapland. *Nature and Culture, 8*(1), 53–73.

Saarikoski, H., Raitio, K., & Barry, J. (2013). Understanding "successful" conflict resolution: Policy regime changes and new interactive arenas in the Great Bear Rainforest. *Land Use Policy, 32*, 271–280.

Saarman, E., Gleason, M., Ugoretz, J., Airame, S., Carr, M., Fox, E., . . . Vasques, J. (2013). The role of science in supporting marine protected area network planning and design in California. *Ocean & Coastal Management, 74*, 45–56.

Sabatier, P. A., Leach, W. D., Lubell, M., & Pelkey, N. W. (2005). Theoretical frameworks explaining partnership success. In P. A. Sabatier, W. Focht, M. Lubell, Z. Trachtenberg, A. Vedlitz, & M. Matlock (Eds.), *Swimming upstream: Collaborative approaches to watershed management* (pp. 173–200). Cambridge, MA: MIT Press.

Sagive, M., Obidallah, M., Al-Asad'd, H., Aberman, M., Khateeb, M. A., Dreiat, A., . . . Milner, M. (2013). *Community based problem solving on water issues.* Tel Aviv, Israel: EcoPeace/Friends of the Earth Middle East.

Salzman, J., & Thompson, B. H. (2010). *Environmental law and policy.* New York: Foundation Press.

Savage, G. T., Nix, T. H., Whitehead, C. J., & Blair, J. D. (1991). Strategies for assessing and managing organizational stakeholders. *Academy of Management Executive, 5*, 61–75.

Schon, D., & Rein, M. (1994). *Frame reflection: Towards the resolution of intractable policy controversies.* New York, NY: Basic Books.

Segev, E., & Baram-Tsabari, A. (2012). Seeking science information online: Data mining Google to better understand the roles of the media and the education system. *Public Understanding of Science, 21*(7), 813–829.

Senecah, S. (2004). The trinity of voice: The role of practical theory in planning and evaluating the effectiveness of environmental participatory processes. In S. Depoe, J. Delicath, & M.-F. A. Elsenbeer (Eds.), *Communication and public participation in environmental decision making* (pp. 13–33). New York: State University of New York.

Senge, P. (1994). *The fifth discipline fieldbook.* New York, NY: Doubleday.

Senge, P. (2006). *The fifth discipline: The art and practice of the learning organization.* New York, NY: Doubleday.

Siegrist, M., Earle, T. C., & Gutscher, H. (2007). *Trust in cooperative risk management: Uncertainty and skepticism in the public mind.* London, England: Earthscan.

Singletary, L., Smutko, L. S., Hill, G. C., Smith, M., Daniels, S. E., Ayres, J. A., & Haaland, K. (2008). Skills needed to help communities manage natural resource conflicts. *Conflict Resolution Quarterly, 25*(3), 303–320.

Singleton, R. A., & Straits, B. A. (1999). *Approaches to social research*. New York, NY: Oxford University Press.

Skewes, J. C., & Guerra, D. (2004). The defense of Maiquillahue Bay: Knowledge, faith, and identity in an environmental conflict. *Ethnology, 43*(3), 217–231.

Speth, J. G. (2004). *Red sky at morning: America and the crisis of the global environment*. New Haven, CT: Yale University Press.

Stanghellini, P. S. L. (2010). Stakeholder involvement in water management: The role of the stakeholder analysis within participatory processes. *Water Policy, 12*, 675–694.

Stenseke, M. (2009). Local participation in cultural landscape maintenance: Lessons from Sweden. *Land Use Policy, 26*, 214–223.

Stone, D., Patton, B., & Heen, S. (2000). *Difficult conversations: How to discuss what matters most*. New York, NY: Penguin Books.

Straus, D. A. (1999). Designing a consensus building process using a graphic road map. In L. Susskind, S. McKearnan, & J. Thomas-Larmer (Eds.), *The consensus building handbook* (pp. 137–168). Thousand Oaks, CA: Sage.

Stringer, L. C., Reed, M. S., Dougill, A. J., Rokitzki, M., & Seely, M. (2007). Enhancing participation in the implementation of the United Nations Convention to Combat Desertification. *Natural Resources Forum, 31*, 198–211.

Sullivan, J., Vasavada, U., & Smith, M. (2000). Environmental regulation & location of hog production. *Agricultural Outlook, September 2000*, 19–23.

Susskind, L., Camacho, A. E., & Schenk, T. (2012). A critical assessment of collaborative adaptive managment in practice. *Journal of Applied Ecology, 49*, 47–51.

Susskind, L., & Cruikshank, J. (1987). *Breaking the impasse: Consensus approaches to resolving public disputes*. New York, NY: Basic Books.

Susskind, L., Levy, P. F., & Thomas-Larmer, J. (1999). *Negotiating environmental agreements: How to avoid escalating confrontation, needless costs, and unnecessary litigation*. Washington, DC: Island Press.

Susskind, L., & Secunda, J. (1998). Environmental conflict resolution: The American experience. In C. Napier (Ed.), *Environmental conflict resolution* (pp. 16–55). London, England: Cameron May.

Susskind, L., & Thomas-Larmer, J. (1999). Conducting a conflict assessment. In L. Susskind, S. McKearnan, & J. Thomas-Larmer (Eds.), *The consensus building handbook* (pp. 99–136). Thousand Oaks, CA: Sage.

Susskind, L., van der Wansem, M., & Ciccarelli, A. (2000). *Mediating land use disputes: Pros and cons*. Cambridge, MA: Lincoln Insitute of Land Policy.

Taneja, H., Webster, J. G., Malthouse, E. C., & Ksiazek, T. B. (2012). Media consumption across platforms: Identifying user-defined repertoires. *New Media & Society, 14*(6), 951–968. doi: 10.1177/1461444811436146

Tayler, S. (1984). *Making bureaucracies think: The Environmental Impact Statement strategy of administrative reform*. Standford, CA: Stanford University Press.

Taylor, B. (2009). "Place" as prepolitical grounds of democracy: An Appalachain case study in class, conflict, forest politics, and civic networks. *American Behavioral Scientist, 52*, 826–845.

Tear, T. H., Kareiva, P., Angermeier, P. L., Comer, P., Czech, B., Kautz, R., . . . Wilhere, G. (2005). How much is enough? The recurrent problem of setting measurable objectives in conservation. *BioScience, 55*(10), 835–849.

Thompson, K., Leintz, P., Nevers, B., & Witkowski, S. (2010). The integrative listening model: An approach to teaching and learning listening. In A. D. Wolvin (Ed.), *Listening and human communication in the 21st century* (pp. 266–286). Oxford, UK: Wiley-Blackwell.

Tippett, J., Handley, J. F., & Ravetz, J. (2007). Meeting the challenges of sustainable development: A conceptual appraisal of a new methodology for participatory ecological planning. *Progress in Planning, 67*(1), 9–98.

Tombouctou2000. (2014). *Edwards aquifer recovery implementation program receives 2013 Partners in Conservation award: Sierra Club Lone Star Chapter's Tyson Broad among recipients honored in Washington.* The Texas Green Report. Retrieved from http://texas greenreport.wordpress.com/2014/01/16/edwards-aquifer-recovery-implementation-program-receives-2013-partners-in-conservation-award-sierra-club-lone-star-chap ters-tyson-broad-among-recipients-honored-in-washington/

Trigger, D., & Mulcock, J. (2005). Forests as spiritually significant places: Nature, culture, and "belonging" in Australia. *The Australian Journal of Anthropology, 16*(3), 306–320.

U.S. Fish and Wildlife Service. (2014). Edwards Aquifer recovery implementation program receives 2013 Partners in Conservation Award press release. http://www.fws.gov/south west/es/Documents/R2ES/EARIP_PIC_AWARD_NR_012014.pdf

Van Kleef, G. A., De Dreu, C. K. W., Pietroni, D., & Manstead, A. S. R. (2006). Power and emission in negotiation: Power moderates the interpersonal effects of anger and happiness on concession making. *European Journal of Social Psychology, 36*, 557–581.

Varasokszky, Z., & Brugha, R. (2000). How to do (or not to do). . . : A stakeholder analysis. *Health Policy and Planning, 15*(3), 338–345.

Vedeld, P., Jumane, A., Wapalila, G., & Songorwa, A. (2012). Protected areas, poverty, and conflicts: A livelihood case study of Mikumi National Park, Tanzania. *Forest Policy and Economics, 21*(0), 20–31.

Vella, P., Bowen, R. E., & Frankic, A. (2009). An evolving protocol to identify key stakeholder-influenced indicators of coastal change: The case of Marine protected areas. *International Council for the Exploration of the Sea (ICES) Journal of Marine Science, 66*, 203–213.

Voinov, A., & Bousquet, F. (2010). Modelling with stakeholders. *Environmental Modelling & Software, 25*, 1268–1281.

Voogd, H. (2000). Urban environmental pollution: Perception and compensation. In D. Miller & G. de Roo (Eds.), *Resolving urban environmental and spatial conflicts* (pp. 91–102). Groningen, The Netherlands: Geo Press.

Waddell, C. (1998). *And no birds sing: Rhetorical analyses of Rachel Carson's Silent Spring.* Carbondale: Southern Illinois University Press.

Wade, S. O. (2004). Using intentional, values-based dialogue to engage complex public policy conflicts. *Conflict Resolution Quarterly, 21*(3), 361–379.

Walker, G. B. (2004). The roadless area initiative as national policy: Is public participation an oxymoron? In S. P. Depoe, J. W. Delicath, & M.-F. A. Elsenbeer (Eds.), *Communication and public participation in environmental decision making* (pp. 113–135). Albany, NY: State University of New York Press.

Walker, G. B. (2007). Public participation as participatory communication in environmental policy decision-making: From concepts to structured conversations. *Environmental Communication, 1*(1), 99–110.

Walker, G. B., Daniels, S. E., & Emborg, J. (2008). Tackling the tangle of environmental conflict: Complexity, controversy, and collaborative learning. *E:CO, 10*(4), 17–27.

Walker, G., Senecah, S., & Daniels, S. (2006). From the forest to the river: Citizen's views of stakeholder engagement. *Human Ecological Review, 13*(2), 193–202.

Walton, R. E, & McKersie. (1965). *A behavioral theory of labor negotiation.* Ithaca, NY: ILR Press.

Webb, T., & Raffaelli, D. (2008). Conversations in conservation: Revealing and dealing with language differences in environmental conflicts. *Journal of Applied Ecology, 45,* 1198–1204.

Weber, E. (2012). Getting to resilience in a climate-protected community: Early problem-solving choices, ideas, and governance philosophy. In B. E. Goldstein (Ed.), *Collaborative resilience: Moving through crisis to opportunity* (pp. 177–206). Cambridge, MA: MIT Press.

Webler, T. (1995). Right discourse in citizen participation: An evaluative yardstick. In O. Renn, T. Webler, & P. Wiedemann (Eds.), *Fairness and competence in citizen participation: Evaluating models for environmental discourse* (pp. 35–86). Boston, MA: Kluwer Academic.

Webler, T., Tuler, S., & Krueger, R. (2001). What is a good public participation process? Five perspectives from the public. *Enviornmental Management, 27,* 435–450.

Weible, C. M. (2006). An advocacy coalition framework approach to stakeholder analysis: Understanding the political context of California marine protected area policy. *Journal of Public Administration Research and Theory, 17,* 95–117.

Weible, C. M., & Sbatier, P. A. (2009). Coalitions, science, and belief change: Comparing adversarial and collaborative policy subsystems. *Policy Studies Journal, 37*(2), 195–212.

Weick, K. (1995). *Sensemaking in organizations.* Thousand Oaks, CA: Sage.

Welton, M. (2002). Listening, conflict, and citizenship: Toward a pedagogy of civil society. *International Journal of Lifelong Education, 21*(3), 197–208.

West, F. (2014). Owyhee desert: Ranching, recreation, conservation, way of life. Retrieved from http://focuswest.org/lands/owyhee.cfm

Westley, F., Miller, F., & Lacy, B. (2003). Far from land: Further explorations in consilience. Paper presented at the 10th International Conference on Multi-Organizational Partnerships, 25-28 June 2003, University of Strathclyde, Glasgow, Scotland.

Wiersema, A. (2008). A train without tracks: Rethinking the place of law and goals in environmental and natural resources law. *Environmental Law, 38*(4), 1239–1300.

Williams, B. K., Szaro, R. C., & Shapiro, C. D. (2009). *Adaptive management: The U.S. Department of the Interior technical guide.* Washington, DC: Adaptive Mangement Working Group.

Williamson, A., & Fung, A. (2004, Winter). Public deliberartion: Where we are and where can we go? *National Civic Review,* 3–15.

Winslade, J., & Monk, G. (2000). *Narrative mediation: A new approach to conflict.* San Francisco, CA: Jossey-Bass.

Wolvin, A. D. (2010). *Listening and human communication in the 21st century.* Oxford, UK: Wiley-Blackwell.

Wondolleck, J., Manring, N. J., & Crowfoot, J. E. (1990). Conclusion. In J. E. Crowfoot & J. Wondolleck (Eds.), *Environmental disputes: Community involvement in conflict resolution* (pp. 254–263). Washington, DC: Island Press.

Wondolleck, J. M., & Yaffee, S. L. (2000). *Making collaboration work: Lessons from innovation in natural resource management.* Washington DC: Island Press.

World Commission on Environment and Development (1987). *Our common future.* Oxford, UK: Oxford University Press.

Yearly, S. (2000). Making systemic sense of public discontents with expert knowledge: Two analytical approaches and a case study. *Public Understanding of Science, 9,* 105–122.

Yukl, G. (2010). *Leadership in organizations* (7th ed.). Upper Saddle River, NJ: Pearson.

Index

About the Authors

Dr. Tracylee Clarke is currently an associate professor and chair of the Communication Program at California State University Channel Islands. Her current research and teaching interests include environmental communication and conflict management; collaborative decision making and policy development; the intersections of narrative, culture, identity, and conflict; and the role of dialogue in conflict prevention and resolution. She is a member of U.S. Institute for Environmental Conflict Resolution, Morris K. Udall Foundation and teaches a course for the Straus Institute for Dispute Resolution at Pepperdine School of Law.

Dr. Clarke worked as an environmental mediator and policy analyst and has over 18 years of experience in environmental conflict management and collaborative policy development. She has managed and directed large, complex stakeholder processes and mediations for federal, state, local, and tribal governments as well as private industry. Controversial issues she has mediated include natural resource management, land use, endangered species protection, water supply and water quality, transportation, energy development, and toxic remediation and cleanup. As an environmental consultant, she has also designed and conducted professional training workshops for government officials and environmental managers to enhance collaborative problem solving, negotiation skills, and communication competency.

Dr. Clarke holds an MA in communication from the Edward R. Murrow School of Communication at Washington State University and a PhD in environmental communication from the University of Utah. She is also certified as a professional mediator.

Dr. Tarla Rai Peterson is professor of communication at the University of Texas at El Paso. She also serves as guest professor of environmental communication at the Swedish University of Agricultural Sciences and as an adjunct professor of communication at the University of Utah.

Dr. Peterson has published several books on communication, technology, and the environment as well as numerous research articles on environmental conflict and public participation in environmental policy making. Her research program explores how the intersections between communication, democratic practice, and policy enable/constrain policy options and public life. She values classroom teaching and serves as a faculty mentor for graduate teaching assistants. She has developed an active theory to practice program that includes design and evaluation of best practices for facilitating public participation in issues related to environmental policy. The program is centered on the critical role of communication in facilitating the emergence and implementation of sustainable environmental policy.

Dr. Peterson's most recent books examine conflict surrounding housing (*The Housing Bomb*, published by Johns Hopkins University Press) and energy (*Smart Grid [R]Evolution*, published by Cambridge University Press) policy. She has worked with environmental conflict in a variety of locations including Australia, India, El Salvador, Sweden, and the United States.